SCIENCE 7
FOR YOUNG CATHOLICS

by

Dr. Kenneth Stein

EDITS BY
SETON STAFF

SETON PRESS
FRONT ROYAL, VA

Written by Dr. Kenneth Stein, based on previous edition by Kathleen and Mark Julicher.
Activities and Experiments by Kathleen and Mark Julicher.
Edits, Chapter Summaries, and Review Questions by Seton staff.

Executive Editor: Dr. Mary Kay Clark
Editors: Seton Staff

© 2014, 2019 Seton Home Study School
All rights reserved.
Printed in the United States of America

Seton Home Study School
1350 Progress Drive
Front Royal, VA 22630
Phone: (540) 636-9990
Fax: (540) 636-1602

For more information, visit us on the web at www.setonhome.org
Contact us by e-mail at info@setonhome.org

ISBN: 978-1-60704-146-7

Cover: *Christ Healing Blind Bartimaeus* by Carl Bloch

DEDICATED TO THE SACRED HEART OF JESUS

Table of Contents

Introduction viii

Chapter 1 - History of Science 1
   I. Introduction 2
   II. Ancient Egypt 5
   III. Ancient Greece 9
   IV. Ancient Rome 11
   V. The Fall of Rome 13
   VI. The Middle Ages 13
   VII. The Birth of Modern Science 16
   VIII. The Renaissance 18
   IX. The Age of Newton: Development of Modern Science 19

Chapter 2 - The Scientific Method 23
   I. Observation, Hypothesis, and Experimentation 24
   II. The Limitations of Science 28
   III. Other Forms of Science 30
   IV. Scientific "Failures" in Our Time 32
   V. Who Wants to Be a Scientist? 34

Chapter 3 - Geology 37
   I. The Unique Design of the Earth 38
   II. Journey to the Center of the Earth 40
   III. Forces and Movements 44
   IV. Land Forms 49
   V. Maps 54
   VI. Rocks 62
   VII. Identification of Minerals 66

Chapter 4 - Flight and Space Travel 75
   I. Discovery and the Hand of God 77
   II. Basics of Flight 77
   III. Lift and Speed 80
   IV. Parts of an Airplane 83
   V. Flight Stability 87

VI. Rockets 91
VII. Parts of a Rocket... 93
VIII. The Difference Between Rockets and Planes 98
IX. The Advancement of Science... 98
X. Orbits and Satellites 99
XI. Space Shuttle Program 100
XII. Space Probes.. 102
XIII. Telescopes.. 107
XIV. Hubble Space Telescope.. 109

Chapter 5 - Energy 113
I. Energy of Motion...115
II. God: The Prime Mover..116
III. God's Laws of the Universe 117
IV. The First Law of Motion 118
V. The Second Law of Motion 118
VI. The Third Law of Motion...119
VII. The Laws of Thermodynamics 124
VIII. Transformation of Energy 125
IX. God: The Creator of the Laws of Energy.. 130
X. The Progress of Science 132

Chapter 6 - Light...135
I. Light Energy...136
II. Electromagnetic Spectrum..137
III. Properties of Light...139
IV. Lenses 149

Chapter 7 - Energy: Heat, Radio, Sound... 155
I. Heat 156
II. Heat Production 160
III. Heat Transfer 162
IV. Radiation.. 165
V. Insulation 166
VI. Radio 168
VII. Sound 169

Chapter 8 - Electricity 177
  I. Introduction 178
  II. Electric Current 179
  III. Production of Electric Current 181
  IV. Electrical Energy 182
  V. Elements of a Circuit 183

Chapter 9 - Chemistry, Part I 193
  I. Matter 194
  II. Observing and Reporting 204
  III. Properties of Matter 208
  IV. Atoms: Protons, Neutrons, Electrons 209
  V. Isotopes 212

Chapter 10 - Chemistry, Part II 215
  I. The Periodic Table 216
  II. Chemical Compounds 218
  III. Reactants and Products 221
  IV. Radioactive Elements 224
  V. The Four States of Matter 226
  VI. Matter and Change: Change of State 235
  VII. Chemical Reactions 239
  VIII. God's World 242

Chapter 11 - The Five Senses 245
  I. The Gift of Sight 246
  II. The Gift of Hearing 254
  III. The Gift of Smell 258
  IV. The Gift of Taste 259
  V. The Gift of Touch 261

Introduction to Science 7

As is the case in all schools, the science curriculum for each grade must be limited. It is impossible to cover all science topics each year. Most schools alternate from year to year between the physical sciences and the life sciences. Our Science 7 book focuses on the physical sciences. The final chapter, however, briefly covers the five senses, for the yearly health requirement.

No single textbook for seventh grade can possibly cover all the physical sciences. In general, the physical sciences include physics, chemistry, earth science or geology, and astronomy. These general topics include a great variety of topics within each one.

In this textbook, a selection of physical science areas of study are included: Geology or Earth Science; Flight and Space Travel, with emphasis on the physics of flight; Energy, Light, Sound, and Electricity, all part of the study of Physics; and two chapters on Chemistry.

The national standardized tests for each grade level cover a variety of science topics. Therefore, it is important to determine what specific topics your child needs to know for the particular standardized test he or she may be taking. First, find out if you need to administer the standardized science test. Because the schools alternate the science topics from year to year, most states do not require elementary students to take the science section of any standardized test.

If you wish your student to take a science standardized test, try to find out what topics might be included on the test. Many elementary-level tests are not requiring specific areas of science knowledge but rather ask questions regarding the process of finding the answer. Check on the Internet for "Standardized Test Questions for Seventh Grade Science."

We believe this textbook will provide your student with a solid foundation in the science topics that it covers. At the same time, we encourage your student to learn more about the topics that he or she finds particularly interesting.

For those enrolled, the lesson plans include optional questions and experiment activities based on the book *The Mystery of the Periodic Table*.

May God and His Mother Mary bless you and your child as you study God's wonderful world of science!

History of Science

I.   **Introduction**

II. **Ancient Egypt**
     A. The Papyrus Plant
     B. Heavenly Constellations
     C. Pyramids

III. **Ancient Greece**

IV. **Ancient Rome**

V.   **The Fall of Rome**

VI. **The Middle Ages**
     A. Legacy of the Saints
         1. St. Patrick
         2. St. Benedict
         3. St. Columbkille and St. Columbanus
     B. Monks' Contributions to Science

VII. **The Birth of Modern Science**
     A. Robert Grosseteste
     B. St. Albert the Great
     C. St. Thomas Aquinas
     D. Roger Bacon

VIII. **The Renaissance**

IX. **The Age of Newton**

History of Science

Chapter 1

"Have you not known? Have you not heard? The Lord is the everlasting God, the Creator of the ends of the Earth. He does not faint or grow weary, His understanding is unsearchable" (Isaiah 40:28).

I. Introduction

God created our world and all of its creatures. Sacred Scripture and Catholic Tradition teach that the world was made to show us the glory of God. Every part of the world was planned and made for us. The creation of the world comes from His love and His goodness: "And God saw that it was good…" (Genesis 1:4).

The Bible, the inspired Word of God, teaches that God created the world from nothing. Not one of us can comprehend exactly how He did this!

As Catholics, believers in the inspired Word of God, the Bible, we know that God created the world because of His love. As we study the world, we see His wisdom in the order that we find in His creatures and creation: "You have arranged all things by measure and number and weight" (Wisdom 11:20). This orderly world reflects His greatness. You don't need to be a scientist to see this order. We see order in the regularity of the day and night, the sunrises, and the sunsets. We see order in the seasons of summer, fall, winter, and spring. We see order in the design and beauty of snowflakes, flowers, birds and other animals, the sun, and the stars. There are countless examples.

"Snowflake" photo, by Wilson Bentley

Some of God's designs are invisible to us. For example, we can't see gravity or electricity, but we know that these exist because we see their results. St. Paul, in his Letter to the Colossians 1:16, wrote, under the inspiration of the Holy Spirit, that God created the visible and the invisible things, noting that He created the invisible angels: "For in him were all things created in heaven and on earth, *visible and invisible*, whether thrones, or dominations, or principalities, or powers: all things were created by him and in him." The thrones, dominations, principalities, and powers are choirs (or kinds) of angels.

We know that the Lord God Almighty is a God of order, because all living creatures seek order. It is natural for them to do so. If you have ever taken a pet to a kennel, you might have noticed that your pet was not happy to go there. You took your pet away from its routine and sense of order. When you brought the pet home, it quickly adjusted back to its routine and habits. Your pet knows when and where to go for food, for sleep, and for play. Even though animals are not capable of thinking and reasoning like human beings, they still seek some kind of order in their lives. It doesn't matter whether it is a dog, cat, fish, or bear.

We, too, are creatures of habit, and we like predictability. With even one little disturbance in our daily life, we feel a sense of disruption. For example, think of what happens when your home loses electrical power during a storm. You are forced to do things with candles or flashlights. You go about your routines, but not as easily! You can't use the computer, the television, or the stove. The frozen food in the freezer begins to go bad! It might be a little fun for a while to use candles and a flashlight, to eat up all the ice cream before it melts … if the power remains off for only a short time. However, if your home loses power for more than a day, it will cause serious disorder in your home.

Since the beginning of time, people have desired order in their lives. Order helps us to live our daily lives calmly, with plans and without frustration. Order is important for planning ahead. For example, farmers know there is a short time in the spring when they must prepare their land for planting crops. If bad weather prevents them from preparing their land during a certain period, they likely will have a smaller harvest. Sailors know that there are specific times each day when ocean tides help them to leave the harbor without trouble. If they are unable to leave during those times, then they might need to wait for the following day. These are only a few examples of how people depend on periods of time, weather, or rhythms of the natural world. Think about some patterns of weather that affect your life and your activities.

We know some things about the material world on our planet. We also know some things about the sun and the moon which affect our planet and our daily weather. What we know has been built on the knowledge and discoveries that have been passed down from our ancestors, people who lived before us, sometimes a long time before we were born. We often think that scientists or inventors have discovered this knowledge through laboratory experiments, but that is not always true. Ordinary people have learned, discovered, or developed much of the knowledge of our material world. Their knowledge was often the result of trying to make their own lives easier or to solve some simple problems they experienced. Most knowledge about the material world has been the result of trial and error. Some people would try to see if something worked, and if it did not, they would try something else again and again until they found something that did work.

What does this have to do with science? What is science? Science has many definitions, and how we define it depends on the situation. Sometimes science describes how we go about studying a subject, how we plan to find out how things work. Science also can mean the subject itself. For example, there are the sciences of geology, physics, chemistry, and biology.

Sometimes science is used to describe orderly methods of discovery or testing: the **scientific method**. Sometimes the word "science" is used rather informally. If your mother is very good at organizing your family's home, your father might describe her method like this: "She has it down to a science."

Many thoughts come to mind when you hear the word "science." Maybe you think of a laboratory with its test tubes, beakers, flasks, and other kinds of laboratory equipment. Perhaps you think of astronauts and space travel, or satellites. Some might think of a favorite science fiction story or movie. Ask anyone, and he will give you his own definition of science. The word "science" has a variety of meanings. Even scientists will have their own definitions of "science."

What then is the "scientific" definition of science? Here is the official definition: **Science is the systematic knowledge or study of the physical or material world gained through observation and experimentation.** (The word "systematic" means an orderly body of knowledge and an orderly and planned study.) This is the way most scientists think of science today.

On the basis of this definition, we can **define a scientist as a person who learns about a subject by collecting data or information through organized observation and experimentation**. When a scientist gains data or information in an organized way or framework, we refer to that data as **empirical data**. Let's say that you collect weather data for one year. Does that mean you are conducting science? Not necessarily. However, if you took that weather data and started developing graphs of temperature and rainfall averages over a period of time, then you would be producing empirical data. You have developed **systematic knowledge** of weather patterns, and you might even be able to make predictions with your data of future weather patterns in a similar time and place. This kind of information could be helpful for those planning outdoor festivals or picnics, or for those who have gardens or farms.

Let's turn our attention now to the science developed by earlier civilizations to find out more about the history of developing knowledge of our material world, knowledge about the planet Earth on which we live, and the processes or workings on our planet. You might find it interesting as we look at the conclusions based on observations of the ancient Egyptians, Greeks, and Romans. Once Jesus came to Earth, and people tried to live the Christian life, even more progress was made in areas of science. We will see what happened when saints and monks observed and gained insights about God's amazing creation. The Catholic Church has often supported scientists and helped expand people's knowledge about scientific discoveries.

So let's take a trip down the lanes of scientific history, shall we?

II. Ancient Egypt

The ancient Egyptian civilization began about 3,500 years before the birth of Jesus Christ. Egypt is a large area in northeast Africa, in the valley regions along the Nile River, south of the Mediterranean Sea. The ancient Egyptians were very religious, and they were preoccupied with death and living in the next world. **They built very elaborate tombs or pyramids for their kings**, queens, and nobles, and for other important people. The detailed drawings on the walls of these tombs illustrate the Egyptians' knowledge of science. There are depictions of **woodworking, hunting and fishing scenes, cattle herding, bread and beer making, beekeeping, and weaving**. There are many other scenes depicted in Egyptian art as well.

The ancient Egyptian religion had regulations for all the tomb-building procedures. First, they had to dig deep underground to find large layers of limestone. Next, stonemasons would measure and then excavate a long hollow chamber from within the rock layer. Artists would then carve detailed scenes and writings into the rock walls and ceilings. Finally, they would paint the carvings. We can say that the ancient Egyptians "had tomb building down to a science."

Egyptian Tomb

Ancient Egyptian paints were simple and known as **tempera** or egg tempera. Color pigments were made from rocks, minerals, plants, and other items. These substances were crushed and turned into fine powder. The colors blue and green were made from copper ores; red, yellow, and orange came from iron ores. The Egyptians used soot to make the color black, and gypsum (plaster of Paris) to produce white. These pigments were mixed in a solution of water, eggs, and sap from plants. Though the Egyptians were ancient people who lived a very long time ago, they took the time to learn and figure out how **to produce colored paints from simple rocks and plants**!

The colors in some of the Egyptian tomb paintings look fresh and bright, like they were recently painted. In some tombs, you can see brush strokes, even hairs from the brushes! It is remarkable that these paintings have lasted thousands of years. Of course, they have been underground and protected from the sun, wind, and rain. What can we make today that can last thousands of years?

We can say that the ancient **Egyptians developed the science of making paint**. Most likely, they passed their science formula for paint on to the Greeks, who in turn passed it on to the Romans. The Romans handed the paint formula down to Western Europe, and so on down to us. Think about that for one moment. Certainly, there have been many improvements, but nevertheless, the paint you see on your walls had its origin in ancient Egypt!

The **ancient Egyptians also practiced the art of medicine**. They were able to treat some diseases, perform some surgeries, and fix broken bones. Egyptian physicians learned through trial and error that extracts from certain plants helped treat diseases. They treated asthma with garlic. Onion was given to those suffering from digestive problems.

The ancient Egyptians also knew that certain spices kept insects away from their stores of food. They learned that spices prevented cooked food from spoiling. Today we know that these spices preserve food by preventing the growth of harmful microbes or bacteria. However, Egyptians did not have the concept of microbes or germs as we do today. A few of their spices included cumin (KEW-min), coriander (KOR-ee-and-ehr) and fenugreek (FEN-you-greek). Because of scientists and inventors, we are fortunate to have refrigerators to keep food from spoiling and do not need to depend on spices. Nevertheless, we still use these same spices for cooking to add unique flavors to our food. Which spices can you find in your kitchen?

Aerial Photograph of the Karnak Complex

The Temple of Karnak is in the city of Luxor, Egypt. It was built over many years, and today is a popular tourist site. The Karnak Complex contains a large section known as the "Botanical Garden." It does not contain living plants, but it contains rock carvings that show more than 275 species of plants! Some of these plants were known for their beauty and were grown in gardens. **The Egyptians used other plants for food, spices, and medicines.**

The **ancient Egyptians made medicines from the extracts of certain plants**. Foxglove was one such plant. It contains a chemical known as digitalis, which is used today to help people with heart problems. Opium poppies were used for sedation and to relieve pain. Poppies contain morphine, codeine, and other important ingredients. Belladonna contains a chemical known as atropine, which has many medicinal uses. Medical clinics and hospitals still use these drugs today. If you ever had a painful tooth, a badly broken bone, or a severe cough, your family doctor may have prescribed medicine that contained codeine.

You can see that some of the most common medications used today are not so modern and were first used by the ancient Egyptians. The ancient Egyptian physicians used trial and error over many, many years to develop or discover their medicines. Much of this medical knowledge has come down to us today.

It is unfortunate that some Egyptians attempted to use "magic" as part of practicing medicine, thus offending God and slowing down the progress of real science. Who knows what other scientific discoveries the ancient Egyptians might have made had they not turned their attention to such grave evils?

Even our modern knowledge of medicine is still far from complete. There remains much that we do not know about the human body and human health.

A. The Papyrus Plant

Perhaps no other plant was as important to the ancient Egyptians as papyrus. The papyrus plant was used to make baskets, bags, ropes, mats, sandals, rafts, and sails. The upper part of the plant was used for making a type of paper. The root was not thrown away, but cooked and eaten. Along with papyrus roots, the diet of ordinary ancient Egyptians included lotus roots, garlic, onions, and lentils. Other foods were available but used mostly by people of higher status.

Today we take printed books for granted. If you think about it for one moment, you can understand that printed texts and books make knowledge portable; knowledge can move from one person to many persons if it is printed. **Paper made from papyrus was important in Egypt for transmitting all kinds of knowledge, especially science and medicine. It made possible the passing of information from one region to another, from one country to another, and from one period of history to another**. The ancient Egyptians used papyrus for describing their religion, their history, and their Pharaohs and other leaders. **Papyrus helped develop an Egyptian civilization of educated people.**

Almost every society has come to know about papyrus, either as single sheets or rolled-up scrolls. Some original papyrus texts can be found in museums. Throughout recent history, however, no one knew how papyrus was made. The ancient Egyptians recorded a great deal about their science, but making

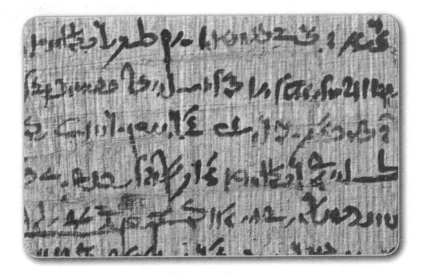

Papyrus Sample

papyrus was not part of it. It wasn't until the 1960s that Dr. Hassan Ragab rediscovered this lost art: how to make paper from papyrus. Since then, small page-size pieces of papyrus have been manufactured and sold as popular souvenir items throughout Egypt and the Mediterranean.

B. Heavenly Constellations

You may be surprised to learn that our knowledge of the heavenly constellations has its origins in ancient Egypt. The **ancient Egyptians made maps of many of the constellations**, including Orion, Ursa Major, Gemini, and Taurus. They used these stars for navigation so that they could travel on the seas by locating the stars and constellations.

The Egyptians used certain placement of the stars to determine times to mark important religious festivals or yearly events. For example, they knew that the rising of Sirius indicated the time for the flooding of the River Nile. This was the beginning of their new year and an important time for farmers. The flooding brought water—but more important, fertile soil and dissolved nutrients—to their farmlands.

C. Pyramids

You are probably familiar with the pyramids. These were **large burial complexes for the Pharaohs**. It has been more than 4,000 years since the pyramids were built. The most famous of the pyramids is known as the Great Pyramid of Cheops (KEY-ops). Some archaeologists believe that this Great Pyramid took more than 80 years to build! If a person had lived in Egypt as a child during the completion of the Great Pyramid, then most likely his father and grandfather would have worked on it.

**Aerial photograph of the Great Pyramids
Giza, Egypt**

We could further explore many other sciences developed by the ancient Egyptians. For example, they domesticated birds and other animals, including the domestic house cat. They pioneered the development of tool-making and of extracting metals from rocks. They developed certain grains for farming.

The ancient Egyptians certainly left a remarkable scientific legacy. They passed their information on to the Greeks and the rest of the world. Other ancient societies, such as the Mesopotamians and Sumerians, had their sciences too, but much of it has been lost.

DID YOU KNOW?

Did you know that a man named Joseph became a prince in Egypt because God's hand was upon him? You can read about Joseph in the book of Genesis in the Bible. Unfortunately, the ancient Egyptians made slaves of many people, including those they conquered in war. Out of jealousy, Joseph's brothers sold him into slavery, and he was made a slave in Egypt. When he was accused of a crime he did not commit, he was even put in prison. However, God's hand was upon him. God rescued Joseph from prison and blessed him with an important position in Egypt. God revealed to Joseph that there would be a famine for seven years. When Joseph told this to Pharaoh, he made Joseph a prince in charge of distributing the whole food supply in Egypt!

Many years later, the descendants of Joseph and his brothers, known as the Hebrew people (the ancestors of the Jewish people of today) were made slaves by the Egyptians as well. The Hebrew people were treated very cruelly. However, just as God had freed Joseph from slavery, He also freed the Hebrew people from slavery. Through His servant Moses, God delivered the Hebrew people out of Egypt and brought them to the Promised Land!

III. Ancient Greece

The ancient Greek civilization began about 2000 B.C. (that is, 2,000 years before Christ). Ancient Greece was in the current area of Greece as well as the current countries of Bulgaria and Turkey. The ancient Greeks had a different approach to science than the Egyptians. They were very logical and even developed logic into a science.

The ancient Greeks contributed many important developments to the **field of mathematics**. They developed the rules of **geometry, mathematical proofs, number theories, and applied mathematics**. What does mathematics have to do with science? Actually, mathematics is a field of science. In this book, we are mainly focusing on one *kind* of science, **empirical science**, in which everything must be demonstrated through experimentation, but most people simply call it "science." This is the predominant form of science that is currently practiced, and thus the most prevalent way in which science is thought of today. However, there are other kinds of science as well, such as mathematics and logic. Sometimes, mathematics is referred to as "the language of science." Scientists use mathematics to study quantities such as length, width, area, volume, and weight or mass. Mathematics can be applied to study patterns and rates of change. The many kinds of engineering could not have come about and progressed without mathematics.

The Greeks also made lasting contributions to the science of **astronomy**. They considered it a branch of "mathematical arts," along with arithmetic, geometry, and music. In the 4th century B.C., the Greeks developed three-dimensional models to explain the motion of the planets. The Greeks thought that the planet Earth rotated on its axis and the planets traveled around the Earth in circles. The Greeks also believed that the Earth was at the center of the universe. This became known as the **geocentric theory**.

Photograph of the Antikythera, by Marsyas

In the 3rd century B.C., a scientist by the name of Aristarchus suggested that the sun, not the Earth, was at the center of the universe. This is called the **heliocentric theory**. Whether the Earth or the sun was at the center of the universe eventually became a serious controversial topic of debate. These two theories would be argued well into the 16th century A.D. (that is, Anno Domini, meaning "in the year of Our Lord").

The ancient Greeks knew that the Earth was a sphere. Their beliefs enabled astronomers to **accurately calculate the circumference of the Earth**. They did this by measuring the angles of shadows in two cities in Egypt, during the summer solstice. They used trigonometry, a branch of mathematics, to compare the angles.

Perhaps one of the most interesting archaeological finds came from a shipwreck that was discovered near an island in Greece in 1900. The ship contained several statues and other items, or artifacts. The most important find was a device for calculating the movements of planets. At first, archaeologists thought that it was a mechanical clock. It took many years before a scientist discovered it was a device for calculating the movement of the sun, moon, and planets. It came to be known as the Antikythera (an-tee-KITH-er-uh) mechanism. Scientists believe that this was the first kind of mechanical computer!

The **most famous scientist of ancient Greece was Aristotle**. He studied and wrote about some aspect or topic in every scientific subject known at that time, such as botany, anatomy, embryology, entomology, geography, geology, meteorology, astronomy, ornithology, physics, and zoology. Aristotle also wrote about one or more aspects or topics in philosophy, politics, theology, education, and literature. Many scholars believe that he truly had "encyclopedic knowledge."

IV. Ancient Rome

The city of Rome was founded (according to tradition) by twin brothers Romulus and Remus in the year 753 B.C. The science of the ancient Romans was very different from that of the Greeks. The Greeks liked philosophy and abstract thought. The **Romans had their philosophers, but used science for practical matters, such as engineering and building**.

The Romans handed down many architectural designs that we still use today. One of these was **the arch**, a design which they learned from the Etruscans. The Etruscans were a civilization of people living in Italy before the Romans came to power. The Romans put the arch to use in new ways. It helped the Romans build bigger temples, amphitheaters, bridges, aqueducts, and the famous Colosseum.

You probably know what arches look like, but most people do not think about how they are used in construction. Take a look at the windows and doors in your home. You will notice that both of these are surrounded by small wooden beams. There may be small beams inside the wall too. Beams give support to the walls and ceiling that surround the windows and doors. If you removed the beams, the weight pressing down from the ceiling would cause these spaces to sag or collapse. Imagine what it would

Photograph of the Porta Maggiore ("Larger Gate") in the Ancient 3rd-Century Aurelian Walls of Rome

be like if you had to make a very large building but couldn't find beams that were large enough. Arches helped solve this problem. That is, arches were built to support weight. Arches can be found around windows, doors, and even roofs of very large buildings. Many churches built before the 1960s used arches in their design. Some of these arches surround and give support to stained-glass windows.

The **Romans are famous for building aqueducts**. Aqueducts are elevated bridges that transport water from mountainous areas into cities. The Romans made use of eleven aqueducts, totaling 500 miles in length! Aqueducts helped the Romans build their cities by providing people with fresh drinking water and bathing water. The science behind the flow of water in an aqueduct was complex. They had to understand the science, or the aqueduct wouldn't work. If the gradient was too steep, water would overflow the channel of the aqueduct. If the grade was too gentle, the water wouldn't flow downhill.

The Romans were the first people to design **indoor plumbing**. They channeled water from the aqueducts into palaces, houses, public fountains, and public baths. They had the best indoor drinking water! Water that wasn't suitable to drink was used in bath houses or for other purposes. Used or waste water was drained into underground sewers. The continuous flow of water from the aqueducts helped carry sewage and waste into the Tiber River, and then to the Tyrrhenian Sea. Many sections of this ancient sewer system still drain rainwater and sewage today!

Photograph of the Appian Way, by Paul Vlaar

The Romans also developed **high-quality bricks and cement**. These two inventions helped the Romans construct cities on a scale that had never been seen before. Bricks were made from molded clay that was heated in kilns. Most modern red bricks in the United States have a rectangular shape that measures 8 inches long by 4 inches wide. Most Roman bricks were very large, measuring 1-1/2 feet long by 1 foot wide. The Romans even made bricks in a variety of shapes and sizes: square, rectangular, triangular, and round. The largest bricks were over three feet in length! Cement was made from a type of volcanic ash called Pozzalana. It was a very durable cement; after more than 2,000 years, it still holds buildings together! Scientists believe that the quality of the Roman cement was similar to the cement we use today.

The Romans built the first paved roads. The **most famous paved road was known as the Appian Way**. The lowest level of the road was a leveled dirt road that was covered with small stones. Then mortar, a cement paste, was laid on top of these stones to hold them in place. Then gravel was placed on top of the mortar-stone foundation. Finally, interlocking stones, large flat stones cut and shaped to fit together, were placed over the top of the gravel. The road had a flat surface but was slightly crested or higher in the center. This allowed for the drainage of water into ditches on both sides of the road.

Many parts of the Appian Way have been preserved, and some parts are still in use today, even for car traffic! It truly is amazing that a road built over three hundred years before Jesus lived has survived for so long. Even our modern roads need regular repairs!

V. The Fall of Rome

The Roman Empire became very powerful and wealthy, but as often happens with such civilizations, the **wealthy and powerful leaders became corrupt in their personal lives and acted unjustly toward others**. The Roman leaders oppressed, overtaxed, and recklessly punished their own people. It was the Romans who had crucified the Lord Jesus Christ. Now, they blamed Christians for the problems of their civilization. They imprisoned and put to death, often by crucifixion, many innocent people, including women and children. Their civilization began to collapse 395 years after the birth of Jesus. Rome was completely destroyed in 476 by barbarians, almost 500 years after the birth of Our Lord. The barbarians were not builders and had no interest in learning, reading, planning, or building cities. They were not interested in science.

Rome had 28 libraries before the collapse and destruction of its empire by the barbarians. That might not seem like many, but this was a time when books were copied by hand! There were no printing presses. At least one library was left standing into the 6th century. It belonged to Pope Gregory, but even that was eventually destroyed by enemies.

Following the end of the Roman Empire, there were no schools or libraries in Europe. Neither was there any formal education or schools. People couldn't read or write, and they sank into chaos, confusion, or barbarianism. For some time, people in Europe would not enjoy the pleasures of living in any kind of civilized society.

VI. The Middle Ages

A. Legacy of the Saints

1. St. Patrick. The recovery of European civilization slowly began with the work of several saints. One of these was St. Patrick, who was born in Scotland in the year 385, about 350 years after the death of Jesus.

**Stained Glass of St. Patrick
Cathedral of Christ the Light
Oakland, CA**

When Patrick was fourteen, he was captured by pirates and sold as a slave in Ireland. He was forced to take care of herds of sheep, and spent most of his time in prayer.

After about six years, Patrick managed to escape and was reunited with his parents. However, Patrick felt sorry for the people of Ireland. He wanted to take the knowledge of God to them, so he attended a seminary in France and became a priest. Then he went back to Ireland to convert the people there. He is known for many miracles there, included getting rid of the snakes, which had so tormented the people. St. Patrick is famous for using a little green shamrock, a three-leaf clover, to teach the truth of the Most Holy Trinity: the Father, the Son, and the Holy Spirit—three Persons in One God. The Irish people loved Patrick, and he eventually became a bishop.

Perhaps most important to our study of the history of science is the fact that St. Patrick **established many churches and monasteries in Ireland. These were the first centers of Catholic thought and learning in Europe. The importance of the Catholic monasteries in the education of the nations of Europe cannot be overemphasized.**

The **monasteries and the schools** in them became very popular, and people from Europe poured into Ireland. **Thousands of foreign students sought an education in** the Irish monastery schools. Some would stay permanently. Others would eventually **pass on this knowledge to other people when they returned to their own country**.

The monks in the monasteries spent their time in study, prayer, farming, and copying books. Not all libraries and books were destroyed by the barbarians. A few libraries survived in both Europe and the Byzantine Empire (the eastern half of the Roman Empire). The Irish monks tried to acquire all the books they could. With great perseverance and determination, they **copied these books and manuscripts by hand**. Among these books were the Bible, literature of the Greeks and Romans, and the writings of Aristotle and other philosophers.

St. Patrick was responsible for the conversion of several European kings and their followers. His monks preached and converted thousands. St. Patrick preached the Gospel for forty years in Ireland, even working many miracles through the grace of God. He died on March 17, 461 A.D.

2. St. Benedict. Shortly after the time of St. Patrick, Europe produced another great saint, St. Benedict. He was born in Italy in 479 A.D. St. Benedict left his home at a young age. He joined a monastery and eventually started his own order of monks. St. Benedict is most famous for writing the *Rule of Saint Benedict*. It contained information on how to grow in the spiritual life and how to run a monastery.

St. Benedict had a strong influence on the nations of the early Middle Ages and is called the "Father of Western Monasticism." Pope Benedict XVI stated in a homily in April 2008 that "with his life and work, **St. Benedict exercised a fundamental influence on the development** of European civilization and culture." Other Catholic scholars credit St. Benedict for helping to **create spiritual and cultural unity**. This unity was responsible for the religious and intellectual development and growth of all of Europe.

3. St. Columbkille and St. Columbanus. St. Columbkille was born in Ireland in 521 A.D. and became a monk in 546. He was one of St. Patrick's successors. St. Columbkille went to Scotland, where he established and developed 60 monastic communities, which became centers of prayer and learning. During his lifetime, the **monasteries trained more than 3,000 monks!** These monks were almost warrior-like and fearless in their determination to convert the barbarians and ignorant people. When they left Scotland, the monks went in many directions.

One of the monks from the Irish monasteries was St. Columbanus. St. Columbanus was born in Ireland in 543 A.D. and, after being trained in an Irish monastery, he traveled across Europe as a missionary priest. He followed the example of St. Columbkille, establishing and developing monasteries. At the age of forty, he sailed with twelve companions to Gaul, or what is now known as France. He became popular for his sanctity and was welcomed everywhere. St. Columbanus **was critical of some Church leaders for their worldliness and laxity**. He eventually left Gaul and traveled to other countries, including Germany, Switzerland, and Italy. During his twenty-five years of service to the Church, St. Columbanus set up more than 60 monasteries and churches, though some believe the total was closer to 100!

B. Monks' Contributions to Science

The Catholic monks built their monasteries in remote areas, away from the towns. These remote areas were on land that many considered unusable. The monks became experts in clearing and greatly **improving these lands**. The monks used most of these lands for farming. They introduced **new crops, especially grains, fruits, and vegetables**. They also developed vineyards, made wine, and produced a new type of sparkling wine that came to be known as champagne. In addition, the monks contributed to the science of **beekeeping**. They kept bees for their honey and beeswax.

The monks reared and **improved the quality of cattle and horses** through controlled breeding and good nutrition. They produced **leather goods** and designed a special harness for horses. The monks learned that **horses could plow land faster** than other animals, such as oxen, which were being used by most farmers. Amazingly, the monks developed the modern **steel plow**. Steel plows easily turned the hard soil that was found throughout most of Europe. Using horses with a steel plow revolutionized agriculture throughout Europe and increased the production of food for everyone.

The monks learned to access **underground springs and developed water power through mills**. Water mills were used for crushing wheat, sieving flour, and tanning leather. They used water mills for a process known as **fulling cloth**. Before wool could be used for making clothing, it had to be pounded with wooden hammers. It was painstaking and time-consuming work. The use of water mills greatly helped **begin the industry of wool processing**.

The monks mined various ores and **made high-quality iron for forging**. They advanced the science known as **metallurgy** and produced a variety of useful **metal tools**. Many timekeeping devices had been made over the centuries, but the monks perfected the art of **clock-making**. They developed two mechanisms in clocks that we use even in our clocks today.

The monks in the Middle Ages **changed the lives of all people in Europe**. All of the above activities made people's lives easier. Improved methods in farming, textile or cloth manufacturing, and other industries, resulted in the growth of trade and commerce. Monasteries, churches, and cathedrals became the centers of learning and industry. Knowledge became organized and systematized and resulted in the **creation of universities**. Catholics established the first university in Bologna, Italy, in 1088.

The science that we have been discussing in this section is properly called **invention**. Most inventions result from people thinking about easier and better ways to perform certain tasks. People invent by using their reasoning skills, along with trial and error. This is not quite in line with the official definition of science we discussed earlier: the systematic knowledge or study of the physical or material world gained through observation and experimentation. People back then had a broader understanding of science than they do today.

In the early Middle Ages, people did not have the **scientific framework** used in modern science to probe, study, and understand the mysteries of the universe through experimentation and demonstration. Most people saw nature as mysterious. Many people believed that earthquakes, volcanoes, and other events could have been the result of some kind of randomness of nature. Most people could observe and study nature, but they did not have formal methods for performing scientific experiments and drawing scientific conclusions. That was about to change, but it would happen very slowly.

VII. The Birth of Modern Science

A. Robert Grosseteste

Robert Grosseteste, who lived from 1170 to 1253, was a graduate of Oxford University in England and was an English Franciscan professor and bishop. He was the **first man to write down the steps that were necessary for performing scientific experiments**. Bishop Grosseteste produced several important scientific works related to astronomy, ocean tides, mathematical reasoning, and optics.

Robert Grosseteste

B. St. Albert the Great

St. Albert the Great, who lived from 1206 to 1280, was a great philosopher, theologian, and bishop, who spent most of his life in France and Germany. He was famous for his vast knowledge of science, possibly from studying the writings of the monks who lived before him.

Strangely, during the time of St. Albert, scientists and religious did not get along very well. St. Albert knew that this was harmful for both the Church and society, especially since the Church was supporting education in the monasteries. As a remedy, he tried to promote harmony **between science and religion**.

C. St. Thomas Aquinas

One of St. Albert's pupils was the great theologian **St. Thomas Aquinas**, who lived from

Saint Albert the Great in His Study

1225 to 1274. St. Thomas Aquinas spent most of his time in France, especially in Paris. He did not give us better ideas about conducting experiments or developing theories. His legacy was more important: he gave the Church a better understanding of God the Creator.

St. Thomas believed that God made an ordered world. Humans were made in the image of God and, for that reason, were **rational** beings. This means people learn through **reason** (logical thinking), in which they think about concepts and put ideas together to solve problems. We can reason about many ideas, such as cause and effect, and the essence or nature of things.

St. Thomas Aquinas believed that God can and does reveal Himself through the natural world, which He created. When we study nature, we can learn about nature's Creator. Thomas believed that **if we use reason to understand the world, we learn more about God**, Who created the world. The more we learn about God and His world, the more we can realize His love for us, which helps lead us to love Him more.

Saint Thomas Aquinas

D. Roger Bacon

Roger Bacon, who lived from 1214 to 1294, was an English Franciscan professor known for his work in mathematics and optics (the study of sight and the behavior of light). Roger Bacon is often called the pioneer of the scientific method. He taught that argument could prove a theory, but experiments led to certainty and removed doubts.

In summary, it is commonly accepted that science had its roots in early civilizations. It moved forward, but was limited by people who did not recognize the true God and believed nature could not be understood. Catholic philosophy changed the way people looked at the world. The Catholic Church affirmed the truth that man is a rational being blessed with the ability to think and reason. Man can learn more about God's world by observing and studying His creation and using the science of logic to draw scientific conclusions. The Catholic Church's saints in Europe helped build the foundation for the science of today.

VIII. The Renaissance

The **Renaissance** was a cultural movement in Europe from about the 14th century to the 16th century. It was a time of change in art, music, and literature. It was a time when people wanted to think for themselves and work only for their own desires. Unfortunately, it was also a time when many people appeared who denied the truths of the Catholic Church and started their own religions. Some people claim that the Church hindered scientific research during the Renaissance. However, the truth is that the Catholic Church often sponsored scientists. It did this in two ways. The first was by **giving financial support to scientists**. The second was by **providing access to the Church's institutions, including the cathedrals, cathedral schools, and libraries where scientists studied**.

Copernicus was a famous astronomer.

Two of the most famous scientists who lived during the Renaissance were both Catholic: Nicolaus Copernicus and Galileo Galilei. Both were astronomers. Copernicus studied the works of the ancient Greek astronomers and began to consider that the planet Earth was not at the center of the solar system. After Copernicus' death, his work was studied by Tycho Brahe, Galileo Galilei, and Johannes Kepler. Their investigations led them to accept the work of Copernicus and the heliocentric theory that the Earth revolved around the sun.

IX. The Age of Newton: Development of Modern Science

Sir Isaac Newton lived from 1642 to 1727. He attended Cambridge University in England and later spent many years as a professor there. He became a member of Parliament, as well as president of the Royal Society of London. He was the most esteemed scientist of Europe at that time because of his discoveries, especially in the area of optics.

Newton was a physicist, mathematician, astronomer, philosopher, and theologian. He developed new theories and laws that completely transformed science. His work was truly revolutionary, and the world would never be the same.

You are probably familiar with the story of Newton watching an apple falling from a tree. He reasoned that the same forces that acted on the apple were the forces that caused the orbits of the sun and planets. This observation and others eventually led to the **formulation of the Three Laws of Motion**, which Newton published in 1657.

Sir Isaac Newton

Newton also made contributions to the study of geometry and algebra. He was the famous **inventor of a mathematical method known as calculus**. Calculus became useful in the sciences for studying rates of change and making predictions. Newton's mathematical discoveries made possible the future developments in modern science and engineering.

Newton also produced a **theory having to do with color**. In a dark room, Newton allowed sunlight to enter a prism. The light split into the colors of the rainbow. Next, he used a small device to allow one of the colors to pass from one prism and on through another. He found that the color remained the same after passing through the second prism. That is, it could not be split further into additional colors.

As Newton became older, he spent more time thinking and writing about religion and became a Biblical scholar. He was a very dedicated Christian and warned against only natural explanations for the working of the universe.

Newton was quoted as saying, "Gravity explains the motions of the planets, but it cannot explain Who set the planets in motion. God governs all things and knows all that is or can be done."

The great philosophers and scientists of the past gave modern science its foundation in reason, investigation, and trial-and-error experimentation. Logical reasoning freed man from the shackles of superstition. Reasoning made possible the many discoveries and advances in all scientific fields. The scientists of today rest on the shoulders of many great Catholic thinkers.

ACTIVITY (OPTIONAL)

Look in an encyclopedia or on the Internet with your parents for the following people listed in this chapter: St. Patrick, St. Benedict, St. Albert the Great, St. Thomas Aquinas, Roger Bacon, and Sir Isaac Newton.

Print out a picture or drawing of each person. Cut out the picture and put it in a scrapbook or paste it onto a 8 ½ × 11 sheet of paper.

Under each person, write at least five important discoveries or inventions. Accompany these with pictures that can be printed and cut out, then pasted next to the name of the person.

Adoration of the Trinity, **by Durer**

Chapter 1 Summary

1. God created the world out of nothing. As we study the world, we see order in His creatures and creation.

2. We see order in sunrises and sunsets. We see order in the seasons. We see order and design in flowers, birds, animals, stars, and everything in nature. We see order in the results of invisible things, such as gravity and electricity.

3. People desire order in their lives.

4. Science is a system of knowledge or study of the physical or material world gained through observation and experimentation.

5. Ancient Egyptians first began assembling bodies of knowledge in the areas of construction, astronomy, painting, and medicine. They found numerous uses for the papyrus plant and made some significant medical discoveries.

6. The Greeks made advancements in math, music, and astronomy. They explained the motion of the planets and even created a mechanical model to calculate their movement. Aristotle, was the greatest of the Greek thinkers, and wrote about everything from the sciences to philosophy and education.

7. The Roman civilization made advancements in architecture and the building of aqueducts and roads. However, when Rome fell to the barbarians, much of this knowledge was lost to Western Europe. Only with the rise of the monasteries did learning in the sciences and humanities once again take root and prosper.

8. The work of many saints, from St. Patrick to St. Thomas Aquinas, contributed greatly to the advancement of this knowledge and the growth of science. Even one of the fathers of modern science, Sir Isaac Newton, owes much of his learning to the achievements made by those who came before him.

Questions for Review

1. What is the official definition of *science*?

   System of Knowledge or Study of the Physical or Material world gained through observation.

2. What is the work of a scientist?

3. What were some ways the Egyptians used the papyrus plant?

To make baskets, bags, Mats, Santals, rafts and Sails,

4. Name three specific examples of Greek and Roman contributions to science.

_____

_____

_____

5. How did the rise of the monasteries of St. Patrick, St. Benedict, and others promote learning in Western Europe?

_____

_____

_____

6. Robert Grosseteste was the first man to do what?

To write down Steps that were necessary to perform Scientif Exprimeny

7. What did St. Albert the Great try to promote?

He Promoted harmony Bewteon Science and religion.

8. What did St. Thomas Aquinas say about the use of reason?

Thomas Said People learn through reason, in which Concepts and Ideas are used to solve Problems.

9. Name two ways the Church helped sponsor science during the Renaissance.

_____

_____

10. What were three of Sir Isaac Newton's achievements?

_____

_____

_____

The Scientific Method

I. **Observation, Hypothesis, and Experimentation**
   A. Method of Agreement
   B. Method of Difference
   C. Method of Concomitant Variation
   D. Experimental Controls
   E. Conclusions
   F. Repeated Trials
   G. Theory
   H. Laws

II. **The Limitations of Science**
   A. Spontaneous Generation
   B. Louis Pasteur
   C. Falsifiability

III. **Other Forms of Science**
   A. Natural Philosophy and Logic
   B. Pseudoscience
   C. Discoveries by Non-scientists

IV. **Scientific "Failures" in Our Time**
   A. Fleischmann and Pons
   B. Peer Review Process Necessary

V. **Who Wants to Be a Scientist?**
   A. Unique Passion
   B. Knowledgeable
   C. Science as a Way of Serving God

The Scientific Method

"And I proposed in my mind to seek and search out wisely concerning all things that are done under the sun…" (Ecclesiastes 1:13).

You read in the previous chapter that, throughout history, people have borrowed ideas and inventions from their ancestors. Advances in science proceeded in the same way. New scientific discoveries didn't just pop up out of nowhere. These new discoveries came from new knowledge, which was always built on an old foundation of past discoveries. If you could examine the historical lives of famous scientists, such as Newton, you would find that his peers were working on the same projects as he was—and at the same time!

At any given moment, many scientists are working on cures for the common cold, for cancer, and for various diseases. Other scientists are attempting to make important discoveries in biology, chemistry, computer science, geology, and physics. How can so many people be working on the same projects at the same time? This happens for two simple reasons. First, for so many scientists to be working on the same project, it must be very important to science, and to many people, to find an answer to a common problem.

The second reason is probably more significant. It takes a great deal of time and work to conduct scientific investigations. Scientists spend years of effort before solving a problem or making a breakthrough, which, within the scientific framework of empirical science, can come about only by using what is called the scientific method. This is a very slow process. When many people work on the same project, discoveries can be made more quickly.

I. Observation, Hypothesis, and Experimentation

The **scientific method** is the framework, or universal language, that enables scientists to gain knowledge, discover new insights, and draw scientifically verifiable conclusions in an organized, reliable way. **Scientifically verifiable conclusions** are formal conclusions that scientists can prove by reproducing their results through repeated experimentation.

The scientific method involves several steps. In the first step, a scientist makes accurate **observations** about a subject or problem. Second, the scientist spends a great deal of time thinking about how to solve the problem. Eventually, his reasoning leads him to describe the problem in a new way. This becomes the next stage and is called developing a hypothesis. A **hypothesis** is a *proposed explanation* (an educated guess) concerning how something works. Next, he or she designs and conducts an experiment, or many experiments, to test whether the proposed hypothesis is true.

You have probably heard about experiments before and may have conducted one in a science class. **Experiments** are a rigorous, precise, accurate, systematic type of trial-and-error process. Experiments involve changing the conditions or environment for the **subject** (whatever is being studied in the experiment). Generally, scientists recognize three types or methods of experiments: agreement, difference, and concomitant variation.

A. Method of Agreement

Scientists use the **method of agreement** to look for factors in which the different cases of a phenomenon or occurrence under investigation agree. They are asking, "What is a common factor present in all cases?" For example, during a flu epidemic in the winter of 2012-2013, the common factors present in the H3N2 strain of virus were a fever, sore throat, and cough.

B. Method of Difference

The **method of difference** is often used to investigate the development of new medicines. For instance, a scientist wishes to use laboratory rats to evaluate a new medicine. Two groups of rats receive the same amount of food and water, and are held under the same conditions. One group receives the drug, and the other doesn't. Any difference found between the two groups indicates that the drug caused the effect. However, to be certain that this conclusion is correct, all other factors must remain constant, except the single factor that is being varied (administering the drug, in this case).

C. Method of Concomitant Variation

So far, we have discussed methods where (1) a factor is present or absent, and (2) an effect does or doesn't occur. Sometimes, though, the scientist finds that either the factors or effects change, or vary. In these cases, the scientist wishes to **measure the amount of change**. He then uses the **method of concomitant variation** to determine whether changes in a factor cause changes in an effect. Using the example of laboratory rats again, in this case the scientist finds that the **effects** caused by the drug **increase** with increasing dosages of that drug.

D. Experimental Controls

Experimental controls are an essential part of all scientific investigations. Scientists use **experimental controls**, or **control groups**, as a basis for studying comparisons. Let's look at the above example with the two groups of laboratory rats. The group that received the drug is called the **experimental group**. The group that did not receive the drug is known as the **control group**.

Now, let's say that you didn't use a control group, and all of the rats became sick, and some of them died. Your first conclusion might be that the drug made them sick and caused death.

However, you do not know this for certain. So, you repeat the experiment, but this time you use a control group. You then observe that these too become sick, and some of them die. You begin to think, "Hmm, maybe they had a virus? Maybe their food was bad? Maybe their water was contaminated?" Clearly, you can see the importance of control groups within experiments. These help scientists determine whether an effect is due to their scientific experimentation or some other factor.

E. Conclusions

Setting up a *good* experiment takes a great deal of thinking and time. You may have noticed the emphasis on the word "good." This is because there are good experiments and bad ones. Good, or well-designed, experiments can lead to **reliable conclusions**. Bad, or poorly designed, experiments will lead to **error** or **faulty conclusions**. Surprisingly, most experiments begin as poorly designed. Almost always, as a scientist experiments, he notices things that he should have done differently. Here is when trial and error comes into the picture. The scientist rethinks his experiments and results, corrects his errors, or makes adjustments or changes.

F. Repeated Trials

The true scientist, the honest scientist, redesigns his experiment and his plans to conduct **repeated trials** or redesigned repetitions of the experiment. It is important that the scientist conducts more than a few trials. In fact, the true scientist conducts many, many trials, maybe even a hundred! Only in this way can the scientist improve his chances of producing consistent results. Many trials mean more data for analysis and improve the chances for reaching a reliable and consistent conclusion. Fewer trials mean less data and could result in the scientist reaching a preliminary or incorrect conclusion.

There have been some scientists who jumped to conclusions too soon, published their results from too few experiments, and were later proven wrong by other scientists who conducted the same experiments many more times, and came to different conclusions. Scientists who publish their conclusions too soon and are proved wrong damage their reputation so severely that they often lose their jobs and sometimes are pressured to move out of their country!

G. Theory

Once the scientist feels confident in his results and in his conclusion from the experiments he conducted, he moves on to the next step. The scientist spends a great deal of time thinking over his results and his conclusions. Perhaps he learns that his hypothesis is true. He uses these results to change the current scientist-accepted **theory**. A theory is another name for a *logical explanation* for how something works. If, on the other hand, his hypothesis was not true, then the current theory would not change. He rechecks his data. He begins to ask himself new questions. "Did I design the best experiment possible? Should I have changed something else?" Maybe the scientist consults with his fellow scientists to see if he overlooked something important. The scientist may continue to pursue his investigation with further experiments.

Now comes the exciting part in science. The scientist develops new concepts about his investigation. He sees some things more clearly, and sometimes in a fleeting instant, he discovers something new about his subject. Suddenly, he thinks to himself, "Aha!" The scientist abandons his old line of thinking and embraces a new one. He returns to his work with zeal!

You can see that discovering something new in science almost always results from so-called "failures." Failures are not really failures at all but the direct result of using the scientific method and proving something is not true. It is the way scientists learn whether something is true or false. Sometimes, too, we say that science is **self-correcting**. If scientists approach their work slowly and cautiously, then in time, they will correct their mistaken theories. This is how theories change, and truths become known.

By now, you can see how the gift of human reasoning is important to scientists. You don't have to be a scientist to use reasoning. We use it all the time. If your parents recently completed a household project, like painting or remodeling a room, ask them if they would have done anything differently if they did it again. Most likely, the answer will be yes. Almost everyone makes mistakes the first time he tries something. We are thinking and reasoning creatures, and we learn from our mistakes. How to deal with mistakes is the most difficult part about learning.

An easy way to summarize the above paragraphs is as follows. A scientist studies a subject and recognizes a problem. It is a starting point for an investigation. Next, the scientist forms a hypothesis, a potential solution. Then he or she tests the hypothesis with experiments, analyzes the data, draws conclusions, and possibly modifies the theory.

H. Laws

We have not yet discussed scientific laws. A **law** is a former theory that has consistently proven to be true over time. Laws are used to explain how something works. For example, we are familiar with the principle or law of gravity. We know that if we toss a baseball into the air, gravity will pull it back down toward the earth. We can even calculate and predict how fast it will fall.

II. The Limitations of Science

The scientific method is a tool for testing hypotheses. If a new hypothesis is true, the scientist develops a new theory from an older one. Does this mean that the older theory was incorrect? Sometimes it does. However, other times, it just means that the older theory did not completely explain something. The new theory may provide a clearer or more complete explanation.

A. Spontaneous Generation

Perhaps some of the above can be explained by a few famous historical examples. For example, for many centuries, people believed in a theory known as **spontaneous generation**. This theory meant that life can rise from non-living matter. In the 17th century, people believed that maggots or fly larvae formed or came to life from rotting meat. In 1668, a physician by the name of Francisco Redi set out to investigate this common theory. Redi placed raw veal and fish in several jars. He left half of these uncovered and exposed to open air; he covered the other half with gauze. In a few days, maggots began to appear on the uncovered meat and fish. He kept some of the maggots and allowed them to turn into adult flies. Maggots, however, did not appear on the jars covered with gauze.

Think about the above experiment for one moment. What did it prove? What didn't it prove? Well, it neither proved nor disproved the theory of spontaneous generation. Redi's work did, however, weaken the theory because it indicated that maggots came from flies—not from meat or dead fish. Despite this, the theory of spontaneous generation did not simply go away.

In the 1750s, a clergyman by the name of John Needham wanted to show that spontaneous generation was true. Like many people during his time, he believed that boiling something killed microorganisms. He boiled a flask of chicken broth and then sealed it. Microorganisms grew in the broth, and Needham believed that this proved spontaneous generation.

In 1768, Father Lazzaro Spallanzani, a Catholic priest, followed up on Needham's work. He believed that microorganisms came from the air. Father Spallanzani conducted the same experiment as Needham but changed one of the procedures. He boiled the broth, but before sealing the flask, he drew off the air by creating a partial vacuum. Then, he let the broth sit, and found that microorganisms did not grow. Again, this work did not satisfy some of those who believed in spontaneous generation. They claimed that his work merely showed that spontaneous generation could not occur without the presence of air.

B. Louis Pasteur

The theory of spontaneous generation continued to remain popular for some time. However, in 1859, a devout Catholic scientist by the name of Louis Pasteur challenged this theory. He repeated the above experiment, using two flasks. However, first, he made an important change to the glass tubes that attached to the flasks. He heated and then folded the flasks into S-shapes, with their ends pointing downward. In this manner, air could leave the flasks, but microorganisms could not fall inside. As you might guess, microorganisms did not grow in either of the flasks. In the next experiment, he removed the top of one flask so that air could enter. In a short period of time, the solution turned cloudy, which was evidence for contamination by microorganisms. Pasteur allowed the other flask to remain intact, and the solution never turned cloudy.

Louis Pasteur

Pasteur's experiment proved that microorganisms do not arise spontaneously. Microorganisms come from other microorganisms. He also demonstrated that a sterile solution will remain that way until it becomes contaminated. Following his experiment, Pasteur kept the flask and its sterile contents for years. It never turned cloudy. His famous experiment changed the way scientists thought about microorganisms.

As this historical example shows, some people will cling to their belief in a scientific theory, even when the evidence shows that this theory is false. Redi had shown that maggots came from flies. Father Spallanzani had demonstrated that boiling the solution and removing air prevented the growth of microorganisms. Pasteur's experiment produced the same results as Father Spallanzani's experiment, except Pasteur showed that microbes could enter a flask that was open. However, people do not like getting rid of their ideas or beliefs. In this case, the incorrect theory of spontaneous generation became an essential part of the theory or argument for those who currently believe in **evolution**. Has the so-called "theory of evolution" ever been proven to be true by the scientific method? No. However, the **theory of spontaneous generation**, upon which this "theory of evolution" rests, has been proven by the scientific method to be false.

C. Falsifiability

Scientists use experiments to reveal scientific truths. But here is a twist to our discussion about hypotheses and truth. It is important to understand that scientists do not discover truth by proving a hypothesis true. Rather, they learn truth by rejecting a hypothesis that has been proven false. This principle is known as **falsifiability**, or disproving. We can restate this as "a scientist gains knowledge *when he tests a hypothesis and it is shown to be false.*" For something to be considered scientific, a hypothesis must be capable of being falsified.

Let's look a little closer at the principle of falsifiability, using weather as an example. Let's say that each time you looked at the daytime sky in April, it darkened, filled with clouds, and then rained. So, you develop a hypothesis that rainfall follows the appearance of dark cloudy skies. During the following week, however, the sky darkens with thick clouds, but it doesn't rain. Your hypothesis, therefore, has been falsified. So, you modify your hypothesis: rainfall does not always follow the appearance of dark cloudy skies. Now, you must develop a different theory about dark cloudy skies and rainfall. You develop a new hypothesis and examine other factors. Hopefully, you now understand that science is the business of testing hypotheses.

III. Other Forms of Science

A. Natural Philosophy and Logic

The scientific method—and, hence, modern science—has its limitations. There are some things it cannot prove. For example, it is impossible to use the scientific method to prove (or disprove) that God exists. We believe in God because of His Revelation and our Faith, but we cannot use experimentation to demonstrate that He exists. This does not mean science has failed; nor does it mean that we cannot know with certainty that God exists. It simply means that proving the existence of God is outside the scope of modern science. We mentioned earlier that the official definition of science given in this book actually describes one kind of science, **empirical science**: "the systematic knowledge or study of the physical or material world gained through observation and experimentation." According to this modern view of science, in order for something to truly be considered science, it must be demonstrated through experimentation using the scientific method.

However, long before empirical science was formally developed, St. Thomas Aquinas defined science more broadly, stating: "it is the definition of science that from some known things other things are necessarily concluded...." If we use this broader definition of science, then we *can* prove scientifically that God exists. In fact, St. Thomas Aquinas did so in five different ways (see http://newadvent.org/summa/1002.htm). These proofs do not fall under the realm of *empirical* science, because they do not use the scientific method. However, they do use the sciences of logic and what is now called natural philosophy. **Natural philosophy** refers to the type of natural science that was practiced before the advent of empirical science, in which natural **reason** (logical thinking) is used to discover new truths on the basis of truths that are already known.

B. Pseudoscience

Some books, TV programs, and Internet sites discuss topics that are dressed up as science for the purpose of entertaining people. Chances are that most of this "entertainment science" contains partial truths, errors, or misleading information. Examples include unidentified flying objects (UFOs), space aliens, the Loch Ness Monster, and Bigfoot. To be fair, it is equally possible that all of these exist or do not exist. Some scientists believe in and investigate such subjects. However, if these scientists fail to test their hypotheses, then they are not using the scientific method. They also are not proving their conclusions using some other form of science, such as logic or mathematics. Therefore, we would refer to their investigations as **pseudoscience** (SUE-doe-sigh-ens).

One professor travels annually to Scotland, where he investigates the so-called "Loch Ness Monster." This professor has never seen the creature; but he has read the reports of those who say they have, and he believes in its existence. This professor is an accomplished scientist, but he will frankly admit that his studies regarding the "Loch Ness Monster" are pseudoscience.

C. Discoveries by Non-scientists

Before we move on to the next section, there is an additional point to be made. Quite often, the advancement of science depends on people who are not necessarily trained as scientists. Consider the following account.

A MAN SKILLFUL IN HIS WORK, BY DR. KENNETH STEIN

When I investigated the distributions of snakes in Egypt, our group hired one of the most knowledgeable "snake biologists" I have ever met. He knew where we had to go to find certain species of snakes. In our Land Rover, we would travel in the eastern Sahara Desert, along the canals of the Nile River, and near the tombs of the Pharaohs. As we drove, he would look for certain areas that, well, looked "snakey." We'd stop, get out of the car, and he would begin his search. He could tell one species from another by their tracks in the sand, and then he tracked them to their burrows. Upon finding a species of interest, he dug them (both poisonous and non-poisonous) from their burrows with great skill and caution. He developed his own techniques and was well-recognized for his abilities in Egypt. Sounds like a pretty accomplished scientist, right? Well, the man I discussed could neither read nor write. Although we wouldn't properly call him a scientist, he was clearly a well-respected expert. Our project would never have been completed without his expertise. This passage from the Bible comes to mind: "Do you see a man skillful in his work? He will stand before kings; he will not stand before obscure men" (Proverbs 22:29).

IV. Scientific "Failures" in Our Time

From what you have read so far, you can tell that science is a complicated subject. Certainly, there is more to it than testing hypotheses, developing theories, and so on. Like anyone else who works for a living, scientists must be good at what they do to earn a paycheck. If scientists are working on something important to those in authority, then pay raises, promotions, and prestige become part of their motivation to prove or disprove, or to make important discoveries. Sometimes these likely rewards put pressure on scientists and their sponsors to "speed up their work." After all, most people want to be popular and wealthy. As a consequence, scientists sometimes report preliminary conclusions without knowing that these conclusions are only preliminary.

In order to prevent preliminary conclusions from being advertised, whenever a scientist discovers something important, he must describe his complete investigation in a scholarly article. This is a very difficult process and occurs in several steps. First, he writes the article, which may take months. Second, he sends the article to the editor of a journal. In turn, the editor sends it to three or four peers, scientists in the same field of science, known as anonymous reviewers. They read, study, and evaluate the article. If the science appears sound, then the editor will publish the article. On the other hand, if the research arouses suspicion, then the editor will reject the article. The peer review process is like a filter. It screens out *faulty science* and allows *sound science* to pass through. This is the way modern science moves forward, that is, through the **peer-reviewed journal**. In the next section, we will review an example of what happens when scientists bypass the peer-review process.

A. Fleischmann and Pons

In March 1989, Martin Fleischmann and Stanley Pons held a press conference to announce that they could produce low-energy nuclear reactions through a small tabletop experiment. It was referred to as "cold fusion" and involved the electrolysis of water on the surface of an electrode. **Electrolysis** is a process by which water is broken down into hydrogen and oxygen. They didn't use ordinary water but water known as *heavy water*. It is rich in deuterium (dew-TEER-ee-əhm), which is a different form of hydrogen. The electrode was made from palladium (pəh-LAY-dee-uhm). This is a rare, expensive metal that is used in many things, including jewelry, collectors' coins, and catalytic converters in cars.

The research presented by Fleischmann and Pons was big news! It was going to solve all of our energy problems! The television and press interviewed scientists from all over the world. Many lay people began talking about their experiments. However, their research was doomed from the start. This was because they presented their findings in public, and not in a peer-reviewed journal. You can imagine that other scientists must have felt offended and angry at the time. Every scientist must go through the difficult process of peer review. Why not Fleischmann and Pons? The problems for these two men were about to begin.

Not too long after their press conference, many scientists tried to repeat the experiments of Fleischmann and Pons but failed. In addition, these scientists found errors. Fleischmann and Pons received much criticism and were ridiculed. They became the laughingstock of American scientists. The criticism continued for years. Both scientists eventually left the United States, humiliated, to work in Europe. This must have been very difficult for both men, especially Fleischmann. He was a past recipient of several awards for his scientific work. Without a doubt, he was an accomplished scientist.

B. Peer Review Process Necessary

Is there anything to learn from the experiments of Fleischmann and Pons? How does the world of science separate the wheat from the chaff, so to speak? In order for science to accept new theories, the results must be **consistent and reproducible**. Scientists who evaluated the work of Fleischmann and Pons found errors and were unable to reproduce their results. For these reasons, these scientists rejected the work of Fleischmann and Pons. But what about all of the time and effort put into this work by Fleischmann and Pons? Why would they spend so much time working on something that was incorrect? Well, this is the way science works. Quite often, scientists do not know enough about something that is new. Maybe Fleischmann and Pons didn't really know as much about their experiment as they led themselves to believe. Maybe they didn't use the best materials and instruments. If there is some truth to a new theory, then scientists will continue their investigations. Discoveries take a lot of hard work and thinking, and much time. In addition, new theories are always met with rejection. They could have spared themselves humiliation if they had followed the peer-review process.

Today, at least twenty science laboratories are working on similar experiments as those conducted by Fleischmann and Pons. These laboratory scientists are approaching their research slowly and cautiously. Many claim that they have observed a significant production of energy. They just haven't been able to produce consistent results. At the moment, no one knows why. It is interesting, though, that despite all the bad publicity, many continue to believe in the theory of cold fusion.

It is possible that sometime in the near future, we will see the fruits from the labor of these scientists and be able to produce power from low-energy nuclear reactions. Such an invention would surely transform our civilization. Can you imagine buying a laptop computer that has its own permanent energy supply? Or what if you could purchase a car that comes with a power supply that lasts three or four years? Once you exhausted the power supply, you would take it in for service and buy a new power supply.

The above paragraph is nothing more than speculation. By now, you can clearly see that it is the business of science to test hypotheses. We cannot predict the future. Only God knows what the future holds. If scientists eventually produce a reliable form of energy, then they will point to Fleischmann and Pons as the "new-energy pioneers." In all likelihood, they will show where they went wrong and what they could have done better. Of course, Fleischmann and Pons sacrificed their careers for their beliefs. Now, perhaps you are wondering, "Who would want to be a scientist?"

V. Who Wants to Be a Scientist?

A. Unique Passion

Most scientists are ordinary people, but they also have a unique passion for learning how something works. Perhaps they are fascinated with chemistry, rocks, birds, or trees. This passion stays with them, until one day they realize it is a calling. They want to study their hobby in a university. Now, they are at a point in which they will often spend ten or more years learning about their subjects. If being a scientist truly is their calling, then they will spend their lives learning about it.

B. Knowledgeable

All scientists must be knowledgeable in their fields. They must spend a good deal of time reading to stay current with various topics. Scientists also must have a unique character that allows them to patiently work through research that is mostly trial and error. As you know by now, scientific discoveries do not happen overnight. A scientist might spend an entire lifetime trying to discover a principle or solve a problem and never do so. This author knew a professor who went to his grave dissatisfied that he wasn't able to solve a certain problem. It is easy to see that months and perhaps years of failure are the result of many scientific investigations. Does that stop them? In most cases, no. For example, the disgraced and humiliated Fleischmann still continues his work on low-energy nuclear reactions. Who has the patience for this kind of work?

C. Science as a Way of Serving God

In your studies, you have learned that **God created us so that we can know Him, love Him, and serve Him, and be happy with Him forever in the next world** (*Baltimore Catechism*). But what exactly does it mean to serve Him? All of our daily activities should glorify Him, regardless of what we are doing and what stage of life we are in. You are probably familiar with the stories of saints who seemed to have worked tirelessly and effortlessly, often without eating or resting.

St. John Vianney comes to mind. His gifts were legendary and helped convert a great deal of people. We really can't compare his work with that of scientists, but there are some scientists who believe that their calling is all about serving God. They try to solve mysteries, work with great fervor, and sometimes give little thought to their own personal well-being. Certainly, these kinds of individuals have a vocation. Perhaps no one said it better than Johannes Kepler, the famous German astronomer. Describing his work, he once said that, "I was merely thinking God's thoughts after Him … it benefits us to be thoughtful, not of the glory of our minds, but rather, above all else, of the glory of God." You read earlier that scientists seek to understand something about the natural world. When we study nature, we can also learn more about God, the Author of all nature. All things were created by Him, and—whether or not they realize it—all scientists are led by His hand.

Chapter 2 Summary

1. Observation, hypothesis and experimentation are the three essential components of the scientific method. This method forms the basis for all scientific inquiry.

2. Scientists use the scientific method to study how data in their experiments agrees, differs, or varies, being careful to take into account each varying circumstance as well as experimental controls. Scientists analyze these results in order to reach a reliable conclusion about the natural world.

3. Through repeated trials and verification of results, scientists begin to form a theory, or logical explanation, about their subject matter. Theories, once shown to be consistently true over time, are considered law.

4. The scientific method, nevertheless, has its limitations; not all questions can be proved or disproved using empirical science. Some questions are better suited to the right use of reason or logic.

5. Some theories take a great deal of time to prove or disprove, since not all scientific experiments are perfectly designed. An example of this is shown by Louis Pasteur, who showed that microorganisms do not arise spontaneously. In so doing, he disproved nearly 200 years of accepted scientific theory.

6. Criticism of an experiment by other scientists, called *peer review*, is necessary. Scientists need to have a passion, knowledge, and a desire to serve God with their science.

Questions for Review

1. Define *observation*, *hypothesis*, and *experiment*.

   _____

   _____

   _____

2. What are the *method of agreement* and *method of difference*?

   _____

   _____

3. What is the *method of concomitant variation*?

   _____

   _____

4. What is an *experimental control*?

_____

_____

5. Explain the difference between a *theory* and a *law*.

_____

_____

_____

6. Who is Louis Pasteur? What did he do? Why is his work significant?

_____

_____

7. Explain the difference between empirical science and natural philosophy.

_____

_____

_____

8. Who were Fleischmann and Pons? What did they do?

_____

_____

_____

9. Why is the peer review process in science necessary?

_____

_____

_____

10. What are three personal qualities a scientist needs to have?

_____

_____

_____

Geology

I.   **The Unique Design of the Earth**

II.   **Journey to the Center of the Earth**

III.   **Forces and Movements**

     A.   External Forces

     B.   Properties of Solutions

     C.   Internal Forces

         1.   Subsidence

         2.   Uplift

         3.   Earthquakes

IV.   **Land Forms**

     A.   Mountains

     B.   Volcanoes

     C.   Plateaus

     D.   Hills

     E.   Plains

     F.   Valleys

     G.   Rivers

     H.   Lakes

     I.   Salt Domes

V.   **Maps**

VI.   **Rocks**

     A.   Sedimentary Rocks

     B.   Igneous Rocks

     C.   Metamorphic Rocks

VII.   **Identification of Minerals**

     A.   Streak

     B.   Luster

     C.   Magnetism

     D.   Cleavage

     E.   Hardness

Geology

"The Earth, though out of it comes forth bread,
is in fiery upheaval underneath" (Job 28:5).

The Earth is the third planet from the sun. Many scientists have spent a great deal of time searching for other planets like ours. These investigations are properly called **space exploration**. Every so often, newspapers and television programs report some new discovery of a planet far away in space. Astronomers, though, have been unable to find life on any other planet.

I. The Unique Design of the Earth

God created the Earth as a truly unique planet. When you examine many of the Earth's features, you can see that these features are in perfect balance. It is precisely the right size and weight. If our planet were smaller and lighter, the forces of gravity would be too weak to hold our atmosphere. The atmosphere is a thick blanket of gases surrounding the Earth. Without the correct force of gravity, the whole atmosphere would simply float away into space. If the Earth were larger and heavier, the gravity would be too strong to keep the atmosphere in its proper location around the planet. Heavier gravity from Earth would result in unbearably heavy pressure from the atmosphere. The planet Earth is exactly the right size and weight for the atmosphere to support human life.

The planet Earth is the perfect distance from the sun. If the sun were even slightly closer, the glaciers on our planet would melt, and too much water would evaporate. We would not have enough water to survive. On the other hand, if our planet were farther from the sun, the atmosphere would become cooler, resulting in extreme amounts of freezing. People, animals, and plants would freeze.

Photo of the Earth, by NASA

God created the speed at which the Earth rotates perfectly. The speed of the Earth's rotation is about 1,070 miles per hour. If our planet rotated any slower, then the days would become longer, and we would have more exposure to sunlight during the day and less during the night. People would be too hot during the day and too cold during the night. If our planet rotated any faster, this would result in very strong winds. In fact, if the Earth rotated too fast, it would break apart!

The moon is not part of the Earth, but the **gravitational pull of the moon** influences the planet Earth in several ways. The first way the moon affects our planet is by **tidal effects**. You are probably familiar with **tides** from the ocean and lakes. Tides, the rising and falling of water levels in oceans and lakes, are caused by the position of the moon in relation to the planet Earth. Have you thought about what happens on the land, on the continents, in response to the forces of the moon? Land cannot simply flow back and forth like water. Earth scientists believe, however, that the **pull of the moon's gravity deforms and changes the surface of the Earth**! Since the land cannot easily move, the energy resulting from the force of the moon's gravity on Earth is converted into heat. This causes **heating of the Earth's surface**.

Tidal effects on the oceans and lakes play an important role in influencing the long-term weather patterns on Earth. The weather that we experience day to day is due to ocean currents. These ocean currents form in the deep ocean, where cool and warm waters mix. Tidal effects from the moon cause the location of these currents to change. When these locations change, so too does the worldwide weather.

Besides the tidal effects, another way the moon influences the Earth is by **helping stabilize the Earth on its axis** and keeping it moving in the same direction. Remember that the axis of a planet is the imaginary line that each planet rotates around. When the Earth makes one full turn on its axis, we call it one day, a 24-hour rotation.

Planets without moons, such as Mercury, have a "wobbly axis." This means that the positions of the poles and axes change from time to time. This would be catastrophic if it happened on Earth. Imagine, for one moment, that you are living in a nice, somewhat temperate area of the eastern United States, such as the state of Virginia. Then one day, without warning, the Earth changes its position on its axis. You wake up and find that Virginia is now at the North Pole, or perhaps at the Equator. The Earth would continue to exist, but all living creatures would face chaos. God has arranged for the moon to prevent this from happening.

In summary, the four **features of the planet Earth—weight, distance from the sun, speed of rotation, and the gravitational pull of the moon—show the design of an intelligent Supreme Being, God**! Truly, the Earth is a remarkable planet and the only one of its kind in the whole universe, as far as scientists can tell. God made the Earth so that it would be perfectly suitable for all human beings, as well as the other living things that God put on the Earth for us.

II. Journey to the Center of the Earth

We can examine anything in nature and find that it is made up of small parts. For example, take something simple like water. A water molecule is made from hydrogen and oxygen atoms in a ratio of 2:1. However, there is more to it than that. If we dig deeper, we could examine the hydrogen bonds that link one molecule of water to another. We could investigate the properties of the atoms. Going one step further, we could examine the forces that hold the atoms together, and so on. Everything in science is like that. There is more to everything than first meets the eye. The planet Earth is no different.

We begin our journey to the center of the Earth with a review of its four layers: crust, mantle, outer core, and inner core. You can think of these as giant shell-like coverings that are sandwiched together in one giant ball. All four layers are distinct from one another. That is, each of these layers has unique structures and properties.

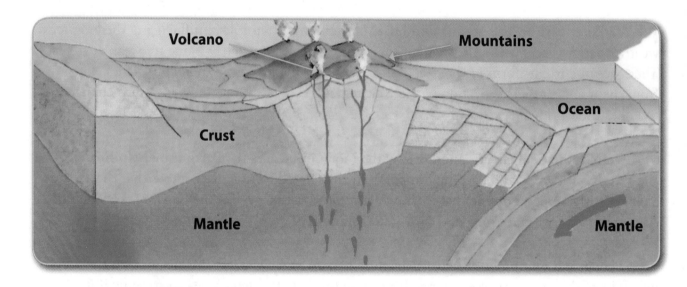

The **crust** is the outermost solid layer. There are two kinds of crust: continental and oceanic. Both of these originally formed from **magma**, or molten rock. We live on the **continental crust**, which ranges in thickness from 20 to 30 miles down from the top. The **oceanic crust** is found at the bottom of the oceans and seas. It is thinner than the continental crust, only about 3 to 6 miles down from the top.

The composition of the crust varies throughout the world, though more than one-half of the crust contains the compound silica, or silicon dioxide. We find silica everywhere on Earth: in sand, soil, sediment, and rocks. Silica is important in our daily lives. It is the main ingredient used to make window glass, bottles, cement, bricks, and the electrical components of computers and televisions.

We tend to think that the continents are covered with soil. Soil, especially fertile soil, is a gift from God. It makes the growth of plants and trees possible, and modern agriculture could not exist without it. Fertile soil is essential for our food and the food of animals. However, in many parts of the world, the outermost part of the crust consists of sand and rocks. These areas are generally very inhospitable—that is, not good for raising crops for food. Some people live in these areas, but they must struggle to find food and water.

Directly beneath the crust is a boundary area that separates it from the mantle. It is known as the Mohorovicic Discontinuity, or the **Moho.** The Moho was discovered in 1909. The Moho is called a boundary because it has a different structure than either the crust above it or the mantle below it. How do scientists know there is a boundary, when it is 20 to 30 miles below the surface of the Earth? They can test this hypothesis by studying earthquakes.

Earthquakes produce seismic waves, or seismic energy, that travel through the Earth. Scientists measure the speed and location of seismic waves with instruments known as seismographs. When a seismic wave travels through part of the Earth, it moves at a certain speed. The seismic wave will speed up or slow down when it enters an Earth layer having a different composition. By measuring these changes in speed, scientists know that the material in which the wave travels is different from the previous material.

Beneath the Moho is the **mantle**, the largest layer of the Earth. It is 1,800 miles thick, down toward the center of the planet. 1,800 miles is a little more than the distance between New York City and Denver, Colorado. The mantle begins beneath the Moho, and makes up 84 percent of the planet Earth's total volume.

The **outer mantle** consists of two layers: upper and lower. The upper layer and the crust together comprise the **lithosphere**. The lithosphere is rocky, hard, and responds to stresses or pressures by bending and breaking. It is not uniform, or one piece, but consists of huge rocky regions known as **tectonic plates**. Scientists recognize seven major tectonic plates within the planet, and several minor tectonic plates. The major plates are huge; some of them are the size of a whole continent, and some are even larger.

The lower layer of the outer mantle is called the **asthenosphere**. It is hotter than the lithosphere, and the rock is almost fluid-like. This property allows the lithosphere rock to "float" on top of the asthenosphere, much as ice floats on water. This fluid-like layer allows for the movement of the tectonic plates. The plates move, slide around, and spread apart on top of the asthenosphere.

Let's use a hardboiled egg to describe what we are talking about in regard to the lithosphere and the asthenosphere. In this example, consider that the eggshell is the lithosphere, and the egg white is the asthenosphere. Think for one moment what would happen if you dropped the egg on a table—say, from a distance of 2 feet. The eggshell would crack into many large and small pieces, yet remain intact, and bind or cling to the egg white. This is how you might think about the lithosphere and asthenosphere of the Earth "working together." Of course, you can see that the Earth is far more complex. Both the lithosphere and the asthenosphere are not stationary and move almost constantly.

The **inner mantle** lies directly below the outer mantle. It extends from 190 to 1,800 miles below the surface of the Earth. It is solid but very hot, with an average temperature of 5,400 °F. How hot is this temperature? Well, modern blast furnaces process iron ore at 3,600 °F. As you can see, the heat of the mantle is tremendous—almost 2,000 degrees Fahrenheit hotter than is necessary to melt iron ore! In some places, the inner mantle exists as a hot liquid known as **magma**. When magma (or molten rock) pushes to the surface of the Earth, it is called **lava**.

The next part of the Earth's interior is the core. The **core** consists of two layers, an outer core and an inner core. The **outer core** is molten rock that contains mostly iron and nickel. The temperature of the outer core is much hotter than the mantle and ranges from 7,200 degrees to 9,000 degrees!

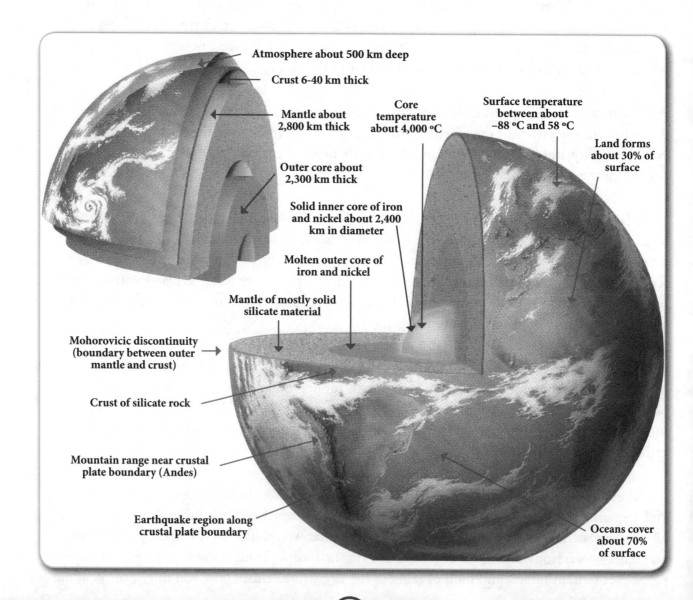

Atmosphere about 500 km deep

Crust 6-40 km thick

Mantle about 2,800 km thick

Core temperature about 4,000 °C

Surface temperature between about −88 °C and 58 °C

Land forms about 30% of surface

Outer core about 2,300 km thick

Solid inner core of iron and nickel about 2,400 km in diameter

Molten outer core of iron and nickel

Mantle of mostly solid silicate material

Mohorovicic discontinuity (boundary between outer mantle and crust)

Crust of silicate rock

Mountain range near crustal plate boundary (Andes)

Earthquake region along crustal plate boundary

Oceans cover about 70% of surface

You may be surprised to learn that the outer core, though deep within the planet, is very important to life on Earth. The outer core produces the Earth's **magnetic field**, which protects us from harmful cosmic radiation. In addition, many living creatures use the magnetic field for navigation. As incredible as it may seem, God gave these creatures internal compasses.

Although scientists do not know much about these internal compasses of creatures, they do know that the brains of some organisms contain **magnetite**. From your earlier science classes, you might recall that magnetite (or lodestone) contains iron and is naturally magnetic. In fact, it is the most magnetic naturally occurring mineral on Earth! This might explain the annual migration of birds that travel long distances between continents to the same locations year after year.

Within the outer core is the inner core. The **inner core** is composed of iron and nickel. These are the same elements that make up the outer core. The temperature of the inner core is very high, varying from 9,800 to 10,800 degrees. Even though these are extremely high temperatures, the tremendous pressures deep inside the Earth keep this inner core layer in a solid state.

ACTIVITY: Scientific Drawing and Model Building of the Earth

Crust

Mantle

Inner Core

Outer Core

DIRECTIONS: First, provide a detailed drawing of the Earth that depicts the four basic parts. Then, take four different colors of **clay**, to represent each section of the Earth, and construct a model of the Earth. When you have the layers built into a sphere, cut into the sphere with a sharp knife and remove a pie-shaped section of the "Earth." The layers should be exposed.

III. Forces and Movements

The Earth's crust is continually exposed to a combination of external and internal forces. The Earth's crust responds to these forces by twisting, folding, breaking, and wearing down. Some forces happen over long periods of time and are gentle forces. Other forces are sudden, immediate, and catastrophic, and sometimes cause the loss of human life.

Folding

A. External Forces

External forces include the actions of water, ice, wind, and gravity that wear down the Earth's surface and change its structure. Perhaps erosion is one of the best-known external forces. **Erosion** is the movement of rocks, soil, and other particles by wind, water, ice, and gravity. **Wind erosion** occurs mainly in desert regions. Powerful winds can carry large amounts of sand and, in the process, wear away rocks. **Flooding** accompanies heavy rainfall. Fast-flowing water travels to lower elevations via ditches, creeks, and rivers. The water carries small particles of sand, gravel, and other debris. The faster the water moves, the more material it can carry. If the volume of water is large, it carries larger materials such as rocks and boulders. All of these water-borne materials may permanently change the surface of the landscape and cause soil loss.

Mudslides are a catastrophic type of erosion that often and suddenly follow heavy rains, spring thaws, or volcanic eruptions. When mudslides happen, the effects can be disastrous. Houses, businesses, and entire communities may be destroyed. An entire mountainside may be lost forever. Although powerful storms such as hurricanes, cyclones, and typhoons are in the news all the time, mudslides take more human lives each year than all of these storms combined.

Mudslide
(Photo courtesy of the US Forest Service)

Weathering is the breaking down of rocks. It is similar to erosion, except that weathering can occur with no movement. There are two kinds of weathering: chemical and mechanical. **Chemical weathering** breaks down rocks by changing their composition. For example, when rainwater falls, it absorbs carbon dioxide from the air and forms a weak solution of carbonic acid. When it falls on the landscape, this weak acid slowly dissolves limestone and other minerals. You may have seen the actions of chemical weathering on old statues, tombstones, or even concrete. These wear down and eventually start to break apart, because they have been chemically weathered or degraded.

Chemical Weathering of Metal Springs

Mechanical weathering involves the freezing and thawing actions of water. When water falls into the cracks of rocks and then freezes, it expands. This causes tremendous pressure on the rock, which then breaks into smaller pieces. You can see the results of mechanical weathering when you travel along roads through passes where large mounds of rock have been removed to make way for the road. As you pass between these walls of rock, you might see small rocks and boulders on the ground. These are the result of mechanical weathering and, of course, gravity.

B. Properties of Solutions

You may conduct the following two experiments or activities. Both of these have to do with the properties of solutions: carbonated water, and water that comes from several sources.

When we study the properties of a solution, we typically wish to know whether it is an acid, a base, or neutral. When we think of an acid, we think of something very sour or sharp in taste, such as vinegar. An example of a base solution is baking soda in water. We can determine whether something is an acid or a base by using a strip of pH paper called **litmus paper**. Litmus paper turns red when dipped in an acid, and turns blue when dipped in a base. Another kind of pH paper is called **alkacid (or universal) paper**. Alkacid paper changes color when dipped in a solution as well. However, in this case, fourteen different colors are possible, each corresponding to a particular pH value.

What then is pH? It is the measure of **hydrogen ions** (electrically charged particles of hydrogen), or H^+, in a solution. Pure water, such as distilled water, is neutral and has a pH of 7. It is neither an acid nor a base. Acids or acidic solutions have a pH of less than 7. Some examples of common acids that you might find in your home include lemon juice and cola. Bases or alkaline solutions have a pH greater than 7. When household items such as laundry detergent and soap are mixed with water, they produce alkaline solutions.

ACTIVITY: Testing the pH of Water from Creeks, Streams, Ponds, and Rain

MATERIALS: alkacid pH paper strips, bottles, glue

PROCEDURE:

1. Collect one bottle of water from each of three to five different locations.

2. On a sheet of paper, write down the source from which you obtained each sample of water and your observations about the water, such as the color and clarity.

3. Dip one strip of pH paper into your first water sample. What color is it? What pH value does it correspond to on the indicator chart? Record your observations and results. Repeat these procedures using a separate strip of pH paper for each water sample.

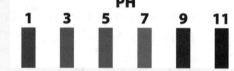

4. Dry and then glue the strips onto this page.

OBSERVATIONS:

1. Paste your dried pH paper strips here. Be sure to record the source of the water.

LOCATIONS: 1.   2.   3.   4.   5.

1. _____

2. _____

3. _____

4. _____

5. _____

DESCRIPTIONS: Describe the water from each location: Hint: Is it cloudy, clear, yellowish, light brown, or greenish?

1. _____

2. _____

3. _____

4. _____

5. _____

C. Internal Forces

1. Subsidence. There are many forces and movements that shape our planet Earth. **Gravity** is the force that pulls everyone and everything on Earth down to the ground—or, to be more precise, toward the center of the Earth. Gravity is a powerful force that works with other processes to shape the Earth. **Subsidence** is the sinking movement of the Earth's surface. Subsidence may result from natural causes. One of these causes involves huge, heavy **glaciers** pressing down on the ground, causing the land to sink far below its normal position on the landscape. Another cause shaping the Earth is the enormous **deposition of silt** along the banks and deltas of rivers. The weight of the heavy silt pushes down and causes the land to sink.

Finally, subsidence is caused by the **chemical weathering** of limestone below the surface of the ground. Through the actions of acidic groundwater, the limestone dissolves, resulting in the formation of **caves**, or caverns. Two popular caves in the United States are Carlsbad Caverns in New Mexico and Mammoth Cave in Kentucky. Sometimes, however, the ground's weight above the cave is so strong that the cave collapses. This results in the formation of a **sinkhole**. You may read about sinkholes from time to time. They sometimes swallow up cars, homes, and entire sections of neighborhoods!

Subsidence is also caused by the **activities of people**. Mining of coal, natural gas, and other materials creates empty spaces underground. Like the above examples, the force of gravity pulls the land above these empty spaces downward, and causes the land to sink. Perhaps the most well-known type of subsidence occurs in areas where farmers use groundwater to irrigate their crops.

Groundwater comes from rainfall that percolates or trickles downward deep into the ground. It accumulates and is stored in natural wells called **aquifers**. In the absence of irrigation, the groundwater remains balanced and gives support to the land above it. Farming, however, changes this balance. The groundwater is removed but not replenished. This causes the land above to sink down into the space below.

Let's explore subsidence using a familiar example. Have you ever dug a hole in the sand at the beach? You started off digging a small hole. As you dug deeper, you noticed that the sand was packed down and very wet. You kept digging until the hole began to fill with water. Without fail, the sides of the hole began to collapse. This resulted in a wider hole. You kept digging, trying to remove as much material as possible. The sides kept collapsing, and you ended up with an even wider hole. Using this example, you can see that the water holds the sand together and supports the sand above it. If it didn't, you would be able to dig straight down without the hole collapsing. This is an example of how subsidence works, but on a very small scale.

2. Uplift. The opposite of subsidence is uplift. **Uplift** is the rising of land and is caused by one of two processes. One process involves the **collisions of tectonic plates**. In this case, the huge plates of rock below the surface of the Earth push against each other, and one plate rises over the other. When this occurs, it increases the elevation of the land. If the increase is great, it causes the formation of mountains or hills.

Uplift can also occur as a result of the **melting of glaciers** or the **erosion of materials from mountains**. In both of these examples, the loss of weight, in effect, causes the surrounding landscape to rise.

3. Earthquakes. Finally, let's discuss **earthquakes**. Earthquakes occur in areas throughout the world where there are **faults** (or cracks) in the Earth's surface. Faults may range in length from several inches up to hundreds of miles. Scientists who study earthquakes believe that earthquakes are the cause of faults. How do earthquakes occur? As large layers of rock move and collide with one another, many under the crust of the Earth, they build up stress. At some point, the rock layers break or fracture, and the result is a fault, or crack, or the sudden release of seismic energy (or earth vibration), which is an earthquake.

The San Andreas Fault of California is a very good example of an area that is prone to having earthquakes. This fault marks the boundary between two tectonic plates: the Pacific Plate and North American Plate. These plates continually slide past each other, moving as much as 2 inches per year. If you ever have the chance to see California from an airplane, perhaps you will take the time to look for this famous fault. It is 810 miles long and runs almost the entire length of California!

The marks on this utility pole indicate the level of the surrounding land in preceding years. Between 1925 and 1977, this part of the San Joaquin Valley subsided almost 9 meters because of the withdrawal of groundwater and the resulting compaction of sediments.

Aerial photograph of the San Andreas Fault
(Courtesy of US Geological Survey)

We have completed our review of the forces that work to **change** the Earth's landscape features. In the next section, you will learn how these forces work to **produce** new land forms, such as mountains, volcanoes, plateaus, hills, plains, valleys, rivers, and lakes.

IV. Land Forms

A. Mountains

Mountains are large land forms that rise above the surrounding land, usually in the form of peaks. Mountains form by several processes but typically result from the collision of two continents or tectonic plates. One continent or plate uplifts (or rises) above the other. How fast these collisions occur will determine the kind of mountain that forms. When the collisions happen over a long period of time, the rocks do not break, but they bend, or fold. These are called **fold mountains**. They have the appearance of a wrinkled carpet when viewed from an airplane. Fold mountains are the most common type of mountain and include the Appalachians in the eastern United States (such as in Virginia and West Virginia), and most of the Rocky Mountains in the western United States.

When collisions between plates occur over a short period, the rocks are unable to relieve the stress. They break rather than fold, and result in **fault-block mountains**. Fault-block mountains look like large blocks, have steep slopes, and are craggy. The majestic Sierra Nevada Mountains of Nevada and California are fault-block mountains.

A good place to view the structure of fold and fault-block mountains is where construction workers have removed parts of mountains to make room for new roads. These areas are treasure troves for geologists because the carved-out walls of rock show excellent detail of the rock layers in mountains. Geologists use the layers to describe the principle of **superposition**. This principle means that layers of rock are deposited in a time sequence, with the oldest on the bottom and the youngest on the

Faulting: Notice that the layers of the dirt and rock are the same on both sides of the fault. By observing these layers, we can see that the fault motion was upward and to the left for the left side, and down and to the right for the right side.

top. This sounds pretty reasonable and is fundamental to studying rock layers. However, recent research following the volcanic eruption of Mount St. Helens in the state of Washington showed that this principle is not always true. Scientists reported finding several large layers that were laid down together – at the same time!

The finding at Mount St. Helens indicates that rock layers can form quickly. In addition, geologists have learned a sequence of layers in one part of the world, yet found the layers reversed in another part of the world. Scientists admit that movements of the Earth's crust, such as folding and faulting, can result in older layers of rock pushing and rising above younger layers. This shows that the principle of superposition is sometimes unreliable as a means of dating rock layers.

**Mount Saint Helens
(Photo courtesy of US Forest Service)**

ACTIVITY: Geology in Your Own State

Many states have books entitled: *Roadside Geology*. Check for a book for your own state at your library. These books are excellent resources for exploring the geology in your area and other areas when you travel.

ACTIVITY: Folding and Faulting

Perhaps you can better understand the processes of folding and faulting with modeling clay. Take the clay and mold it into three small rectangles, say, 4 by 6 inches. It might be helpful if you have three different colors of clay. Lay these rectangles on top of each other. Now, slowly push the long ends toward each other and observe how wrinkles or "folds" begin to appear. This demonstrates the process of folding. Next, take the wrinkled clay layers and stretch these out to their original, rectangular shapes. Obtain a small wooden block or brick and place it on the table. Position one part of the clay on the block and leave the other part hanging down. With your hand, push down on the layers, near the edge of the block. For a short period, the clay stretches and folds. Eventually the layers break apart, and a "fault" appears.

B. Volcanoes

Volcanoes are openings in the Earth's crust that allow magma (molten rock), ash, and gases to escape to the surface from far below the surface of the Earth. Once magma escapes through a volcano and flows down to the surrounding land, it eventually cools and hardens. The volcano then becomes a **depositional mountain** that forms by the accumulation of once-melted rock on the Earth's surface. When magma forces its way to the Earth's surface, it pushes the rocks above it upward. This process may occur repeatedly over a long period of time.

Sometimes a volcano explosively erupts and leaves a large gaping hole known as a central vent. The vent is surrounded by rocks and debris, which create a formation known as a **cinder cone**. Once the volcano has erupted, it may stay active, or it may become dormant. In either case, it remains a mountain. Mount St. Helens in the state of Washington erupted on May 18, 1980. At that time, few people could have imagined the possibility of such a catastrophe happening in the United States. In fact, 57 people died from the eruption. Although this was a terrible disaster, scientists did learn a great deal about many geological processes by studying the area around Mount St. Helens.

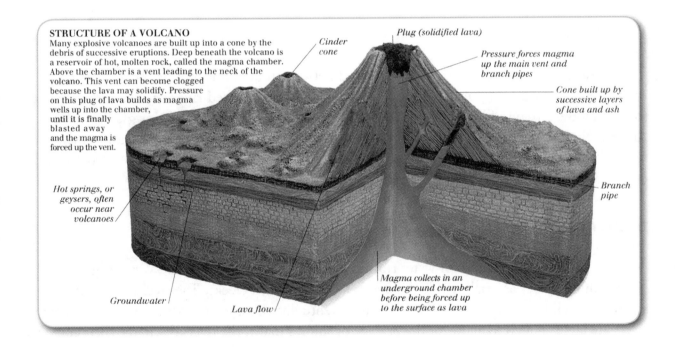

STRUCTURE OF A VOLCANO
Many explosive volcanoes are built up into a cone by the debris of successive eruptions. Deep beneath the volcano is a reservoir of hot, molten rock, called the magma chamber. Above the chamber is a vent leading to the neck of the volcano. This vent can become clogged because the lava may solidify. Pressure on this plug of lava builds as magma wells up into the chamber, until it is finally blasted away and the magma is forced up the vent.

Cinder cone

Plug (solidified lava)

Pressure forces magma up the main vent and branch pipes

Cone built up by successive layers of lava and ash

Branch pipe

Hot springs, or geysers, often occur near volcanoes

Groundwater

Lava flow

Magma collects in an underground chamber before being forced up to the surface as lava

C. Plateaus

Plateaus are regions of flat rock that are found at high elevations. Sometimes plateaus have steep slopes. In the geological past, erosion removed sections of plateaus, resulting in two distinct formations: **mesas** (MAY-suhs) and **buttes** (byootz). Both of these are flat-topped hills having steep, vertical walls. They differ in that mesas are broad and buttes are narrow.

D. Hills

Hills are like mountains and form from similar processes. In fact, most people cannot tell the difference between the two. Not geologists but botanists (plant scientists) tell us whether a land form is a mountain or a hill. If the kinds of plants at the bottom of the land form are different from those at the top, it is a mountain. If the kinds of plants at the top and bottom are the same, it is a hill.

E. Plains

Plains are flat or mostly flat regions of land. They are found in coastal areas but also may be located inland. Plains form by several processes, including the erosion of mountains and hills. The products of erosion, sand, and rocks and debris are transported and deposited at lower elevations. The Atlantic Coastal Plain in the eastern United States formed in such a manner. The Atlantic Coastal Plain is a very large plain, which ranges from Nova Scotia in Canada down to the state of Florida. The Great Plains region is another large plain of the United States. This region extends from the Mississippi River to the Rocky Mountains and up through Canada. The fertile soil in the Great Plains supplies a large part of the world with food.

F. Valleys

Valleys are long, low areas, usually located between mountains or hills. There are two types of valleys: V-shaped and U-shaped. V-shaped valleys are called **river valleys** and were once formed by the erosion of land by flowing rivers. U-shaped valleys are known as **glacier valleys**. At some time in the past, a glacier covered the entire valley. When the glacier began to melt and retreat, or move, it carved out the valley. Besides the U-shape of the valley, boulders, rocks, and other debris deposited by the melting glacier are signs of past glacier activity.

G. Rivers

Rivers are the pathways for water running from high to low elevations. Water begins its downhill journey as small trickles before collecting in small creeks. The creeks empty into streams, which then gather into larger streams. Eventually, the streams empty into rivers. Some rivers are large enough to allow for the passage of ships. Finally, the rivers discharge their contents into mouths or deltas. These are the entry points for water into lakes or oceans. The Mississippi River is the third largest river in the world and drains 40 percent of the continental United States.

H. Lakes

Lakes are depressions in the land that hold either fresh water or salt water, in addition to many life forms. Some lakes are man-made, usually for the purposes of supplying electric power, drinking water, or recreation. However, most lakes are natural, and there are more than fifty ways in which they can form! Many lakes, including the Great Lakes in the eastern United States, were produced by the actions of glaciers. Imagine, for one moment, a huge mountain of ice that was capable of scooping out the very large region that we know as the Great Lakes. This area is not only wide but deep as well. Lake Superior is the largest of our five Great Lakes and has a maximum depth of 1,332 feet! Look at a map to see the five Great Lakes.

Some natural lakes are made when a **rock slide** dams a stream and water fills in the cavity or hollow. Filling a hollow with water does not necessarily result in the formation of a lake. The area must have a suitable clay or rocky bottom to hold the water and keep it from leaking out. Another way by which lakes form is through the actions of one of God's creatures: the beaver. With their razor sharp, chisel-like teeth, beavers cut down trees and shrubs. These float to specific areas of a stream, and the beavers pack these materials with mud. In a short time, they build their dam and a lake forms. Sometimes this causes trouble with homeowners.

Dr. Kenneth Stein relates the following story: "I remember living in an area where beavers constructed a dam. Within a short time, the water in a very slow moving creek backed up and formed a small lake. It caused flooding on the roads and properties of several families. The homeowners destroyed the dam, but the beavers rebuilt it once again. This happened several times until they trapped the beavers and relocated them elsewhere. However, the beavers journeyed back to the same area and continued the job for which they were designed, making lakes!"

ACTIVITY

You can experiment with different materials to see which would make a good lake bottom. Use a flat piece of clay to make a bowl. Does it hold water? Try the same with sand. Does it hold water? For a lake to form, the bottom must be sufficiently solid to hold the water. Also, with your parents, find and print out colored photos of each kind of land form.

I. Salt Domes

Salt domes are land forms that appear as hills on the landscape. Many years ago, salt water became trapped within areas known as marine basins. Salt crystals began to form when the water in the basins dried up. Again and again, the basin filled with salt water and dried up. This cycle may have happened many times. Over time, the salt was buried under other sediment, such as sand and debris. However, because salt is lighter than the sediment or land surrounding it, the salt pushed up to the Earth's surface while the heavier sediment pushed down. This produced a shape like a dome. Salt domes contain more than salt, however. They possess large quantities of sulfur, crude oil, and natural gas. Because of the oil and gas, salt domes are a very important natural resource.

V. Maps

Mapmaking (or **cartography**) has its roots in ancient times. It involves methods for displaying information and features about a landscape. Cartographers use the term **spatial representation** to describe these displays. Today, nearly all maps are produced by computers using software that is known as **Geographic Information Systems** (**GIS**).

Relief is the measure of elevation differences in a region. Mountains are described as having high relief, and plateaus and plains as having low relief. We can better understand this concept by viewing **relief maps**. These maps show changes in elevation by curved or wavy lines known as **contours**. Each contour represents a collection of points for a given elevation. Sometimes, too, relief maps depict changes in elevation by colors or shading. Users can view a map and understand not only its elevation but also its ruggedness. Relief maps are important tools for surveyors, engineers, foresters, geologists, the military, and hikers. Geologists use maps that show the elevation of land but also the locations of ores, minerals, mines, wells, soil type, archaeological sites, and water. Because of the demand for less expensive fuels, geologists are very much in demand by governments.

You will learn to make two types of maps: a flat distance map and a topographical map. The **flat distance map** is used for describing local, small distances among features on a landscape. Typically, the flat distance map shows a point of view that "looks down" from above the mapped region. The neighborhood pictured below is an example of a flat distance map. It might look like this:

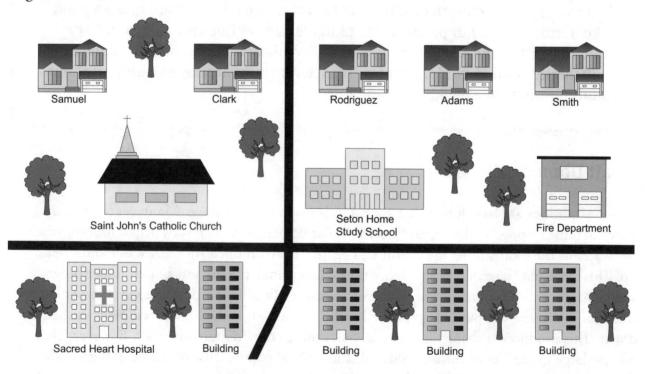

Example of a Flat Distance Map of a Neighborhood

In the next activity, you are to make a map of your room using a ruler and graph paper. This is fairly easy to do. In the second activity, you will need a different technique called **pacing.** To pace accurately, you will need to know the average length of your stride. Geologists who must measure a large distance sometimes use pacing for measuring.

ACTIVITY: Making a Map of Your Bedroom

Make a map of your bedroom on a separate sheet of paper, preferably a sheet of graph paper. Use a ruler to figure out the actual size of your bedroom. Then figure out how many inches, or part of an inch, or squares on the graph paper, would represent a foot of your room. Then draw the walls of your room. Then measure your closet, your bed, your dresser, or other furniture. Figure out what fraction of an inch these items would measure on your ruler in relation to the size of the room. If you are using graph paper, it is even easier to figure out the number of squares you need to represent the closet and the furniture.

ACTIVITY: Making a Map of Your Yard

MAP MAKING: Pacing

DRAWING: Your yard

Begin at a sidewalk or other straight path. Make a mark on the ground with chalk at your toes. Take ten normal steps. It is important that you walk with an even stride and in a straight line. Begin walking with your left foot, walk ten paces, and end with your right foot. Mark the ground at your toes at the end of your tenth step. Measure the distance between the two marks. Divide this number by ten. This is the average length of your stride. Now, you are ready to do the next activity.

The distance of ten of my paces equals how many feet: _____

My average pace is how many inches: _____

Draw a map of your yard using your average pace. After you pace off the boundaries of the yard, you will know the dimensions of the yard in feet. Convert the feet into inches or fractions of inches for the map paper. Next, fill in the major parts of the yard like plants, lawn furniture, and toys. Include your gardens. If the yard is too large, map only a portion of it.

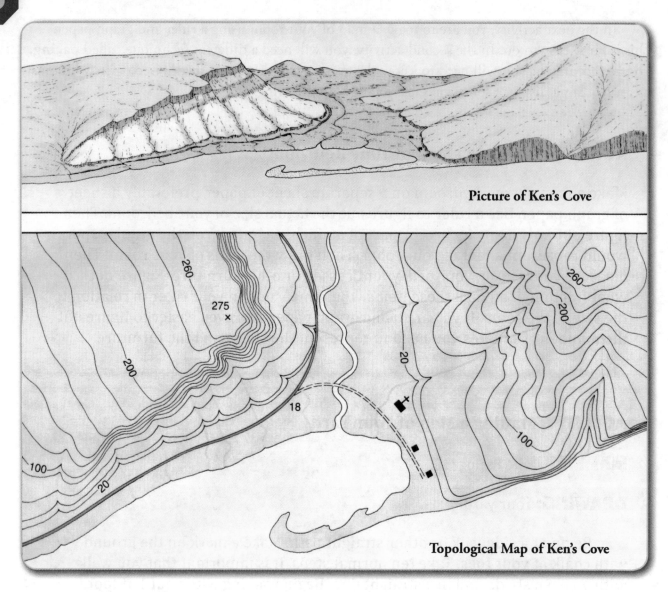

Picture of Ken's Cove

Topological Map of Ken's Cove

The illustration above shows the use of contour lines. To draw a topographical map, you must follow a certain set of rules. These rules guide the placement of the contour lines:

1. Contour lines connect only points of equal elevation.

2. The lines must point up toward the source of a stream. You can understand this if you imagine what it would be like to walk along a stream in a hilly area. If you walked upstream, you would walk toward the source. On the other hand, if you walked downstream, you would walk away from the source.

3. Concentric circles begin to increase in number toward the top of a hill, or hilltop.

4. When the slope of a hill is very steep, we say that it is a cliff. Cliffs are shown on a topographical map by several contour lines that are close together.

5. With your parent, find a topological contour map of a familiar location.

Muir Inlet, Alaska. What do you think the topological map might look like for this inlet?

Contour Line Exercises

The next four pages contain points with numbers. Keep the following steps in mind when you complete the topological maps for these four pages:

1. In the first exercise, you will connect the points of similar elevation to form contour lines.

2. In the second exercise, you will connect the points of similar elevation to form contour lines with hills and dips.

3. In the third exercise, you will connect the points with like numbers to form contour lines with cliffs and beaches.

4. In the fourth exercise, you will connect the points with like numbers to form contour lines with streams, cliffs, beaches, hills, and dips.

As you complete each of these four exercises, notice the geographical feature shown by the contour lines.

J.M.J.

MAPMAKING: Contour Lines

DIRECTIONS: Connect the points of similar elevation to form contour lines.

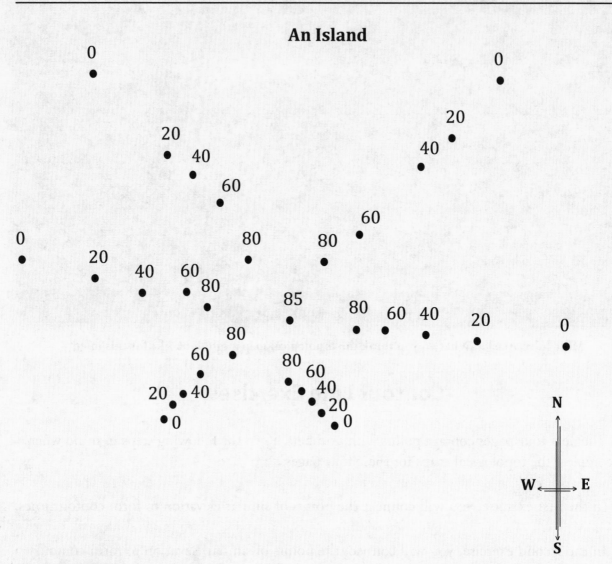

An Island

QUESTIONS:

1. Where is a good beach for swimming? *Hint: Use the directions of the compass or label the area.*

_____

2. How high is the top of the hill?

_____

3. Where is a cliff which goes down to the sea?

_____

GEOLOGY   58   SCIENCE 7 FOR YOUNG CATHOLICS

MAPMAKING: Contour Lines

DIRECTIONS: Connect the points of similar elevation to form contour lines with hills and dips.

"I lift up my eyes to the hills" (Psalm 121:1)

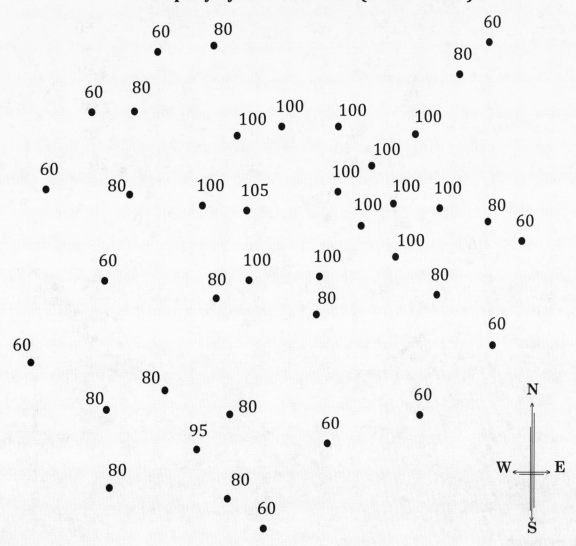

QUESTIONS:

1. How many hills are on this map?

   _____

2. Are there any depressions? Did you remember to put the depression marks around it?

   _____

3. What is the highest feature at this location?

   _____

MAPMAKING: Contour Lines

DIRECTIONS: Connect the points with like numbers to form contour lines with cliffs and beaches.

Jonah's Beach

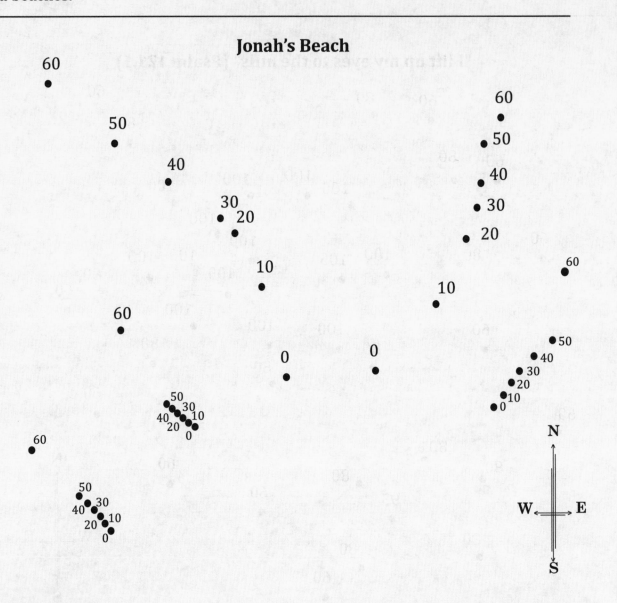

QUESTIONS:

1. Where is a good beach for swimming? *Hint: Use the directions of the compass or label the area.*

_____

2. How high is the top of the hill?

_____

3. Where is a cliff that goes down to the sea?

_____

MAPMAKING: Contour Lines

DIRECTIONS: Connect the points with like numbers to form contour lines with streams, cliffs, beaches, hills, and dips.

Glasswater Brook

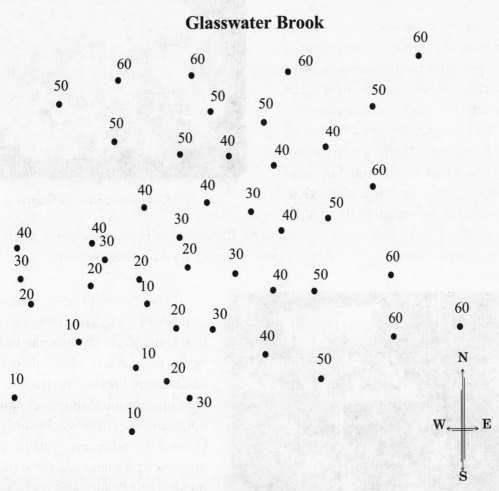

QUESTIONS:

1. Where is the highest point on this map?

_____

2. Where is the lowest point on this map?

_____

3. Do you have any V's on your map? *Hint: You should.*

_____

4. Which way do they point: upstream or downstream?

_____

5. Are there any level places where you could build a house? If you spot one, mark the location by placing a little house on that spot.

_____

J.M.J.

VI. Rocks

Rocks tend to be very durable. Most rocks are hundreds or even thousands of years old. Some rocks, however, are new. New rocks result from the buildup of sediment and the forces of pressure. In addition, a number of rocks continue to be produced by magma flows, both above and below the surface of the Earth. For example, Dr. Stein happened to be in Sicily one month after the eruption of Mount Etna, a famous volcano. Dr. Stein writes: "I collected two rock specimens that came from a one-month-old lava flow. At the time, these pieces of rock were warm to the touch. The elements in the rocks were as old as the Earth but were repackaged in a new form, so we can truly say that they were new rocks."

Gold Embedded in Quartz

Underground Silver Mine in Baden-Württemberg, Germany

There seem to be an infinite number of rocks and minerals. You can find some above the ground and others below the surface. Many of these lie in undiscovered mines, perhaps never to be seen by a person. Some rocks are dull, but many are strikingly beautiful. Our Creator has taken every element in the universe and then used these to make rocks. Their beauty and usefulness truly shout out in praise to Him. If you ever have the chance to visit a natural history museum, make sure that you browse the rock and mineral collections. You may find yourself wanting to become a geologist!

Before we further discuss rocks, it is important to understand what we mean when we use the term *rock*. This is because people sometimes use the term rock when they are talking about minerals or ores. Each of these is different.

Rocks are composed of several materials. A rock may have one or more minerals but it also has other materials. Rocks do not have a specific chemical composition or crystalline structure. Sometimes you can see the different minerals that make up the rock, but in other rocks, the pieces of the different minerals are so small that you cannot see them without a magnifying glass.

Coal is a unique rock that is made from the remains of plants. These plant remains are changed into a variety of mineral crystals by pressure and temperature. Coal is a combination of the different mineral crystals.

Ores are types of rocks from which we extract important metal elements, or metals—for example, gold, silver, copper, iron, and aluminum. Most ores are usually found below the ground where they are concentrated in areas known as deposits. When industries remove ores from the ground, the deposit is called a mine, and the removal process is known as mining. Mining is difficult, expensive, and sometimes dangerous work that occurs far below the Earth's surface.

If you have an interest in mines, you might want to check with your state's department of natural resources. Sometimes they have a list of local mines. You can contact various mines and possibly arrange for a tour. Mines are fun to visit, especially if they contain gems or semi-precious stones. For a nominal fee, some mines will let you dig through their scrap or tailings and allow you to keep what you can find.

© TJ Blackwell. Used with permission.

Morenci Mine

There are three kinds of rocks: sedimentary, igneous, and metamorphic. Each of these is made in a different way, and because of this, each one looks different. Even within one group of rocks, you may find that no two rocks look the same. For example, not all sandstone looks alike. Its crystals vary in both size and color: light yellow, tan, brown, pink, and purple. The same holds true for granite and marble. You can almost say that rocks are like people – no two are exactly alike!

A. Sedimentary Rocks

Sediment results from the erosion and weathering of rocks and soil. Sediment consists of clay, silt, sand, and fragments of rock. Wind, water, and ice carry and deposit sediment to many locations. The sediment accumulates and then sits on the bottom of low-lying areas, often areas underwater, such as stream beds and bottoms of lakes. Over time, the pressure of the accumulating layers of sediment can cause the lower layers to harden into rock. The word sediment comes from the Latin word, *sedere,* which means *to sit.*

Shelly Limestone

You are probably most familiar with sedimentary rocks such as sandstone, shale, and limestone. **Sandstone** is composed of sand-sized minerals or tiny rock grains. **Shale** is made from mud, clay, and small rock grains. **Limestone** consists mostly of the mineral calcite, which is calcium carbonate. Calcite is the primary mineral that is found in the shells of shellfish. If you have ever examined limestone, you may have noticed that it contained small pieces of shells.

B. Igneous Rocks

Igneous rocks are formed by hot and fiery magma. In fact, the term igneous comes from *ignis*, the Latin word for fire. When magma flows out of a volcano, it is called lava. As the lava cools, it results in igneous rocks of various shapes, sizes, and colors. The speed at which it cools determines the size of the crystals that make up the rock. If the magma cools slowly, the rock forms with large crystals. If it cools rapidly, the rock forms with small crystals. Many igneous rocks are also formed from magma below the surface of the Earth.

Granite

You may be familiar with igneous rocks such as granite and obsidian. **Granite** is often used in construction because it is very hard and resists weathering. **Obsidian** is also known as volcanic glass and is dark black in color. The American Indians prized obsidian for its sharp edges and used it for making arrowheads, spearheads, and scraping tools. They would often travel long distances to obtain it. **Pumice** is a rock that contains air trapped within its crystals. For this reason, it floats on water.

C. Metamorphic Rocks

Metamorphic rocks are rocks that have been transformed by heat and pressure. The term metamorphic, or metamorphism, is Greek and means *changing form*. Our spiritual lives can be compared to this process. God allows various trials to transform us into new beings. At one time, metamorphic rocks were

Marble

sedimentary or igneous rocks. Common examples of metamorphic rock include marble, slate, and gneiss. **Marble** comes from the conversion of limestone, and **slate** comes from shale. **Gneiss** is a beautifully layered rock that often contains many colors and patterns. Gneiss is produced by the transformation of both sedimentary and igneous rocks.

Gneiss

ACTIVITY: Rock Collection

DIRECTIONS: Fill in this data about your rocks. Place each rock and a number in one of the depressions in an egg carton.

	List of samples	Location found	Description of sample	Identification
1.				
2.				
3.				
4.				
5.				
6.				
7.				
8.				
9.				
10.				
11.				
12.				

VII. Identification of Minerals

Minerals are naturally occurring substances that have a unique chemical composition and crystalline structure. For example, table salt is known as the mineral **halite** (HAY-lite) and consists of sodium chloride. **Calcite** (CAL-site) is a mineral that is composed of calcium carbonate. Both halite and calcite are examples of minerals that contain two elements.

Some minerals are fairly easy to identify. However, some minerals look similar to others. Because of this, geologists often must conduct various tests to identify minerals. For example, pyrite (or "fool's gold") looks like gold. Both are heavy and have the same color and luster. In this case, geologists can perform tests to determine whether it is gold or pyrite. There are several techniques for identifying various minerals.

The color of a mineral may be the first thing you notice about it. Minerals get their colors in two ways. The first way is through **interaction with light**. Opals get their color this way; if you look at an opal while moving it around under a bright light, you will see it change color. The second way is through the **chemical properties** of the mineral itself. Minerals of copper are green or blue in color, for example, malachite. Sometimes, though, color is caused by minor impurities that are a part of the mineral. The soft pink color of rose quartz is due to small amounts of titanium. Likewise, the purple found in amethyst is due to the effects of potassium. These minerals would be colorless in the absence of the impurities of titanium or potassium.

A. Streak

Streak tests are used to determine if the color within a mineral is real, that is, it comes from the mineral itself and not from an impurity in the sample. A streak test involves rubbing a mineral specimen against an unglazed piece of porcelain. The rubbing causes a streak and powder to form on the plate. In most cases, the color of the powder should be similar to the color of the mineral. However, there are exceptions. The streak of pyrite ranges in color from green to black. Pure gold produces a gold streak. This is a quick, easy way to tell pyrite from gold.

B. Luster

Luster is the way light interacts with the surface of a mineral. Geologists recognize several kinds of lusters, ranging from brilliant to dull. Diamonds are the most brilliant and radiant minerals. They possess a luster known as **adamantine** (add-uh-MAN-tin). On the other hand, kaolinite (KAY-uh-luh-night) is a clay-based mineral and has a dull luster. Opal has the appearance of fat or grease and has a **greasy luster**. Pyrite looks like polished metal and has a **metallic luster**. Gypsum often appears to be layered in fibers and has a **silky luster**. Some minerals such as jade have a waxy appearance, which is called a **waxy luster**. Minerals that resemble glass are said to have a **vitreous luster**. These include quartz, topaz, tourmaline, beryl, fluorite, and others. Other lusters include pearly, resinous (like plastic), and submetallic (rusty).

C. Magnetism

There are more than a dozen minerals that are **magnetic**. Lodestone (or magnetite) is one of these. You can test the magnetic properties of lodestone by holding a paperclip next to it. When you bring the paperclip close, it will move toward the lodestone. Lodestone had its first practical use by navigators who used it in magnetic compasses. Pieces of lodestone were suspended so that these could orient toward the Earth's magnetic poles. In this way, the navigators could always tell direction. The name lodestone is an ancient term that means "course stone" or "leading stone."

D. Cleavage

Cleavage is the tendency of crystalline minerals, when struck with an object, to split along definite structural planes. When you strike a crystal, how it cleaves will be related to the properties of its molecules. Some crystals break in flat sheets and others in planes. Mica cleaves in wafer-thin sheets. You can peel these apart with your fingernails. Halite will always cleave in three directions. It forms cubes that can easily be viewed with a hand lens or microscope. Diamonds and fluorite always cleave in eight directions.

Some minerals do not break along cleavage lines but **fracture** instead. There are several kinds of fractures. The fracture of obsidian and flint is called **conchoidal**. The edges of these materials are curved, smooth, and sharp. They look like concentric circles and ridges. Sometimes, the fracture patterns resemble the shell of a clam. **Earthy fractures** appear as freshly dug soil and seem to have powdery edges. An example of an earthy fracture is seen in the mineral kaolinite. **Hackly fractures** can be seen in metals such as copper and silver. These fractures result in jagged, sharp, and uneven edges. The fractures of slate or asbestos are known as **splintery fractures**. These fractures result in the production of long, sharp edges. Finally, cleavage of minerals such as pyrite results in **uneven fractures** that leave rough, irregular, and uneven surfaces.

Mohs Scale of Hardness

1. Talc
2. Gypsum
3. Calcite
4. Fluorite
5. Apatite
6. Orthoclase
7. Quartz
8. Topaz
9. Corundum
10. Diamond

3

E. Hardness

Geologists also characterize minerals by conducting tests for **hardness**. They use the **Mohs scale**, which is a series of numbers ranging from 1 (very soft) to 10 (very hard). Minerals such as talc or soapstone have a hardness of 1. This mineral is so soft that, when handled, it leaves fine powder in your hands. Gypsum has a hardness of 2. You can easily scratch it with your fingernail. On the other end of the scale, corundum (rubies and sapphires) has a hardness of 9. Diamond is the hardest of all substances and has a hardness of 10.

You can test minerals for hardness by making comparisons. Minerals on the higher end of the scale will scratch those on the lower end of the scale. For example, quartz, which has a hardness of 7, can scratch feldspar, which has a hardness of 6. In turn, feldspar can scratch apatite, which has a hardness of 5. Your teeth are made from the mineral apatite and are quite hard.

You can use the following scale to determine the hardness of minerals.

	CHARACTERISTICS	TYPE OF MINERAL
1	Rubs off on fingers	Talc
2	Scratches easily with fingernails	Gypsum
3	Scratches by rubbing with a copper coin	Calcite
4	Scratches easily by rubbing with a nail	Fluorite
5	Scratches with difficulty by rubbing with a nail	Apatite, Glass
6	Scratches when using the blade of a stainless steel knife or quartz	Feldspar
7	Scratches by rubbing with a crystal of topaz	Quartz (Amethyst)
8	Scratches by rubbing with a crystal of corundum	Topaz
9	Scratches by rubbing with a crystal of diamond	Corundum (Ruby, Sapphire)
10	Cannot be scratched	Diamond

Common Minerals

Calcite: calcium carbonate
- Hardness - 3
- Luster - vitreous to earthy
- Streak - white
- Fracture - concoidal
- Color - colorless, white, gray, green, red, purple, blue, brown
- Comment - This mineral is water soluble and usually white or clear in color.

Calcite

Chalcopyrite: copper and iron sulfide
- Hardness - 3.5 - 4
- Luster - metallic
- Streak - greenish black
- Fracture - concoidal
- Color - brass yellow
- Comment - usually in veins, copper ore

Dolomite: calcium and magnesium carbonate
- Hardness - 3.5 - 4
- Luster - vitreous to pearly
- Streak - white
- Fracture - concoidal or uneven
- Color - white, colorless, yellow, brown, pink
- Comment - somewhat water soluble

Feldspar: silicate of aluminum and potassium, sodium, or calcium
- Hardness - 6 - 6.5
- Luster - vitreous to pearly
- Streak - colorless
- Fracture - prismatic
- Color - pinkish
- Comment - This is the pinkish mineral in granite.

Feldspar

Fluorite: calcium fluorite
- Hardness - 4
- Luster - vitreous
- Streak - white
- Fracture - uneven to concoidal
- Color - purple, white, clear
- Comment - usually in veins

Galena: lead sulphide
- Hardness - 2.5
- Luster - metallic (may be tarnished)
- Streak - lead gray
- Fracture - flat
- Color - silvery gray
- Comment - nice cubic crystals

Galena

Hematite: iron oxide (Fe_2O_3)
    Hardness -5.5 - 6.5
    Luster - metallic
    Streak - bright red
    Fracture - uneven
    Color - black, gray, brown, red
    Comment - slightly magnetic; magnetism becomes stronger if heated to 120 °F.

Halite: salt, sodium chloride
    Hardness - 2 - 2.5
    Luster - vitreous
    Streak - white
    Fracture - concoidal, cleavage is cubic
    Color - clear or white
    Comment - water soluble

Halite (Photo by Didier Descouens)

Magnetite: iron oxide (Fe_3O_4)
    Hardness - 5.5 - 6.5
    Luster - metallic
    Streak - black
    Fracture - concoidal
    Color - iron black
    Comment - magnetic

Mica: silicate of potassium, aluminum, iron, or magnesium
    Hardness - 2 - 3
    Luster - pearly
    Streak - colorless
    Fracture - splits into sheets
    Color - white, silvery, black
    Comment - sheets sparkle in the sun

Pyrite: iron sulfide
    Hardness - 5 - 6
    Luster - metallic
    Streak - greenish or brownish black
    Fracture - concoidal
    Color - brassy gold
    Comment - cubic crystals, "fool's gold"

Quartz: silicon oxide
    Hardness - 7
    Luster - vitreous
    Streak - colorless
    Fracture - concoidal
    Color - clear when pure, many different colors with impurities
    Comment - found in veins, sand, and igneous rocks

Quartz (Photo by Didier Descouens)

OPTIONAL ACTIVITY: Setting Up Your Geology Lab

DIRECTIONS: Perhaps now is a good time to set up your geology lab. You will need a few things to get started.

MATERIALS: Ask your mom or dad to help you find the following:

- An egg carton
- Vinegar (to discover how certain minerals react with vinegar)
- Piece of white tile or a broken dinner plate
- Penny
- Nail
- File
- Hammer
- Hand lens or dissecting microscope

The identification of rocks is really a way to practice your observation skills. All of the characteristics of rocks are observable using your senses. Think of all the things you might be able to observe by using your senses. Color, luster, fracture, cleavage, hardness, density, size of particles, and reactivity with vinegar. Find out which minerals react with vinegar! How do they react? These are all characteristics that you may be able to observe.

Begin collecting rocks and minerals and place them in your egg carton. From what you read in this chapter, conduct several tests to see if you can determine the kinds of rocks and minerals in your collection. If you need more specific instructions, ask your parents to help you look on the Internet. You will find interesting ideas under "science projects for rocks and minerals."

Cliffs of Étretat (Photo by Peco)

Chapter 3 Summary

1. The planet Earth has characteristics that were designed by God to provide a place for us to live. The **external characteristics** are as follows: moderate temperature, energy from the sun, breathable atmosphere, a moon, and many types of elements in the rocks.

2. **Internal characteristics** are as follows: layers of different types of rock, **inner core**, **outer core**, which provides our magnetic field to protect us from the harmful rays of the sun, **mantle**, and **crust**.

3. We live on the **crust**. Crustal rocks are two types: **continental** and **oceanic**. Continental crustal rocks are lighter than the oceanic rocks and move around.

4. The **oceans** of the Earth cover **about 70 percent** of the Earth's surface. **Islands** and **continents** cover the rest. **Land forms of the Earth include mountains, plains, valleys, lakes, volcanoes, and rivers**. You should know the characteristics and an example of each.

5. Types of **Earth movements** are as follows: **earthquakes, folding, faulting, subsidence, uplift,** and **erosion**.

6. Mapmaking is an ancient and useful skill. A **flat distance map** shows local details. A global map must account for the curvature of the planet, whereas a flat distance map does not.

7. To determine the length of your **pace**, measure ten of your normal strides and divide this number by ten. This is the **average length** of one of your paces.

8. **Topographical maps** give information about the contours of the land. Lines connecting points of equal elevation are called **contour lines**.

9. **Rocks are made up of minerals and other materials.** Rocks are formed in three ways and are classified according to these ways. **Igneous rocks** are produced by the cooling of melted rock. **Sedimentary rocks** are the accumulation of sediment that has been transformed into rocks by pressure. **Metamorphic rocks** are rocks of the other two types that have been changed by heat, pressure, or both.

10. You can identify rocks and minerals by their characteristics. Some of these characteristics are **luster, color, magnetism, hardness, streak,** and **fracture**.

Questions for Review

1. What is so special about the planet Earth?

   _____

   _____

2. List some of the external characteristics of the Earth that make it habitable for humans.

   _____

   _____

3. What are the parts of the inside of the planet Earth?

   _____

   _____

4. List nine land forms of the Earth.

   _____

   _____

5. List the types of movements of the Earth.

   _____

   _____

6. Name two famous geological phenomena. (Hint: Some are pictured in this chapter.)

   _____

   _____

7. Two types of maps are _____ and _____.

8. Contour lines are

   _____

9. The three basic types of rocks are _____,
   _____, and _____.

10. What are some of the characteristics used to identify rocks?

   _____

   _____

Thinking about Science

1. Which of the Earth's characteristics are most important to our survival? Why?

   _____

   _____

2. Look up Psalm 18:7 (Psalm 17:8 in the *Douay-Rheims* translation). Explain the "foundations of the mountains." What are they and what does this verse mean?

   _____

   _____

3. Which of the types of Earth movements is the most significant to us today? Explain your answer by referring to the other types of movements.

   _____

   _____

4. What large geographic feature is often thought to be a result of erosion from the aftermath of the Great Flood?

   _____

5. Why do you think we have names for all the different rocks and minerals and their characteristics?

   _____

   _____

Early Mosaic of Noah Releasing a Dove from the Ark

Flight and Space Travel

I.   Discovery and the Hand of God
II.   Basics of Flight
    A.   Lift
    B.   Thrust
    C.   Drag
    D.   Weight
III.   Lift and Speed
IV.   Parts of an Airplane
V.   Flight Stability
VI.   Rockets
VII.   Parts of a Rocket
    A.   The Structural System
    B.   The Payload System
    C.   The Guidance System
    D.   The Propulsion System
VIII.   Rockets and Planes
IX.   The Advancement of Science
X.   Orbits and Satellites
XI.   Space Shuttle Program
XII.   Space Probes
    A.   Flyby Missions
    B.   Rover Missions
XIII.   Telescopes
IV.   Hubble Space Telescope

Flight and Space Travel

Chapter 4

"The heavens are telling the glory of God; and the firmament proclaims His handiwork. Day to day pours forth speech, and night to night declares knowledge" (Psalm 19:1-2).

Since the beginning of time, people have viewed flight with a sense of wonder and awe. Flying was a special part of the myths of early civilizations, including the Egyptians, Greeks, and Romans. The ancient Egyptians saw flight as supernatural. Hawks, vultures, owls, and other birds adorned the tombs of the Pharaohs. Quite often, these birds were depicted as guardians with their wings embracing and protecting a Pharaoh.

There are more than fifty references to cherubim angels in the Old Testament. The **cherubim** represented the power and glory of God and were described as having wings. You may recall that God placed cherubim at the entrance to the Garden of Eden (Genesis 3:24). In addition, when God told Moses to build the Ark of the Covenant, He directed him to place one cherubim on each end of the ark (Exodus 25:19). Angels, the messengers of God, are almost always pictured with wings.

Guardian Angel,
by Bernhard Plockhorst

Modern flight has its roots in the first manned glider. A glider is an aircraft with no engine that flies on air currents. Elmer of Malmesbury was an 11th-century Benedictine monk who constructed a set of feathery wings. He put these on and jumped from the roof of his abbey. His trip was shorter than he expected. He glided only 220 yards before crashing and breaking both of his legs.

Leonardo da Vinci was a true genius from the Renaissance period in Italy with a keen interest in flight. He studied the structure of birds and how they flew. In 1485, Leonardo da Vinci produced detailed plans for an **ornithopter** (or-nith-OPP-tuhr), a wing-flapping device that he believed would allow humans to fly. Although his plans have survived, there are no records of his having actually built the device. Like others during that time, da Vinci failed to realize that because human beings are not built like birds, it is not possible for humans to fly like birds. Birds have hollow bones, are very light in weight, and have strong wing muscles for flapping their wings in the air.

Nothing major happened regarding other attempts at aviation until September 1783, when the French produced the first hot air balloon. They put hot air inside a huge balloon, causing it to rise above the ground and lift an attached basket. Breezes moved the balloon around in the air, but it could not be steered. Its first passengers were a sheep, a duck, and a rooster! The three animals were in the air for fifteen minutes before crashing to the ground. Nevertheless, the desire to put people in the air continued. By November of 1783, two French human passengers manned a **hot air balloon** that flew for twenty minutes.

More than one hundred years passed, with many people experimenting, before human flight made history on **December 17, 1903, in Kitty Hawk, North Carolina. Orville and Wilbur Wright**, popularly known as "the Wright brothers," designed and flew a fully controlled, heavier-than-air, flying machine. They made four flights that day, with the longest flight, conducted by Wilbur, covering a distance of 852 feet and lasting 59 seconds. The world of aviation and our civilization would never be the same! Today, it has been estimated that daily worldwide airline flights number in the high ten thousands.

I. Discovery and the Hand of God

God made the world and all things in it so that we would come to know Him and to love Him. His creations in the world reflect His beauty, His intellect, His love, and His majesty. Everyone has enjoyed watching an eagle swoop through the air or a colorful butterfly flapping its wings on a soft flight from flower to flower. It is easy to become aware of God and His great intelligence when we study His creatures in flight.

When we study flight, which is also known as **aeronautics**, we begin to unfold mysteries about the planet Earth and its surroundings. The pioneers of aviation knew they needed to study God's Earth and the winds above the Earth. They began studying flight but ended up learning about the atmosphere. They came to understand that the Earth's atmosphere was designed in such a way as to make flight possible. This is typical of God's unfolding mysteries that we learn through human reasoning. That is, whenever we study one part of His creation, we come face-to-face with other parts of it. In this way, we discover new information about our world. Let's turn our attention now to the basics of flight.

II. Basics of Flight

Imagine a plane taxiing down the runway and preparing to take off. Four invisible forces will enable it to fly: lift, thrust, drag, and weight.

A. Lift

As the plane begins moving faster, its wings encounter greater resistance with the air. Some of the air flows above the wings, and some of the air flows beneath the wings. The upper part of the wing is curved and, in cross-section, looks like a stretched out water droplet. This aerodynamic shape is referred to as an **airfoil**.

Air flows quickly across the airfoil and results in less pressure in the space above the wing. At the same time as the air flows quickly above the wing, the air flows at a consistent speed and steady rate of pressure along the bottom of the wing. We can restate the above: The air stream flowing over the wing is split into two speeds and pressures, respectively: **fast speed and low pressure above the wing; slow speed and high pressure below the wing**. These differences in pressure result in **lift**, which is the force that pushes the wing upward into the space where there is less pressure.

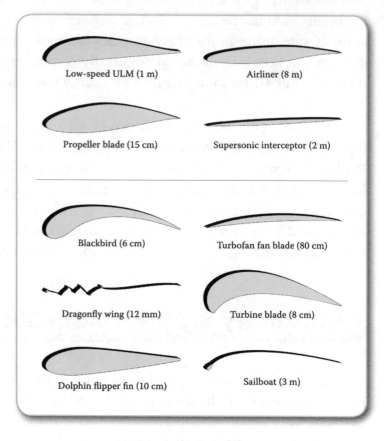

Example of Airfoils

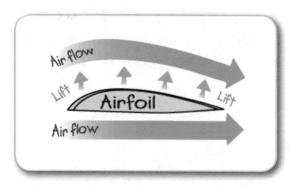

Perhaps a good way to understand **lift** is by recalling a time that you placed your hand outside the car window when the car was moving. When you kept your arm and hand parallel to the road, you felt the air rush across your hand and arm. The air was moving fast, met with little resistance from your arm, and created an area of low pressure. Your hand moved easily through the air. When you cupped your hand or held it upward, the air quickly pushed your hand and actually *lifted* your arm.

B. Thrust

Thrust is the second force that makes flight possible. Thrust is best explained by **Sir Isaac Newton's Third Law of Motion: For every action, there is an equal and opposite reaction. Simply put, thrust propels the plane forward** by pushing air backward. The engines of a plane accomplish this with a propeller or by releasing hot gases. In both cases, the backward action on the air causes an equal reaction that propels the airplane forward.

Another way to think of thrust is by swimming. As you extend your arm and pull your cupped hand back alongside your body, you push against the water, and your body moves forward.

C. Drag

Drag is the force caused by friction with air. You can easily understand drag if you have ever tried running or riding your bicycle in a strong wind. You may recall that the wind slowed you down and made you work harder. You had to overcome the friction of the air molecules pushing against your body. Similarly, as a plane moves forward because of thrust, the plane encounters strong resistance, or drag. Drag acts to hold the plane back.

Flying a plane involves the challenging relationship between *thrust* and *drag*. A pilot must be an expert in understanding and mastering these two principles to maintain both the speed and the control of the flying airplane. Understanding these principles is like a tug-of-war with three possible outcomes:

(1) If thrust is greater than drag, the airplane accelerates or gains speed.

(2) If drag is greater than thrust, the airplane decelerates or loses speed.

(3) If the forces of thrust and drag are equal, the airplane continues moving forward at a constant speed.

D. Weight

Weight is the last of the four forces involved with flight. **Weight** is the constant, downward pull of gravity upon the mass of the plane. Gravity is constantly trying to pull the plane downward toward the Earth. During takeoff and flight, the propulsion forces (thrust) must be strong enough to move the plane fast enough in order for the forces of lift to overcome the forces of weight. Here again, we have another tug-of-war with three possibilities between *weight* and *lift*:

(1) When weight (the force due to gravity) is greater than lift, the airplane sinks.

(2) When lift is greater than weight, the airplane climbs.

(3) When the pilot balances these two forces, the airplane flies steady and level.

You can see that flight is the result of opposing forces that work in pairs. Thrust counteracts drag; lift counteracts weight. The engine provides the thrust to keep the plane moving forward, but the wings do the lifting.

The above principles are universal and apply also to aircrafts without engines, such as **gliders**. An airplane tows a glider, which is attached to the plane by a tether (a rope or chain). Once the airplane reaches a certain altitude, the glider detaches from the tether and flies (glides) back to the earth on air currents. Once again, we can look to nature and find that many birds glide. For example, eagles, hawks, vultures, and other birds use thrust or movements of their wings to fly to a certain altitude. It is at this high altitude point that they lock their wings *open* and glide in the air currents. These birds occasionally flap their wings when gliding to change their position in the air currents.

K21 Glider
(Photo courtesy of www.flightbox.net)

The principles of flight also apply to space shuttles. Space shuttles begin their journey by using powerful rocket motors. Upon completion of a mission, however, the space shuttle descends into the Earth's atmosphere and no longer needs its rockets. The space shuttle uses its "wings" to fly or glide until it lands. The wings support the entire weight of the spacecraft! This is no small feat. The space shuttle weighs 172,000 pounds (or 86 tons) upon its return into the Earth's atmosphere! You will learn more about space shuttles later in this chapter.

III. Lift and Speed

A sparrow, hummingbird, and falcon all possess similar features that enable them to fly. Each of these species has been uniquely designed for specialized behaviors besides ordinary flight. Here we see the creative and infinite genius of God. God took a basic design, for example, wings, and then modified the design of wings for different purposes. The sparrow flies and hops about using its average-sized wings. The hummingbird hovers in the air, not by flapping its wings but by rapidly rotating them. The peregrine falcon is the fastest bird on Earth! It has short, pointed wings that enable it to reach speeds of almost 200 mph! Each of these birds is specialized by God for different kinds of flight. **Each kind of wing provides lift, but the shape of the wing determines the kind of flight and, more importantly, the speed.**

ACTIVITY: Demonstrating Lift and Air Pressures

MATERIALS: Paper, scissors

PROCEDURE:

1. Cut a strip of notebook paper 1 inch wide and 8 inches long.
2. Hold the strip of paper by one end so that the paper extends lengthwise in front of your mouth. It should hang down.
3. Blow just below the paper. Record the action of the paper.
4. Blow just above the paper. Record your observation.
5. Cut two pieces of notebook paper into 5 x 5 inch squares.
6. Hold both squares of paper next to the corners of your mouth.
7. Blow into the corridor you have made with the two squares.

QUESTIONS:

1. When you blew below the paper, where did the air go? How did that air affect the paper? Did you observe the same thing about the other blows?

   _____

   _____

2. Of the four forces of flight, which one applied to the paper?

   _____

OBSERVATION:

Direction of blow	What happened to the paper?
Above the paper	
Below the paper	
Between the paper	

J.M.J.

PROBLEMS: Identify which of the four forces are present in each picture:

We can look at the relationship between lift and speed in another way. Imagine, for one moment, a seagull and a robin, and that each weighs only 1 pound. The wings of each bird must provide 1 pound of lift in order to fly. The seagull has long slender wings and glides majestically. On the other hand, the robin flaps its wings rapidly and flies very fast to stay aloft. In this case, the robin with smaller wings must fly faster to achieve the same amount of lift as the seagull!

The **relationship between lift and speed** holds true for airplanes. Planes that have been designed for rapid flight have smaller wings than those that have been designed to fly at average and slow speeds. Indeed, the shape or design of a plane's wings can tell you a great deal about the purpose of the plane and how it will fly. **Short, stubby wings** provide great maneuverability, which is necessary for **aerobatic** or **stunt planes**. **Delta wings** are triangle-shaped and are used by jets that fly near and above the speed of sound. **Long, wide wings** provide great lift for airliners that transport passengers and cargo. Finally, **long, thin wings** allow gliders or sailplanes to soar.

Here is another way to think of the relationship between lift and speed. You are all set to travel in a plane that weighs 1,000 pounds. Its normal takeoff speed when you are the only additional weight in the plane is 90 miles per hour. Your friend asks for a ride to Dallas along with four heavy suitcases. The combined weight of your friend and his suitcases is 400 pounds. Dallas is a long trip, so you must put 200 pounds of extra gas in the plane. You decide to take Spot, your 100-pound St. Bernard. Now your plane needs an additional 700 pounds of lift. To lift your plane, your takeoff speed must be faster than 90 miles per hour!

Many different kinds of airplanes exist in the world. Although each of these has a similar design, the planes will be constructed differently, based on their intended purpose. For example, a plane that holds two passengers and flies short distances will be constructed differently than a plane that holds 350 passengers and flies across oceans.

IV. Parts of an Airplane

So far, you have read about the four forces involved with flying. Now we will investigate the parts of an airplane that make flying possible.

All planes share a similar design, with some variations in their construction and appearance. To better understand the design of planes, you can think about the design and appearance of birds.

Aeronautical engineers (engineers who design planes) and pilots must be familiar with each and every part. You already know that the wing provides lift, and the propeller or jet engine provides thrust. These parts are essential for flying but represent only a very small fraction of the entire plane.

The **fuselage** (FYOO-suh-lahj) is the body of the airplane and the central structure that holds everything together. The fuselage contains all of the important electrical circuits, controlling cables and structures, and landing wheel wells. For one moment, think of how we refer to the human body. We mostly understand it by thinking about its many parts and how these work together. Think of the fuselage in the same manner. It contains many parts that all work together for its larger purpose. Perhaps it has been designed to hold passengers. Maybe it has been constructed to carry mail, packages, or other cargo. Maybe its purpose is the defense of our skies and contains specialized surveillance systems.

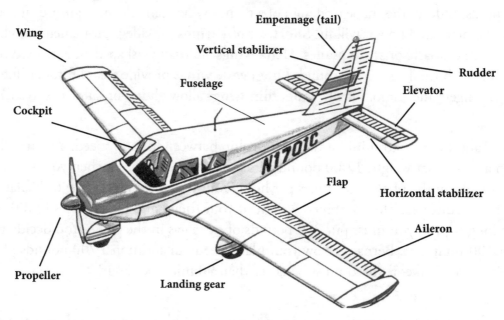

Typical Airplane

The **cockpit** is where the pilot sits near the front of the plane. Quite often, the pilot may have a copilot with him to help perform all tasks necessary for safe flight. The cockpit holds all of the **important navigational controls, instruments, gauges, and communication equipment that make flying possible and safe**.

The **empennage** (em-pen-AHJ) is the tail section of the plane. The tail section helps make the aircraft stable in flight, much like the feathers on an arrow. The empennage contains several important parts: the horizontal and vertical stabilizers, the rudder, and the elevators.

The **horizontal stabilizer** helps the plane fly level and move forward in a straight line. Without it, the plane's nose and tail would pitch up and down, and possibly cause a crash.

Elevators are flight-control parts attached by hinges to the horizontal stabilizer. The pilot uses the elevators **to control the pitch of the airplane**. The pitch is the lift and descent of the nose and tail of the plane while flying. When the pilot pulls back on the flight controls, the elevator deflects upward, which causes the airplane to nose up.

The **vertical stabilizer**, or **fin**, works to keep the plane flying in a straight line, without side-to-side movement known as **yaw**. The **rudder** attaches to the vertical stabilizers. The rudder enables the pilot to change the yaw of the plane. When the pilot depresses one of the rudder control pedals, the plane turns to either the left or the right.

In summary, you can see that the stabilizers work to keep the plane flying straight. The elevator and rudder give the pilot the means to change or correct the up-and-down and side-to-side movements.

The wings of the plane do more than lift the plane. The wings contain additional control surfaces that are located on the back of both wings. This area is referred to as the "trailing edge."

Ailerons (AY-luh-rons) are movable parts **on the trailing edge of the wings** (close to the wing tips), used to control the plane's flight. **Ailerons work together to control the rolling movement of the aircraft**, especially in banking for turns. Both ailerons are interconnected so that when one goes down the other goes up. The aileron that moves down *increases* the lift on its wing. The up-going aileron *reduces* the lift on its wing. Together, these movements produce a *rolling or turning movement* for the aircraft. A roll to the left turns or steers the aircraft to the left. Conversely, a roll to the right turns the aircraft to the right.

Flaps are also found on the trailing edge of the wings, but closer to the body of the plane. Flaps perform two functions during takeoff and landing. When the pilot *extends* the flaps during takeoff, this *increases the curvature* of the wing, resulting in **greater lift capacity**. In this manner, the flaps enable the plane to achieve *lift at slower speeds*. After takeoff, the flaps add too much drag, so the pilot raises them shortly afterward.

The de Havilland D.H.9, an Early Biplane. Notice the open cockpit, large landing gear, and empennage control surfaces.

4

J.M.J.

ACTIVITY: Control Surfaces on a Balsa Glider
PROCEDURE:

1. Purchase a toy balsa wood glider from the hobby shop. If a glider is unavailable in shops, you can make your own paper glider. Instructions are on the Internet.
2. Assemble the glider and throw it a few times to see how it flies.
3. Cut five rectangles as shown out of a 3 x 5 index card or stiff paper.
4. Tape your card stock "control surfaces" to the balsa glider as shown.
5. Bend the left aileron down and the right aileron up. (Recall that the ailerons are movable parts on the trailing edge of the wings, used to control the plane's flight.) Throw the glider. Record your observations.
6. Bend the left aileron up and the right aileron down. Throw. Record.
7. Bend the elevators (both sides) up. Throw. Record.
8. Bend both elevators down. Throw. Record.
9. Bend the rudder left. Throw. Record.
10. Bend the rudder right. Throw. Record.

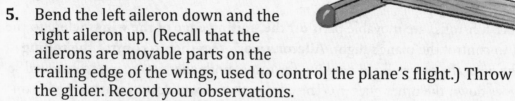

OBSERVATIONS:

Change in Control Surface	Flight Path
Left aileron down, Right up	
Left aileron up, Right down	
Elevators up	
Elevators down	
Rudder left	
Rudder right	

The pilot, once again, **uses the flaps during landing**. He engages the flaps, increasing drag and slowing down the plane, so that it can easily land on its landing gear. In both of these examples, the flaps enable takeoff and landing to occur on short runways.

When we consider all of the structures and processes involved in flight, it cannot compare to our Creator's perfectly efficient design of birds. Birds do not require runways and need only a small hop or run before they take off. Likewise, when birds land, they require little extra room to do so. It is no surprise that birds have served as a model for aviation pioneers throughout history.

Most airplanes have all the parts shown in the drawing shown earlier. Sometimes the parts may not look the same, but every plane needs an engine, wings, controls, and landing gear. Many airplanes have additional attachments or parts to help them perform special tasks such as fire fighting, crop dusting, or aerial photography. If you wish to learn more about planes, there are many books about the history of aviation at your local library. In addition, many towns throughout our nation have aviation museums.

V. Flight Stability

Imagine for one moment that you were designing an airplane. What would be one of your most important considerations? Of course, you would want it to be as light as possible. You would want it balanced, both from side to side and from front to back. While you ponder these concepts, think about how a seesaw works.

A seesaw is a long narrow board that balances or pivots on a support beam. If two people of similar weight sit on its opposite ends, the seesaw balances at its center. We refer to this balance point as the **center of gravity**. If one person is heavier than the other, then that person must shift his end of the seesaw closer to the support beam. Without such an adjustment, the heavier person would cause his end of the seesaw to slam down to the ground.

Seesaw: Balanced Forces

An airplane is balanced in a similar fashion to the seesaw pictured in the illustration. The <u>center of gravity</u> for an airplane is located near the front or leading edge of the wings. The <u>center of lift</u> is farther back, about one-fourth of the way from the leading edge. Try to visualize the balance point and the force of lift pushing upward. However, the plane also needs a **balancing force** to counteract the force of lift. This is because the lift provided by the wings of a plane do not lift the plane straight up but rather lift the rear of the plane higher than the front. Without a balancing force, the plane would pitch forward and enter into a steep dive. The horizontal stabilizer provides this force, which pushes downward on the tail.

It does not take a large force to balance the plane, because the horizontal stabilizer is a long way from the center of lift. This situation is like having several people on one end of a seesaw and one small person at the other end. The balance point would be very close to the end that has several people.

The balance achieved while flying can be summarized as follows:

(1) the center of gravity or balance point is located near the leading edge of the wing,

(2) lift pushes upward at the wing, and

(3) the horizontal stabilizer provides the downward balancing force.

Boeing 787 Dreamliner

J.M.J.

ACTIVITY: Center of Gravity Shift on Balsa or Card Stock Glider

PROCEDURE:

1. Be sure your glider is balanced correctly to start, by resting it on your fingers such that it does not tip over (see photo on right). You will know it is balanced if it makes long smooth glides.

2. Tape a penny (or paperclip) to the nose of the glider. Mark the new balance point on a sketch of your glider. Throw it. Record the results.

3. Add a second penny and repeat step two. Continue to note the balance point and any change in flying performance.

4. Remove the pennies from the nose.

5. Tape one penny on the top of the fuselage behind the wing. Sketch the glider and mark the new balance point on the sketch. Throw it. Record flying performance.

6. Repeat step 5 until the glider will not fly.

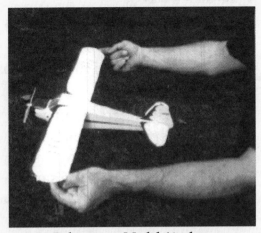

Balancing a Model Airplane

OBSERVATIONS:

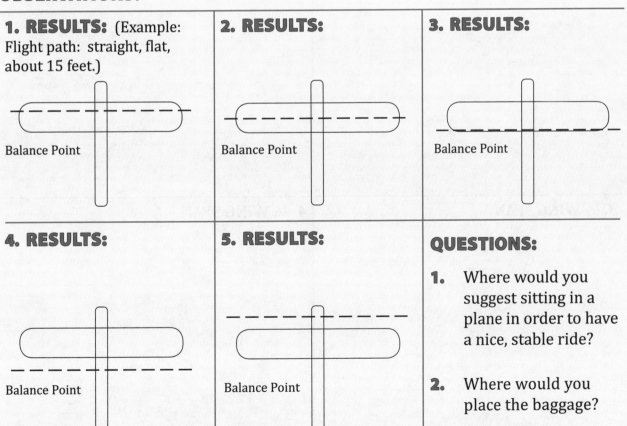

1. RESULTS: (Example: Flight path: straight, flat, about 15 feet.)

Balance Point

2. RESULTS:

Balance Point

3. RESULTS:

Balance Point

4. RESULTS:

Balance Point

5. RESULTS:

Balance Point

QUESTIONS:

1. Where would you suggest sitting in a plane in order to have a nice, stable ride?

2. Where would you place the baggage?

4

ACTIVITY: Wing Size and Speed Experiment

PROCEDURE:

1. Throw your glider to make it go as far as you can. Do not throw it so hard that it climbs steeply or loops.

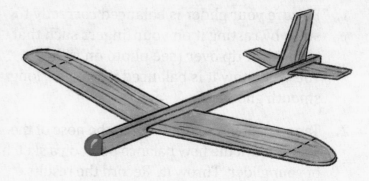

2. Use scissors to cut off a quarter of each wing's span. Throw your glider again. Try to make it go the same distance as in step 1. Observe and record any difference in glide speed.

3. Cut the wings to ½ their original span. Repeat step 2.

4. Cut the wings to ¼ their original span. Repeat step 2.

OBSERVATIONS:

1. FULL WING SPAN	2. ¾ WING SPAN
3. ½ WING SPAN	4. ¼ WING SPAN

VI. Rockets

A Brief History of Rockets

We typically think of rockets as a way to launch people or things into space. This hasn't always been the case. The Chinese were the first to develop and use rockets, and they used them for fireworks and wars as early as the 13th century. During the next 700 years, people continued to build bigger and better rockets; however, most of these were used in warfare. That began to change in the 1900s, when a few people proposed that rockets could eventually carry people into space.

Robert H. Goddard, an American professor, scientist, and inventor, experimented with rockets during the 1920s and 1930s. He developed rockets that were powered by gasoline and liquid oxygen. These rockets could fly higher and faster than rockets that burned solid fuel. Goddard's contributions to rocket science were

Robert H. Goddard

legendary, and he was awarded 214 patents during his lifetime. For these reasons, he is referred to as the "Father of Rocketry."

The Germans took the lead in rocket development during World War II. They designed and produced the V-1 and V-2. The V-2 was a large. liquid-fuel rocket that served as an important weapon. It carried a ton of explosives. Control was minimal, however; they crashed when fuel ran out.

Following the defeat of Germany, **Wernher von Braun** and his development team came to the United States to share knowledge with the Americans. This led to the development of long-range weapons known as **intercontinental ballistic missiles**, or ICBMs.

Wernher von Braun

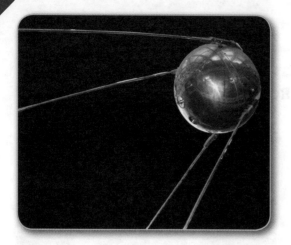

Sputnik 1

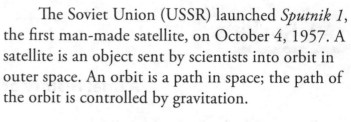

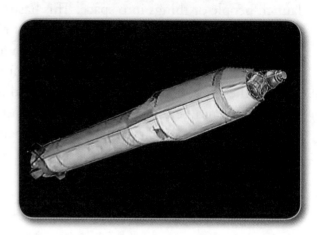

Sputnik 2

The Soviet Union (USSR) launched *Sputnik 1*, the first man-made satellite, on October 4, 1957. A satellite is an object sent by scientists into orbit in outer space. An orbit is a path in space; the path of the orbit is controlled by gravitation.

One month later, the Soviet Union launched another satellite, *Sputnik 2*. This satellite carried the first living creature ever to go into space in orbit. The living creature was a dog named Laika. These two satellites, *Sputnik 1* and *Sputnik 2*, started the "race" into space between the Soviet Union and the United States.

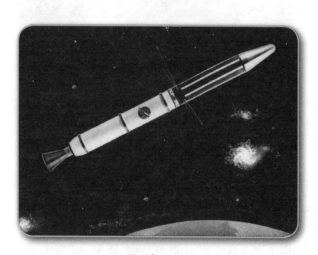

Explorer 1

In a very short time, on January 31, 1958, the United States launched its first satellite, *Explorer I*. The world would never be the same. Both the Soviet Union and the United States would continue to advance rocket science.

The United States National Aeronautics and Space Administration (**NASA**) began human space flights. We put men into space with *Project Mercury* and then *Project Gemini*. In June 1965, on board the *Gemini 4*, Edward White became the first American to walk into space. He enjoyed his walk into space so much that his fellow crew member had to plead with him to return to the space capsule. A total of ten Gemini missions were conducted before plans were made for a moon landing.

The **Apollo Program** began with an address to Congress by President John F. Kennedy on May 25, 1961. He proposed the goal of "landing a man on the moon and returning him safely to the Earth." The first several missions of the Apollo Program were designed to test equipment that would fly to and eventually place men on the moon.

It was July 16, 1969, when the United States placed men on the moon using the rocket known as *Saturn V*. This was a very big event in our nation's history. About 600 million people tuned into the television to watch Neil Armstrong set foot on the moon and say, "That's one small step for man, one giant leap for mankind!"

Today, NASA uses rockets to launch satellites and space probes to areas both inside and outside of the Earth's atmosphere.

Neil Armstrong on the Moon

Sounding rockets collect information during all parts of their flight, including going up and coming down. This information includes the areas of radiation, temperature, magnetic fields, and numbers of meteors in outer space and closer to our planet.

VII. Parts of a Rocket

There are many parts that make up a rocket. These are organized into four major systems: structural, payload, guidance, and propulsion.

A. The Structural System

The **structural system** or frame is similar to the fuselage of an airplane. The body is cylindrical and contains fairings and fins. **Fairings** are structures that work together to produce a smooth outline of the rocket and thus reduce drag. The fairings cover gaps and spaces between the parts of a rocket and provide it with an aerodynamic shape. **Fins** are typically attached to the bottom of the rocket and provide stability during flight.

The **frame** of a rocket is made from strong, lightweight materials, such as titanium and aluminum. These materials run from the top to the bottom of the frame and are known as **stringers**. In turn, the stringers are connected by **hoops**, which run around the circumference of the frame. Try to think of the stringers and hoops as an **internal skeleton**. This internal frame is covered with a metal **skin**, which gives the rocket its basic shape. The skin is coated with materials that serve the important function of keeping out heat that builds up from friction with the air.

B. The Payload System

The **payload system** is the carrying capacity of the rocket. Payload may include cargo, instruments, and extra fuel. The payload system will depend on the mission of the rocket. Some examples of payloads include satellites that have a wide range of missions—for example, communications, weather monitoring, surveillance, and planetary exploration. The payload may even refer to people who are launched into the Earth's orbit or to the surface of the moon, although NASA's missions are now entirely unmanned. For military purposes, sometimes the payloads are munitions that are referred to as warheads.

C. The Guidance System

The primary purpose of the **guidance system** is to control the rocket in flight. Guidance systems are very complex and contain a great deal of specialized equipment: computers, radar, communications equipment, and sensors. **Sensors** are devices that convert information into electrical signals, for example, information about temperature and pressure. All of this information is fed directly into a computer, which is then used to control the rocket, so that it travels with some level of stability.

D. The Propulsion System

The **propulsion system** occupies a significant portion of the total volume of the rocket. It launches the rocket and keeps it in flight using either liquid or solid fuels. **Liquid rocket engines** contain fuel and oxidizer that are contained in separate tanks. These liquids are pumped into a **combustion chamber** where they are mixed and burned.

Solid rocket engines contain fuel and oxidizer mixed into one cylinder tank. A hole in this cylinder serves as the combustion chamber. Once the fuel mixture has been ignited, a **flame front** is produced, which burns directly into the combustion chamber. In both liquid and solid engines, the burning or combustion of fuel produces tremendous amounts of **exhaust gases**. These gases pass through a nozzle, which speeds up the flow and produces thrust.

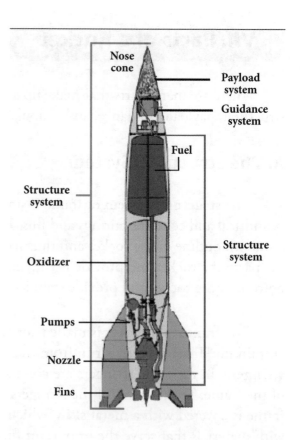

Parts of a Rocket

PROBLEMS: Answer the questions for each picture below.

1. Is the motion in the picture toward or away from the Earth?

2. Is gravity the greater pull in this picture?

3. When will the force of gravity stop acting upon the object, if it will stop?

4. Draw arrows to show the forces at work on these objects.

5. Make the arrow which shows the strongest force bigger than the other arrows.

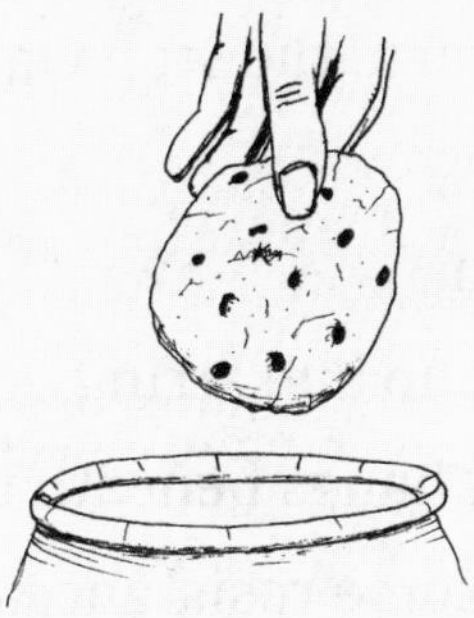

Taking a Cookie out of a Jar

1. _____
   _____

2. _____
   _____

3. _____
   _____

1. _____
   _____

2. _____
   _____

3. _____
   _____

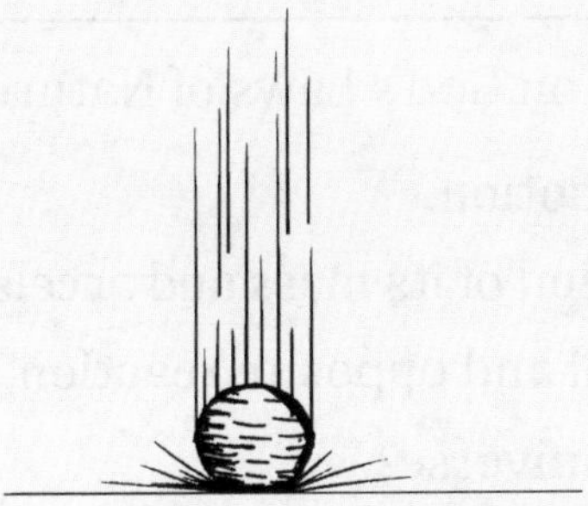

1. _____
   _____

2. _____
   _____

3. _____
   _____

4

ACTIVITY: Balloon Rockets

MATERIALS: Balloon, monofilament (or thread), drinking straw, tape, paper cup, nuts and bolts, stopwatch

PROCEDURE:

1. Pull a piece of monofilament or sewing thread through a straw.
2. Tape the monofilament or thread to the floor and ceiling, straight up and down.
3. Blow up a large balloon, but do not tie off the end.
4. Tape the balloon, end facing down, lengthwise to the straw.
5. Hold the balloon near the floor.
6. Release the neck of the balloon when your partner starts the stop watch.
7. Time the balloon until it touches the ceiling.

Optional: You may wish to test the strength of your balloon.

1. Build a basket underneath the balloon from a paper cup and string.
2. Tape the string to the bottom of the balloon so that it hangs beneath the balloon.
3. Put nuts and bolts in the cup so that the balloon has some resistance to lift.
4. Time the balloon again. Did the weights make any difference in the time to the ceiling?

QUESTIONS:

1. Which direction did the balloon go: toward the ceiling or toward the floor?

   _____

2. Was this the direction of the escaping air? In other words, did the balloon travel in the same direction as the escaping air did?

   _____

3. Which of "Newton's Laws" explains this event?

   _____

4. Would you have been surprised if the balloon went in the same direction as the escaping air? Why?

   _____

5. Memorize Newton's Three Laws of Motion based on God's Laws of Nature:

   First Law: Objects in motion tend to stay in motion.

   Second Law: An object's force is the combination of its mass and acceleration.

   Third Law: For every action, there is an equal and opposite reaction.

6. Why do you think God made laws to govern the universe?

   _____

DIAGRAM ANALYSIS

DIRECTIONS: Look at the images below. Label them as to the type of propulsion they must use to go forward. If you can, identify the type of fuel they use.

PROPULSION:

_____

FUEL:

_____

PROPULSION:

_____

FUEL:

_____

PROPULSION:

_____

FUEL:

_____

PROPULSION:

_____

FUEL:

_____

VIII. The Difference Between Rockets and Planes

The forces that enable a rocket to fly are the same as those that enable a plane to fly: lift, thrust, drag, and weight. The primary difference between rockets and planes lies in their propulsion systems. Both planes and rockets push air backward to produce thrust. Unlike planes, however, rockets do not require air to burn fuel in their engines. Rockets contain their **own supply of oxygen**, which enables the combustion of fuel to produce thrust. For this reason, rockets can fly **outside** of the Earth's atmosphere. Planes, however, can travel only **in** the Earth's atmosphere where the engines have access to oxygen in the air.

Furthermore, planes require the presence of an **atmosphere** to generate lift. Planes are capable of flying at high altitudes until the air becomes thinner and almost a vacuum. At these altitudes, there are few air molecules to hold a plane up, and thus planes cannot fly here. Rockets, on the other hand, can fly in the absence of an atmosphere. Once again, a rocket's propulsion system plays an important role. It produces the force of thrust to overcome the force of weight.

IX. The Advancement of Science

So far, you have learned that flying developed through human reasoning and experimentation. It began with men producing crude flapping wings and then became a reality with the Wright brothers. Scientists and engineers began to look at the atmosphere in a new way. They discovered new information and scientific principles that enabled them to improve the design of aircraft.

Rocket flight developed similarly. Initially, rockets were crude and limited to flying within the Earth's atmosphere. Scientists learned more about the Earth's atmosphere, and engineers improved the design and performance of rockets, until they were able to place people into outer space and even on the moon.

The science of **aeronautics** provides a good example of how science advances. For example, you might think that we know all that there is to know about flying. Yet, scientists continue to study aeronautics and outer space, and engineers continue to improve the designs and the performance of planes and rockets. They keep developing new generations of aircraft and spacecraft. The thirst for new knowledge has not stopped, and never will stop, because God created man with an intellect that is, by nature, interested in learning more and achieving more.

X. Orbits and Satellites

What do we mean when we use the term orbit? An **orbit** is a gravitationally curved path of an object moving around a point in space. For example, the Earth orbits the sun. Most orbits, including the planets' orbits, are **elliptical**, or shaped like a slightly flattened circle. In a **circular** orbit, the object remains at the same distance from the center of its orbit at all times. The speed will remain the same at all points of the orbit.

Objects that revolve around a large primary body are called **satellites.** There are two kinds of satellites: artificial satellites and natural satellites. **Artificial satellites** have been placed into orbit by humans, namely space scientists.

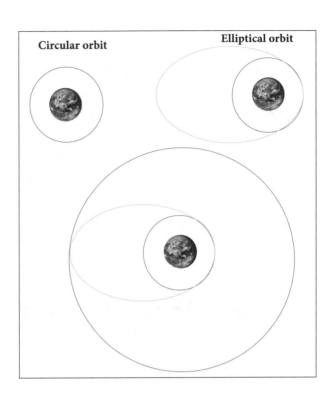

Circular orbit   Elliptical orbit

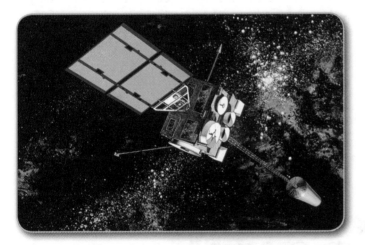

GOES-8 Weather Satellite

Natural satellites are **celestial bodies** that orbit around another body. Of course, celestial bodies were put into orbit by God. The moon is a satellite or celestial body that orbits the Earth; the planets are celestial bodies or satellites of the sun.

The names or kinds of orbits are based on how and where they revolve. **Equatorial orbits** are those in which a satellite revolves around the Earth above the Equator. We refer to all other orbits as **inclined orbits**. A satellite that orbits over the North and South poles travels in a **polar orbit**. For example, **weather satellites** in polar orbits pass over the Earth's poles so that the Earth rotates under the satellite once each day.

Satellites in **circular orbits** 24,000 miles above the Earth revolve at the same rate as the Earth rotates. These satellites remain over the same geographical locations and are called **geosynchronous** or **geostationary satellites**. We use these for many purposes, including communication, navigation, research, and weather monitoring.

As mentioned before, in 1957, the Soviet Union launched *Sputnik I*, the first artificial Earth satellite. Since then, more than fifty countries have placed satellites into orbit. Not all countries have the ability to launch their own satellites, and many rely on the capabilities of other countries. Currently, there are hundreds of satellites orbiting the Earth, but more than a thousand unused ones remain aloft! These unused satellites and their fragments orbit the Earth as **space debris**. Some old satellites were designed to remain permanently in their orbit. However, concern about clutter and crashes with other spacecraft has led to the creation of a **graveyard orbit**. This orbit lies high above the other orbits, and most satellites are sent there at the end of their operational life.

There are many examples of **spacecraft that are satellites** and capable of traveling far into space. These include space shuttles, space stations, and probes. These vehicles help scientists collect information about the moon, planets, and outer space, continually providing us with new information.

XI. Space Shuttle Program

The space shuttle was a spacecraft that could be reused. It was designed to transport people and cargo between Earth and space. It was composed of two solid rocket boosters and an external fuel tank, both of which were jettisoned or released into space after takeoff. The first mission of the U.S. space shuttle program began in 1981, with the launch of *Columbia*, the first of six space shuttles.

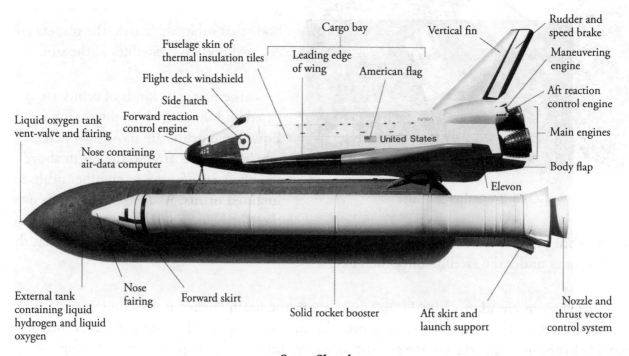

Space Shuttle

The space shuttle was very unique in that it could conduct different kinds of missions. These included launching and recovering satellites, serving as a science laboratory, and working on and repairing other spacecraft. The most notable of its repair work involved fixing the Hubble Space Telescope. In addition, the crew of a space shuttle helped assemble the International Space Station. For one moment, think about what an extraordinary achievement that was! A space vehicle traveled into space where its crew of several people helped assemble a larger space vehicle. No one could have conceived of such an endeavor 100 years ago!

Space Shuttle Columbia

The space shuttle consisted of three parts: orbiter, external tank, and solid rocket boosters. The **orbiter** was a large, white space plane. The crew members lived and worked in the orbiter, and conducted many scientific experiments in the orbiter. The orbiter was the only part of the shuttle that traveled into space. The other parts of the shuttle were jettisoned after launching was complete.

The second part, the **external tank,** contained fuel, and attached to the bottom of the shuttle during takeoff. The two **solid rocket boosters** were much thinner than the external tank. These solid rocket boosters provided most of the thrust for the first two minutes of the launch into space. Additional thrust came from the engines on the orbiter. Once the boosters and external tank ran out of fuel, they were released from the orbiter and fell into the ocean. A special boat and crew retrieved the tanks for future use.

During a thirty-year period, the space shuttles flew 135 missions, totaling 542,398,878 miles, and 21,152 Earth orbits. *Columbia* was the first shuttle, reaching space in 1981. For twenty years, *Columbia* carried dozens of astronauts into space. As years passed, the technology advanced, and *Columbia* was upgraded. There were remarkable achievements.

However, as with any successful enterprise, there were major setbacks. In 2003, *Columbia* burned up during re-entry from outer space over Texas. The seven members of the crew were killed. The *Challenger*, another shuttle, blew up on takeoff in 1986. The crew was killed. This was filmed live on national television and affected the whole nation.

The president, Ronald Reagan, addressing the NASA workers after the loss of the seven crew members of *Challenger*, made the following statement:

"We shall never forget them nor the last time we saw them, as they prepared for their mission and waved good-bye and slipped the surly bonds of Earth to touch the face of God."

The loss of *Challenger* was especially memorable because its mishap occurred only 73 seconds after liftoff, and was broadcast on live television. People throughout the United States and the world were devastated by this event. The loss of *Columbia* was no less tragic. It began to disintegrate during its reentry into the Earth's atmosphere. Parts of *Columbia* were scattered over the states of Louisiana, Texas, and Arkansas.

The final space shuttle mission flew in July 2011, before the program was terminated one month later, on August 31, 2011. Many people lamented the loss of the Space Shuttle Program, not only for the end of space travel, but also for the end of the important inventions that were developed in connection with the program.

It has been estimated that more than 1,500 technologies developed by NASA, the National Aeronautics and Space Administration, have benefited U.S. industries, improved the quality of life, and created meaningful jobs. We call these technologies **spin-offs**. Spin-offs are things that happen to arise from other things; so these spin-offs have been produced as a result of space exploration, but are not for outer space uses, but rather for everyday use for people on Earth.

Some of these spin-offs seem out of the ordinary, but they are very real. For example, the technology used in the space shuttle fuel pumps led to the development of a miniature heart pump by the renowned heart surgeon, Dr. Michael DeBakey. Another spin-off began as a device that measured the equilibrium or balance of astronauts when they returned from space. These are now used by medical centers to treat patients suffering from head injuries, strokes, chronic dizziness, and other disorders of the central nervous system. There are too many spin-off examples to list here, but hopefully you can see that there is more to space programs than simple exploration.

XII. Space Probes

You have learned that rockets launch people and things into space and that rockets travel in orbits. Now we will discuss space probes. Space probes were originally used to explore the moon, beginning in 1958. Within the first few years, however, space probes met with a mixture of failures, partial successes, and very few *complete* successes. This is typical of the way science works. Failures are not really failures at all, but lessons to be learned on the pathway to success.

What are space probes? **Space probes** are unmanned robotic vehicles that travel into deep space. These vehicles possess their own **power supplies**, either **nuclear generators** or **solar panels**. These power supplies allow space probes to remain in space for a long time. There are several space probes that have been in space for over 30 years! These probes have completed their missions but continue to travel into deep space. We have lost communications with them but assume that they are continuing their journey.

Unlike satellites, space shuttles, and space stations, space probes do not travel in orbits around the Earth. Astronomers send space probes to investigate and collect information from far-away **astronomical objects** or **celestial bodies**, such as moons, asteroids, comets, planets, the sun, and other stars. These investigations are made possible by the variety of scientific instruments the probes contain. These scientific instruments measure gravity, radiation, magnetic fields, and the composition of surface materials. In addition, some space probes possess instruments for mapping surfaces and geological features. This is done with a type of camera on the space probe, so that the hills and valleys of the various planets and other objects in space can be studied. All of this information is sent back to Earth by a **radio system** within the probe.

The Internet (www.solarviews.com) reported the following after Pluto was mapped: "This is the first image-based surface map of the solar system's most remote planet, Pluto. This map was assembled by computer image processing software from four separate images of Pluto's disk taken with the European Space Agency's Faint Object Camera (FOC) aboard NASA's Hubble Space Telescope. Hubble imaged nearly the entire surface, as Pluto rotated on its axis in late June and early July of 1994.

"The map, which covers 85% of the planet's surface, confirms that Pluto has a dark equatorial belt and bright polar caps, as inferred from ground-based light curves obtained during the mutual eclipses that occurred between Pluto and its satellite Charon in the late 1980s.

"The brightness variations in this map may be due to topographic features such as basins and fresh impact craters. However, most of the surface features unveiled by Hubble are likely produced by the complex distribution of frosts that migrate across Pluto's surface with its orbital and seasonal cycles. Names may later be proposed for some of the larger regions."

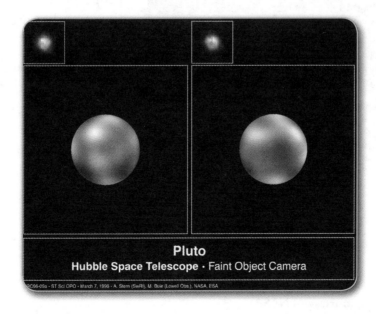

Pluto
Hubble Space Telescope · Faint Object Camera

C96-09a · ST ScI OPO · March 7, 1996 · A. Stern (SwRI), M. Buie (Lowell Obs.), NASA, ESA

A. Flyby Missions

Space probes have two kinds of missions: flyby and rover. In a **flyby mission**, the probe orbits the planet, collecting data without landing on the planet. Venus was the first planet reached by a space probe, *Mariner 2*, in 1962. This was the first of several flyby missions to Venus. The *Magellan* probe was launched from the Space Shuttle *Atlantis* in May 1989. It reached Venus by August 1990, and was able to map 98% of its surface by radar. This means that we know what the surface of Venus looks like!

Mariner 2
(Image courtesy of NASA)

B. Rover Missions

Rover missions use specially designed robotic vehicles known as rovers. They explore and make records of the surface of planets as they move across them. Rovers require another vehicle to land on a planet. A **lander** is placed on the surface of a planet. The first successful rover and lander to explore Mars was *Sojourner/Pathfinder*. These probes were launched on December 4, 1996, and landed on Mars on July 4, 1997. *Pathfinder* opened and allowed *Sojourner* to exit and roam over the surface, recording surface features. Hundreds of thousands of people watched this event, which was broadcast live over the Internet.

Sojourner and *Pathfinder* worked as a team to learn about Mars. They "investigated" (or recorded) the atmosphere, the climate, the geology, and the composition of the rocks and soil. *Pathfinder* had a camera and its own meteorological station. It was able to collect data about air pressure and temperature. The meteorological station also contained three windsocks to measure wind speeds.

Sojourner
(Image courtesy of NASA)

Pathfinder recorded winds that mostly came from the west. *Sojourner* was far smaller than *Pathfinder* and weighed only 23 pounds! *Sojourner* had black-and-white cameras, color cameras, and a device known as an Alpha Proton X-ray Spectrometer (APXS). Together, these instruments were able to analyze the rotation and orbit of Mars, and to analyze its rocks and soil and the magnetic properties of its dust.

Voyager 2
(Image courtesy of NASA)

One of the most successful space probes was Voyager 2. This space probe visited four planets: Jupiter, Saturn, Uranus, and Neptune. It made many important discoveries. As Voyager 2 flew by Neptune, it revealed six unknown moons of the planet and three rings. As with most space probes, it carried many instruments, including cameras. The information from the instruments was sent back to the Earth by radio signals, which were detected by radio telescopes.

Another space probe, Galileo, traveled to Jupiter and gathered much information about the planet and its moons. It also sent a small descent probe into the atmosphere. It was eventually destroyed by the pressure of Jupiter's atmosphere.

The Viking landers, which were sent to Mars, used robotic arms to collect rock and soil from the planet. Space probes have landed on the moon. Some space probes have left our solar system, and it is unlikely they will ever be found again.

Probes remain in use today as we study the moon and the planets and send probes farther into deep space. It is amazing that man's ingenuity and knowledge of science, as well as God's blessings, enabled these kinds of spacecraft. Most amazing is God Himself, Who created the universe and gave people the means and intellect to explore it!

It is impossible to present all of the discoveries made by space probes in one chapter. Indeed, these would make for a very large book. The following table summarizes a few of the key trips. As you read through this list of findings, you should know that this list will become larger with each passing year. With each discovery, we learn more about the heavens and are reminded about our Creator, Who is infinite in knowledge and wisdom.

PLANET/MISSION TYPE	NAME OF PROBE/ LAUNCH YEAR	MISSION DURATION	FINDINGS
Jupiter/Flyby	Pioneer 10 1972	2 yr, 1 mo	Temperature map of Jupiter and two moons, Ganymede and Europa, and presence of magnetic fields. Jupiter produces more heat than it receives from the sun.
Mercury/Flyby	Mariner 10 1973	1 yr, 4 1/2 mo	Moon-like surface, strong magnetic field, iron core, and helium atmosphere.
Venus/Flyby	Mariner 10 1973	1 yr, 4 1/2 mo	Rotating clouds and weak magnetic field. Atmosphere of carbon dioxide and nitrogen.
Saturn/Flyby	Pioneer 11 1973	6 yr, 6 mo	Temperature and magnetic field measurements. Found new moon and a new ring on Saturn.
Uranus/Flyby	Voyager 2 1977	8 yr, 6 mo	Discovery of a magnetic field. Rings have different composition than Saturn's rings.
Neptune/Flyby	Voyager 2 1977	12 yr, 2 mo	Atmosphere consists of hydrogen, helium, and methane. Gases absorb red from sun and reflect blue
Mars/Rover	Sojourner 1996	7 months	Rocky surface, evidence of catastrophic flood, red atmosphere due to presence of iron particles.

XIII. Telescopes

Think about a microscope and a small telescope side-by-side. What is the difference? They are pretty much the same thing: a hollow tube with an objective lens on one end and an eyepiece on the other end. The main difference between the two lies with the design of the lens and its location on the tube. The microscope magnifies close-up objects, and the telescope magnifies far-away objects.

Telescopes are simple tools that astronomers use to discover more about the universe. We use them here on Earth and in vehicles in outer space. We tend to think that telescopes are a new invention, but they have their origin in the 17th century. Galileo Galilei has been credited with developing the first telescope in 1609. Since then, technology has improved upon his first homemade instrument. We continue to develop telescopes, and our knowledge of the heavens has grown rapidly.

The **refracting telescope** was the first and most popular kind of telescope. It is a hollow tube with two lenses. Light enters an **objective lens** at one end of a tube and then bends or refracts the light toward a **focal plane**, a single point where the image is located. An **eyepiece** is located directly behind the focal point of this image. The eyepiece enlarges the image. Once again, we look to God's creatures and find the telescope. The eyes of hawks have long focal lengths with their lenses positioned far back in the eyes. This enables them to see small objects at great distances. You may occasionally see a hawk circling overhead and looking down. It is scanning the area at a great altitude, perhaps scanning a field or a forest, and looking for movement indicating the presence of possible prey.

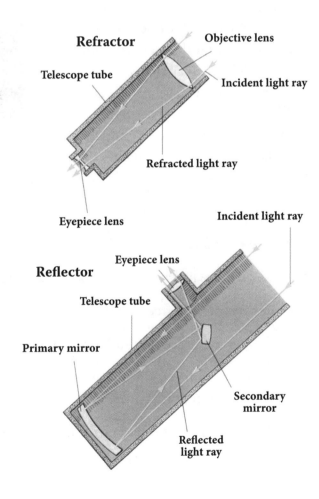

Refracting telescopes are adequate for most purposes. However, they have limits that have to do with their design and construction. Scientists have found that it is difficult to obtain perfect glass without air bubbles. In addition, glass blocks certain wavelengths of light. Because of this, the lens produces degraded images and color shifts. What an astronomer sees may be blurry or not real.

4

There are size constraints to lenses of refracting telescopes. We tend to think that glass is solid and stable. It is for the most part. In time, though, large pieces of glass begin to sag and deform. Lenses greater than 40 inches in diameter begin to sag and produce a distorted image.

The largest refracting telescope in the world is in the **Yerkes Observatory** in Wisconsin. It was designed and built in the 1890s. The objective lens is 40 inches across and weighs about 440 lbs. The tube is 63 feet long. A 75-foot diameter floor works as an elevator and raises astronomers to the telescope eyepiece.

Reflecting telescopes collect light and form images by using concave mirrors. The initial image that forms is small. The image (light) travels to a second mirror, which reflects the image to the eyepiece, where it is magnified. One of the largest reflective telescopes in the world is found in the Canary Islands, Spain. It is known as the Gran Telescopio Canarias (Great Telescope of the Canaries), and its aperture (opening through which light passes into the telescope) is 410 inches (34 ft., 2 in.) in diameter.

Great Telescope of the Canaries
(Photo courtesy of Pachango)

Nearly all large, research-grade astronomical telescopes are reflectors. There are several reasons for this:

• Mirrors are much easier to make than large lenses.

• Lenses must be free of defects and imperfections.

• Only one surface on the mirror must be "perfect."

• Lenses absorb certain wavelengths (colors) of light, whereas mirrors enable passage or transmission of the entire light spectrum.

• Sagging is not a problem with mirrors. Currently, the largest mirror is more than 34 feet in diameter.

XIV. Hubble Space Telescope

The Hubble Space Telescope cost millions of dollars because it is so large and the scientists who produced it were trying to create a flawless mirror. The Hubble Space Telescope is a reflecting telescope; it produces images using a large mirror. The image is magnified by a smaller eyepiece lens, which has a short focal length. The Hubble Space Telescope has provided astronomers with exciting new discoveries about star formations. It has produced amazing photographs of bodies within our solar system.

If you have an interest in astronomy, you will find that you can purchase an adequate telescope at a modest price. These can be a lot of fun, and you may become hooked on a new hobby. Do not rule out using binoculars to explore the heavens.

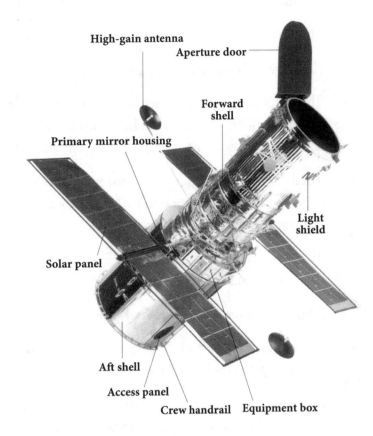

Hubble Space Telescope

Some binoculars are very powerful. One problem with binoculars is that it is difficult to hold them steady. You can solve this problem by resting the binoculars on a steady surface as you look through them. Finally, many science museums and universities have observatories with occasional programs that are open to the public. Looking through a telescope at an observatory can be amazing!

As we think about the heavens and all the wonderful stars and planets and discoveries, it is good to think about an event we can read about in the Bible when the heavens opened up and showed us more than stars and planets. As Jesus was being baptized, we read in Matthew 3:16-17 about the Three Persons of the Blessed Trinity coming together: "And Jesus being baptized came forth out of the water; and lo, the heavens were opened to Him, and He saw the Spirit of God descending as a dove, and coming upon Him. And behold a voice from heaven saying, 'This is My Beloved Son in Whom I am well pleased.'"

Chapter 4 Summary

1. Orville and Wilbur Wright designed and flew the first airplane in 1903.

2. The forces that enable airplanes to fly are **lift, thrust, drag,** and **weight**.

3. An increase in **speed** results in greater lift.

4. The parts of an airplane include the **fuselage, cockpit, empennage** (or tail), and **wings**. The empennage includes the **horizontal stabilizer** with the **elevators** and the **vertical stabilizer** with the **rudder**. The wings include the **ailerons** and the **flaps**.

5. The balance point, called the **center of gravity**, on an airplane is located near the leading edge of the wings. The **center of lift** is located about one-fourth of the way back from the leading edge.

6. The primary function of a rocket is to get as high off the ground as it can. In order to do this, the rocket must fight **gravity**.

7. A rocket engine must have **fuel,** a **spark** to start the fire, and **oxygen** to burn the fuel.

8. The **exhaust** is the real driving force behind the rocket. It provides the opposing force propelling the rocket forward.

9. During World War II, **Germany** did much research on rockets. After the end of the war, many of the researchers came to the United States to work on the space program.

10. Planetary orbits are **elliptical**, rather than circular.

11. **Circular orbits** are even, and the satellite or moon remains at the same distance away from the planet at all times.

12. **Elliptical orbits** are not even, and the satellite or moon does not remain at the same distance away from the planet. Sometimes it passes close to the planet, when it travels the fastest.

13. **Space probes** are unmanned space vehicles sent out to gather information about planets. Because they have robots, they are able to land on a planet that mankind has yet to visit. The most famous and successful space probe is *Voyager 2*.

14. Scientists have long used **telescopes** to view stars and planets. The **aperture** is the opening of the telescope which lets in light. It resembles the eye. It is the most important part of the telescope, even more important than the **magnification**, because some stars are so far away that they only appear as a point of light, no matter what the magnification.

15. A **reflecting telescope** uses a large mirror. The Hubble Space Telescope is an example of a reflecting telescope.

16. A **refracting telescope** produces images using only lenses (usually two of them).

Questions for Review

1. What force makes the plane go up? _____
_____

2. How must the air stream flow around the wing of a plane to create lift?
_____
_____

3. How does the force of drag work? _____
_____

4. How is drag helpful to pilots?
_____
_____

5. Explain how the flaps work in landing. _____
_____

6. What is the purpose of ailerons? How do they differ from the flaps?
_____
_____

7. What are elevators and how do they work?
_____
_____

8. What is yaw? Which airplane part controls yaw?
_____
_____

9. How do planes turn? _____
_____

10. Does a plane need an engine? Why?
_____
_____

J.M.J.

Thinking about Science

1. What would happen to an airplane if you could reduce its drag?

   _____

   _____

2. An airplane can move in six different ways. List these six ways.

   _____

   _____

   _____

   _____

   _____

3. Does an airplane wing have lift when the engine is off? Why? Hint: What generates lift?

   _____

   _____

4. Must a bird flap its wings in order to fly?

   _____

   _____

5. Have you ever seen a buzzard or eagle gliding high up in the air? As the bird glides, its wings are not flapping. How do the wings produce lift without flapping?

   _____

   _____

   _____

Energy

I.   **Energy of Motion**

II.   **God: The Prime Mover**

III.   **God's Laws of the Universe**

IV.   **The First Law of Motion**

V.   **The Second Law of Motion**

VI.   **The Third Law of Motion**

VII.   **The Laws of Thermodynamics**

VIII. **Transformation of Energy**

     A.   Green Plants

     B.   Electricity from Coal, Oil, Nuclear Reactors

IX.   **God: The Creator of the Laws of Energy**

X.   **The Progress of Science**

Energy

Chapter 5

"For what can be known about God is plain to them, because God has shown it t Ever since the creation of the world His invisible nature, namely, His eternal pow deity, has been clearly perceived in the things that have been made" (Romans 1:

The passage above from St. Paul's Epistle to the Romans describes how we understand God through creation: His divinity and power are revealed through His visible creations.

When we hear the word *creation*, we may think of many things: lush tropical jungles with all kinds of animals and birds, sparkling waterfalls set against majestic mountains, or perhaps Adam and Eve in the Garden of Eden. But there is another part of creation that we often don't think about: the invisible world of God's creation. Let's review several examples.

Example 1: You are listening to your favorite music. What you hear comes from instruments or human vocal cords that produce various sound waves. These sound waves are one type of invisible energy. You don't even think about it while you are listening. You only know that you like the music.

Example 2: It's summertime, and the windows are open. Your family is having a backyard cookout, and you are busy cleaning up your room. As you begin to put things away, the aroma of food comes through the window. You can smell the hamburgers and chicken cooking on the grill. The chemicals that you breathe in through your nose are another type of invisible energy. You don't even need to ask your mom, "What's for dinner?"

Example 3: You're on the tail end of a roller coaster car heading down the biggest hill on the track. Your stomach tightens, your heart speeds up, and then—Whoosh!!!—you travel down the track at a high speed. Your inner ear and eyes sense the motion of the coaster, as does your skin, which is bombarded with air molecules. Both the motion and the air are invisible, but you like the feeling and find it exciting.

Example 4: You are visiting a butterfly garden. Your eyes focus on one striking butterfly that displays a combination of vivid colors: maroon, gold, blue, and black. These colors come from pigments in the scales on the wings of the butterfly. The pigments absorb white light and reflect color. You cannot see these invisible processes at work; the results are all you can see.

In the above examples, you may have noted that it is our God-given senses, along with our minds, that help us understand or make sense of the invisible world. You already know that our bodies are made of matter, and we live in the physical world. Yet it is a world not only of solid matter but of invisible things as well. In fact, it is a world filled with invisible energy.

So, what do we mean by the word energy? Energy comes to us from the Greek word *kinein*, which means to move. **Energy** has a simple definition: the ability to do work. Work is accomplished when an object moves or changes, so energy is the ability to move and change things. Scientists recognize two classifications of energy: *potential* energy and *kinetic* energy.

I. Energy of Motion

Potential energy is known as **stored energy**. The word *potential* means having a capability or power to move or do work. Potential energy means that an object has the power to do work but is not doing it yet.

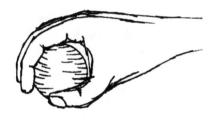

A hand holding a ball above the ground. The ball has potential energy, but no kinetic energy.

Let's look at an example of potential energy. Suppose that you and your family are walking along a winding trail at the top of a ridge. You see a boulder sitting on the edge of the cliff. You don't know how long it has been sitting there or how it came to its present resting spot. Somehow, though, gravitational forces put it there. Does the boulder have energy? Yes, it has potential energy. Suddenly, the part of the cliff on which it is sitting breaks away, and the boulder begins to fall downward toward the river.

Let's stop the boulder for a brief moment and think about what is happening. In terms of energy, what has just happened? As long as the boulder sat there, it had potential energy. When it began to fall because of the force of gravity, its potential energy was turned into kinetic energy. **Kinetic energy** is called the **energy of motion**. Let's continue to let the boulder fall. The force of gravity pulls downward on the boulder, increasing its speed as it falls. After three seconds, the boulder strikes the river. The kinetic energy of motion quickly converts to sound, so you hear the loud bang and splash as it hits the river! Finally, the boulder comes to rest on the river bottom, and it now has no energy. It has no kinetic energy because it is not moving, and it has no potential energy because it is resting on the surface of the Earth. In order to have potential energy, an object must be held up above the surface of the Earth. The higher it is, the more potential energy it has.

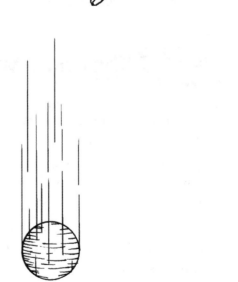

The hand has released the ball. The ball still has potential energy, although less than it did. It has increasing kinetic energy.

Let us study a bouncing ball. Hold a ball out and then drop it without applying any extra force. As you hold the ball up, it has a significant amount of potential energy. When you drop it, the ball starts moving down. During this motion, the ball has increasing kinetic energy and decreasing potential energy. Suddenly, the ball hits the ground, and the ground compresses the ball so that it is flat on one side. When the ball springs back and moves upward, it has decreasing kinetic energy and increasing potential energy.

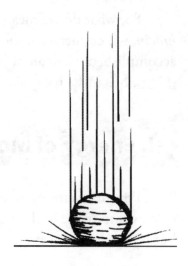

The ball is hitting the ground. It has great kinetic energy, but no potential energy. It will lose some of its total energy as heat from the impact. When it bounces, it will not go as far into the air as before.

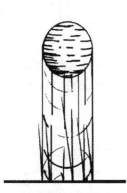

The ball is returning to the air after bouncing. It has increasing potential energy, and decreasing kinetic energy.

As the ball continues to bounce, the energy it possesses changes from potential to kinetic and back again. At each bounce, the ball releases a little of its energy as heat energy. This energy is lost by the ball. So, on the next bounce the ball cannot go as high as it did before. Each bounce is lower until the ball stops bouncing.

When the ball stops bouncing and lies still on the floor, it has no energy. All the potential energy it had at the beginning of the experiment has been used up, and the ball remains still on the floor. All the kinetic energy is gone.

II. God: The Prime Mover

Everything around us is moving. Even as you sit reading this book, your eyes are moving, your hands are turning the pages or moving the computer mouse, and your brain is actively processing words and information. You can go a step further by considering the printed words on a sheet of paper. The chemicals or molecules in both the ink and the paper are moving also! There is nothing in the universe that is not in motion, though we don't always see it. But what exactly is motion? This concept has puzzled scientists and philosophers for centuries. It wasn't until the time of **Sir Isaac Newton in the 17th century** that we really began to understand the complexity of motion. Let's review an example to see what we are talking about.

The illustration above is an example of a pushing or pulling force exerted on an object. In this case, it is the wind blowing on the leaf.

Imagine that you are riding a bicycle. What moves the bike forward? Is it you? Yes, it is you, but how does it move? It moves by its wheels. What moves the wheels? A pair of pedals are attached to cranks on a chain wheel. Your feet push downward on the pedals that rotate the chain wheel. A chain connects the chain wheel in the front with a sprocket in the rear. The chain rotates the sprocket, which in turn rotates the wheel. What moves your feet? Your muscles do, through your mind and will, and kinetic energy. But where does the kinetic energy come from? It comes from chemicals, the products of food you digested. Where does the food come from? All food has the sun as its source. Where does the sun come from? Our Creator God. Where does God come from? **God does not come from anything; He simply always was and always will be, and He owes His existence to no one but Himself.**

Most people do not give this type of systematic reasoning much thought when they ride a bike. However, if you examine the motion of any object, you can see that motion is due to another motion that preceded it. However, eventually, there must be Someone Who moves but is not moved by anything else. For this reason, the great thinkers or philosophers have referred to God throughout the ages as the **Prime Mover or the First Cause**. In fact, St. Thomas Aquinas wrote, "Therefore, it is **necessary** to arrive at a First Mover, put in motion by no other; and this everyone understands to be **God**."

Note the significance of this great saint's words: it is necessary to arrive at a First Mover, Whom we all call God! If we did not have a First Mover, nothing at all would exist! How would anything move at all? There must be a First Mover, God.

III. God's Laws of the Universe

God gave us moral laws so that we might be happy with Him in this world and share eternal life with Him in the next world, in Heaven. This means that He knows the things we should do and the things we should avoid in order to be happy. As Catholics, we know that these laws were given to us by God to help us to grow in grace and spend eternity with Him in Heaven.

God knows what is best for His creation. God gave physical things **physical laws** in order for each of His creatures to operate properly. These laws of physics, or laws for the physical universe, have been in existence since the beginning of creation, since God created the physical world. These physical laws govern everything within the physical universe. They prevent the universe from slipping into total chaos and disorder. None of us can imagine what the world would be like without the laws of nature, the laws of the physical world, which can help us to predict how everything will work.

When we hear the term *scientific laws*, most people think of the Laws of Motion. God is the Author of the Laws of Motion, just as He is the Creator of everything. History books give Sir Isaac Newton credit for describing the Laws of Motion; therefore, they are usually called **Newton's Laws of Motion**. Of course, in reality, they are God's Laws of Motion, but Newton discovered them.

IV. The First Law of Motion

The First Law of Motion states: **an object at rest tends to stay at rest, and an object in motion tends to stay in motion**, with the same direction and speed. This could be restated as: *an object moves or stops moving when acted upon by an outside force.*

Using the First Law of Motion, let's take a closer look at the previous example of the boulder sitting on the cliff. When you first saw the boulder, *it was at rest*. It could have stayed at rest until the end of time. However, the cliff gave way, and the force of gravity caused the boulder to move. *It stayed in motion*, falling until it met the irresistible force of the river bottom. You can see that the boulder obeyed the First Law of Motion. It remained at rest until acted upon by an outside force (gravity).

V. The Second Law of Motion

The Second Law of Motion states: **the acceleration (increasing speed) of an object is directly related to the force that moves or pushes the object and inversely related to the mass of the object.** This law can be expressed as a mathematical equation: the force moving an object is equal to its mass times its acceleration, or $F = MA$.

Let's put this another way. The greater the mass of the object, the greater the amount of force needed to accelerate it, to make it move.

Perhaps acceleration may be a new term for you. Think of a time that you and your family were running late to go somewhere. Your dad may have driven a little faster than normal. Then you had to sit and wait at a traffic light. As soon as it turned green, your dad pushed down on the gas pedal or accelerator, and your car quickly lurched forward; the car was accelerating, or gaining speed rapidly. The acceleration caused you to feel pushed against the back

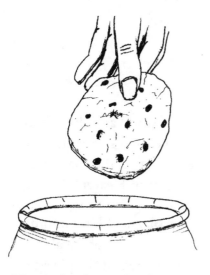

The cookie has some forces acting upon it. The hand picking up the cookie is applying force in an upward direction. The Earth is also acting upon the cookie. The Earth is applying a force called gravity, which acts in a downward direction. What other forces may be acting upon the cookie?

of your seat. Once your car was traveling at a constant speed, say 55 miles per hour, your car was no longer accelerating; it was no longer necessary to give it extra push. It was still moving, but it was not *gaining* speed. You no longer felt pushed against the back of the seat.

Let's take a closer look at acceleration, as it relates to force and mass. We'll use two familiar objects, a baseball that weighs 5 ounces and a bowling ball that weighs 12 pounds. It is clear that the bowling ball has a larger mass than the baseball. You take the baseball and throw it overhand as far as you can, perhaps 200 feet or so. Next, you take the bowling ball and try to throw it in the same manner. Maybe someone can throw it overhand, but you would be lucky to throw it any distance. What happened?

The Second Law of Motion tells us that if you place the same force on two objects having different masses, it will result in two different accelerations. In this example, the acceleration was more noticeable with the baseball. It has a smaller mass. It would take tremendous force or acceleration to throw the bowling ball as far as the baseball.

VI. The Third Law of Motion

Finally, we come to the Third Law of Motion: **for every action, there is an equal and opposite reaction**. We can think of examples of the Third Law in relation to an airplane. First, the force of thrust pushes air backward, which propels or pushes the plane forward. Second, as the plane moves forward, it encounters drag or resistance with air.

That is, the air pushes back or resists the plane as it moves forward. You can also consider the above example with your family car. As the car quickly moves forward, an equal and opposite force pushes backward on you sitting safely in the back seat!

J.M.J.

PROBLEMS: Study these situations and answer the questions.

1. Does the object have the energy to move?

2. Is energy active in this case? Is work being done?

3. Must the object have a source of energy to move? What might that be?

Image by NASA

1._____
_____

2._____
_____

3._____
_____

1._____
_____

2._____
_____

3._____
_____

Image by USFS

Image by Caelio

1._____
_____

2._____
_____

3._____
_____

PROBLEMS: Identify the type of energy present in each of these pictures: potential or kinetic.

1. _____

2. _____

3. _____

4. _____

5. _____

J.M.J.

DIAGRAM ANALYSIS

DIRECTIONS: Look at the images below. Analyze them for all the forces acting on the objects pictured. List the forces acting upon the objects.

Note: To analyze something means to study the subject, make observations of it, and draw conclusions about it.

LIST OF FORCES:

_____

_____

_____

_____

LIST OF FORCES:

_____

_____

_____

_____

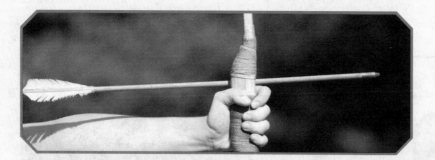

LIST OF FORCES:

_____

_____

_____

_____

LIST OF FORCES:

_____

_____

_____

_____

DIAGRAM ANALYSIS

DIRECTIONS: Look at the images below. Analyze them for all the forces acting on the objects pictured. Using arrows, label the forces that represent those forces.

VII. The Laws of Thermodynamics

Energy is a topic that you may see or read about in the news. Typically, these stories involve oil and gas, but sometimes other types of energy like solar power and windmills. Energy is a popular topic because it affects our way of life. Our entire world runs on energy.

The Laws of Thermodynamics best explain what we know about energy. The First Law of Thermodynamics, also known as *Conservation of Energy*, states that **the amount of energy in the universe always remains constant**. It can be transferred from one form to another form, and from one location to another location. However, we cannot add to or remove energy from the universe. For this reason, the First Law of Thermodynamics is sometimes stated: **energy can neither be created nor destroyed.**

The Second Law of Thermodynamics is often referred to as the Law of Entropy (EN-tro-pee). This law states that **everything in the universe moves from higher energy levels to lower ones**. Remember our example of the bouncing ball: at each bounce, the ball lost some of its energy in the form of escaping heat, until finally the ball lost all energy and stopped moving.

You can see another example of this law if you take a trip in the country. If you have ever seen an "old family farm," you may have noticed tractors and wagons with rust, and a barn that looked like it needed paint. The materials in these items have lost some of their energy and have begun to decay. It's the normal way of nature; it is the Second Law of Thermodynamics. Looking at this from the large scale of the universe, the Second Law of Thermodynamics means that **energy transfers to less usable forms**.

Let's examine the First and Second Laws of Thermodynamics using your family car, which uses gasoline as its energy source. A device called a fuel pump inside the car pumps gasoline from the fuel tank and into the engine. The gas mixes with air and, through the process of combustion (the burning of fuel to provide power), is explosively converted into kinetic energy. The kinetic energy, the energy of motion, is transferred from the engine to the drive shaft and the car moves forward, by the energy of motion. We can use the following notation to represent this process:

Potential Energy → Kinetic Energy

What happened to the potential energy of the gasoline in the car? Through combustion, it was immediately transformed into kinetic energy. Slightly less than 1/3 of the kinetic energy was useful. It powered or moved the car. The remainder was converted into less useful forms, including heat energy and exhaust gases (carbon monoxide, carbon dioxide, and water). Both the heat and gases escaped and became part of the atmosphere. In this example, you can see that energy wasn't created. The energy came from the gasoline. You can also see that energy wasn't destroyed. The energy from the gasoline was converted into less usable forms, but none of it was destroyed.

When an object is not moving, it is said to be **at rest**. God has designed our bodies in such a way that they require rest. He has given us an example of how we should treat our bodies. He spent six days creating the whole universe and then spent the seventh day resting. So important is this rest that God has made it a requirement to keep holy the Lord's Day, Sunday, and rest as He rested after His labors.

VIII. Transformation of Energy

The Laws of Thermodynamics apply to all types of energy use, not just to gasoline-powered engines. Energy use results in (1) a change from one form to another and (2) lesser forms of energy. Let's review some other examples.

A. Green Plants

Perhaps the best example of **energy transformation** comes from green plants. The leaves of trees and other plants contain the green pigment chlorophyll. This pigment works just like the solar cells in your calculator. **Chlorophyll converts light energy or sunlight into electrical energy.** In plants, the electrical energy converts carbon dioxide and water into glucose, simple sugar. The plant uses the chemical energy of glucose to grow and reproduce. All plants, including our very tall trees, result from the transformation of energy. Living things provide great examples of converting energy from one form to another.

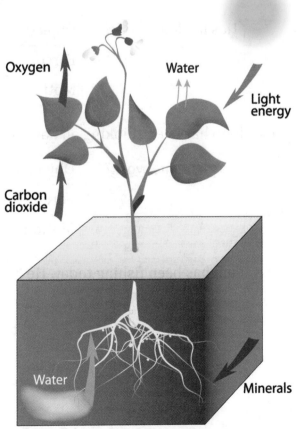

ACTIVITY: Understanding Work as the Action of Making an Object Move

The definition of **work requires an object**, **a force**, and **motion**. Work is said to have been accomplished when the object has been moved.

When determining if work has been done, look for these three components: an object, a force, and motion.

PROBLEMS:

1. Tom is very tired. He has been raking leaves all day. The first one has been done for you.

Has he done work? Yes. Tom moves the rake, so that the rake moves the leaves.	Object: Rake (primary) and leaves (secondary)
	Force: Tom (primary) and rake (secondary)
	Motion: Raking

2. Sally is also tired. She has been bagging those leaves.

Has she done work?	Object:
	Force:
	Motion:

3. Larry is tired. He has been pushing a wall. It has not moved.

Has he done work?	Object:
	Force:
	Motion:

4. John has been thinking all day. He has solved several major problems.

Has he done work?	Object:
	Force:
	Motion:

5. Paul has been fishing today. He has caught several fish.

Has he done work?	Object:
	Force:
	Motion:

ACTIVITY: Analysis of Forces Acting on a Balance

PURPOSE: You will observe the force of gravity on each arm of a balance.

PROCEDURE:

1. Set up the balance by placing a ruler atop a pencil so that it is stable.
2. Place a quarter on the ruler at two inches from the pencil on each side.
3. Observe the result and record further balances on the chart below.

QUESTIONS:

Left side		Right side	
1 quarter	2 inches	1 quarter	2 inches
2 quarters	2 inches	1 quarter	_____
1 quarter	5 inches	2 quarters	_____
1 quarter	6 inches (approx.)	3 quarters	_____
_____	_____	_____	_____
_____	_____	_____	_____

1. Draw a force diagram with one quarter at two inches on each side.

2. When the ruler was balanced, why did it not move?

   _____

3. What force(s) operated on both sides of the balance?

   _____

4. The balance point is said to be an **equilibrium**. What does this word mean? Look it up. Why is the word used for your balance?

   _____

   _____

B. Electricity from Coal, Oil, Nuclear Reactors

We are very familiar with electrical energy in our homes. It is difficult to imagine life without electricity. **Coal** and **oil** are burned in most power plants to produce heat energy. The heat converts water into steam, which turns very large turbines that attach to generators. The generators produce sufficient electricity to supply the energy needs of large cities and even counties. Here we see coal and oil transformed to heat, which is transferred to water, which is transformed to steam to move turbines, which move generators to produce electricity. **Electricity is a form of energy that flows through wires to provide power to machines, lights, many appliances, and so on.**

© airphoto.gr. Used with permission.

Coal-Burning Power Plant

Nuclear reactors are a common source of electrical energy in many cities and countries throughout the world. Here in the United States, nuclear reactors provide about 20% of all electricity. The two most common fuels used in nuclear power plants are uranium and plutonium. These materials undergo nuclear fission, a process by which the nuclei of atoms are split into smaller parts. Nuclear fission produces tremendous amounts of energy. This energy, in the form of heat, boils water, which is transformed into steam. In turn, the steam drives turbines and electrical generators.

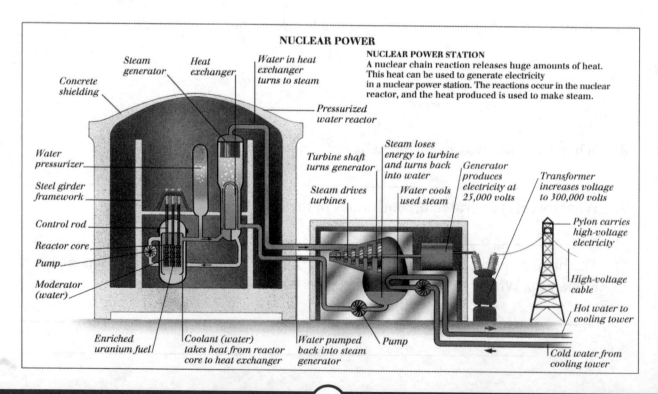

NUCLEAR POWER

Concrete shielding
Steam generator
Heat exchanger
Water in heat exchanger turns to steam

NUCLEAR POWER STATION
A nuclear chain reaction releases huge amounts of heat. This heat can be used to generate electricity in a nuclear power station. The reactions occur in the nuclear reactor, and the heat produced is used to make steam.

Pressurized water reactor

Water pressurizer
Steel girder framework
Control rod
Reactor core
Pump
Moderator (water)

Turbine shaft turns generator
Steam drives turbines

Steam loses energy to turbine and turns back into water
Water cools used steam

Generator produces electricity at 25,000 volts

Transformer increases voltage to 300,000 volts

Pylon carries high-voltage electricity

High-voltage cable

Hot water to cooling tower

Enriched uranium fuel
Coolant (water) takes heat from reactor core to heat exchanger
Water pumped back into steam generator
Pump
Cold water from cooling tower

Perhaps you have heard about **nuclear power**. Nuclear power is a very efficient energy source, but there are concerns about its use. These include the storage and disposal of radioactive waste, and the possibility of releasing radiation through accidents. For example, in March 2011, an earthquake and tsunami struck Japan. A nuclear power plant in the city of Fukushima was severely damaged and partially destroyed. Leaking radiation created a crisis, and the Japanese government ordered a zone of evacuation. Except for workers, people were not allowed within 30 kilometers (18 and 3/4 miles) of the facility. Japan is a densely populated country, so this caused tremendous hardship for many people.

Electricity or electrical energy comes into your home through wires. You flip a light switch in the kitchen, and the light bulb converts electricity to both light and heat energy.

Suppose you decide to grab a snack from the refrigerator. How is food kept cold in your refrigerator? Well, think about what it means to be "cold." To be "cold" is to lack heat; the less heat there is, the colder something becomes. Therefore, if we want to make something cool, we must remove the heat from it. That's the principle behind refrigeration. Electrical energy powers a device that removes heat energy from inside the refrigerator. As the heat energy is removed, the air within the refrigerator becomes cool.

In both of these examples, the energy stored in coal or oil is transformed into electricity, which then passes into your home to conduct useful work, providing light or cooling.

Other examples of one type of energy being transformed to another type of energy include the following:

(a) A telephone converts sound energy into electrical signals that pass through a wire. These signals are turned back into sound energy inside the phone at the other end of the line.

(b) Cell phones work similarly but without a wire to conduct the signal. In this case, sound is converted to electrical energy and transmitted by radio waves or electromagnetic energy.

(c) In televisions, both pictures and sound are turned into electrical signals by a device known as a transmitter. A transformer changes the signals into radio waves. In broadcast television, the signals are sent out by cable or satellite.

IX. God: The Creator of the Laws of Energy

We know that God created the universe and all things in it: matter, space, energy, and all of the laws that govern the universe. God created all the laws that change one form of energy into other forms of energy. Best of all, He created human beings and gave us the ability to understand His laws. How fortunate that we are able to take this knowledge and develop many useful tools, instruments, and modern conveniences! God creates from nothing; we invent based on our knowledge of God's gifts of water, coal, gas, and many, many other gifts we see in the natural world.

You have already learned about changing from potential energy to kinetic energy. There are many energy changes that occur all around us. In plants, **solar energy** is changed into **chemical energy**. We use chemical energy to move our muscles. We use **mechanical energy** to move our bicycles. **Electrical energy** is changed to **light energy** so we can read at night. Electrical energy is also converted into **heat energy** so that we can be warm in the winter and cook our food.

During each one of these transformations, a little energy is lost. This energy is lost because no energy transformation is a perfect 100 percent conversion. Usually, this lost energy is **heat energy**. When we use a light bulb to provide light, we also notice that the bulb gets very hot. This is an example of heat loss in the process of light production.

"So the heavens and the earth were finished, and all the furniture of them. And on the seventh day God ended His work which He had made: and He rested on the seventh day from all His work which He had done. And He blessed the seventh day, and sanctified it: because in it He had rested from all His work which God created and made" (Genesis 2:1-3).

ACTIVITY: Energy Transformation

PURPOSE: Production of heat energy from a transformation of chemical energy into mechanical energy

DIRECTIONS:

1. Hammer a nail halfway into a board.
2. Feel the nail. Is it hot?
3. Feel the board. Is it hot?
4. Feel the hammer. Is it hot?

Materials:

Nail
Board
Hammer

QUESTIONS:

1. Did the nail get hot? _____ Did the board? _____

   Did the hammer? _____

2. From where did the heat come? _____

   _____

3. What provided the energy to this system? _____

   _____

4. Can the heat energy be used? _____

5. Tighten your arm muscles several times. Do your arms feel any warmer? _____

   They should. Can this heat be useful? _____

Athletes "warm up" before working out to protect their muscles. There is an old trick used to warm up a cold sleeping bag while camping. A few minutes of flexing the arms and legs will warm up a very cold bag. Another use for muscle-generated heat is for arthritis-stiffened hands. A few exercises at the piano will warm up hands and relieve some of the pain and stiffness.

X. The Progress of Science

There are two great principles that helped Newton and other great scientists make their discoveries.

The first principle is that **God made a law-abiding universe.**

The second principle is that **people can discover those laws.**

In ancient times, many people had a superstitious view of the universe; they saw nature as a mysterious, magical power, not something that obeyed ordered laws. In the Bible, people learned that God created the universe, and that the universe has its roots in physical creation, not some magical legend. The early Catholic scientists argued that the physical universe obeyed physical laws and that we could understand them.

St. Albert the Great, a theologian and scientist who lived in the thirteenth century, is considered one of the precursors of modern science. In his writings, he frequently said, "*Fui et vidi experiri*" to prove the truth of his observations. This

***Creation*, by Gustave Dore**

is a Latin sentence which means, "I was there and saw it happen." This means that scientific knowledge is obtained through sense experience. St. Albert experimented and saw the results of his experiments.

Sir Isaac Newton, the discoverer of Newton's Three Laws of Motion which we are studying this year, knew of the wonderful contributions of the great Catholic scientists who had gone before him. He said, "If I have seen further, it was only because I was sitting on the shoulders of giants." One of those giants was a theologian and philosopher named **Jan Buridan**. In the fourteenth century, 300 years before Newton, Buridan came very close to describing Newton's First Law of Motion.

Chapter 5 Summary

1. Potential energy means stored energy. Kinetic energy is the energy of motion.

2. God does not come from anything. He always was, is, and always will be. We call God the Prime Mover, because nothing moved or existed before Him. All things that move can ultimately be traced back to God, the First Mover.

3. The First Law of Motion: An object at rest tends to stay at rest; an object in motion tends to stay in motion.

4. The Second Law of Motion: The acceleration or increasing speed of an object is directly related to the force that moves or pushes the object. The greater the mass of the object, the greater the amount of force needed to make it move.

5. The Third Law of Motion: For every action, there is an equal and opposite reaction.

6. The First Law of Thermodynamics: The amount of energy in the universe always remains constant; energy can neither be created nor destroyed.

7. The Second Law of Thermodynamics: Everything in the universe moves from higher energy levels to lower ones.

8. Transformation of Energy: An example comes from green plants, where chlorophyll in plants converts sunlight into electrical energy, which converts carbon dioxide and water into glucose, simple sugar.

9. Coal and oil are burned to produce heat energy. Electricity is a form of energy that flows through wires to provide power to machines, lights, appliances, and more.

10. Nuclear reactors are a common source of electrical energy.

11. God is the Creator of the laws of energy. He created all the laws that change one form of energy into other forms of energy.

12. Energy changes occur all around us, such as solar energy changing into chemical energy, or electrical energy changing into light energy or heat energy.

13. Great scientists accept the fact that God made laws about the way things work in the universe and that people can discover those laws.

Questions for Review

1. What is *potential energy*? _____

   _____

2. What is *kinetic energy*? _____

   _____

3. Who is the *Prime Mover*? _____

   _____

4. What is the *First Law of Motion*?

   _____

   _____

5. What is the *Second Law of Motion*?

   _____

   _____

6. What is the *Third Law of Motion*?

   _____

   _____

7. Energy can neither be created nor destroyed, but it can be _____.

8. What is an example of the Law of Entropy?

   _____

   _____

9. What is electricity? What are two fossil fuels used to create energy?

   _____

   _____

10. What are the two great principles that helped Newton and other great scientists make their discoveries?

    _____

    _____

    _____

Light

I.   **Light energy**
II. **Electromagnetic spectrum**
     A.   Visible Light
     B.   Invisible Electromagnetic Radiation
III. **Properties of Light**
     A.   Transparency and Translucence
     B.   Reflection
     C.   Refraction
IV. **Lenses**

Light

And God said, "Let there be light"; and there was light (Genesis 1:3).

I. Light Energy

When we think of the word *light*, we may think of the sun, light bulbs, candles, oil lamps, or maybe even fireflies. Well, what exactly is light? Light is a type of energy that has a double nature. Light is a combination of two perpendicular waves traveling together. One of these waves is an **electric field**; the other is a **magnetic field**. For this reason, scientists refer to light as **electromagnetic energy**.

Our eyes receive natural light from the sun, and artificial light from incandescent or fluorescent light bulbs. Light can pass through objects or be reflected off objects. How light is affected by objects or how objects are affected by light determines how we see objects.

Light is a form of energy that can be seen by our eyes. Within the retina of the human eye are special sensors that can detect very specific wavelengths of light. Each different wavelength is a different color. These sensors transmit *electrical impulses* (which are like special messages) to the visual centers of the brain through what are called optic nerves. The brain then processes these signals and produces an image of what we are seeing.

The light bulb was invented by Thomas Alva Edison in 1879. When a light bulb in a lamp is turned on, an electrical signal is sent to the lamp. The electricity travels through wires in the lamp. Inside the light bulb is a wire which is different from the other wires. The wire inside the light bulb is **tungsten** (though Edison used carbon). Tungsten is not efficient at passing electricity, so some of the electrical energy is converted into light. This tungsten element also releases heat energy. So when you turn on a light, you are making both light and heat energy.

Illuminated Tungsten Light Bulb

Compact Fluorescent Light Bulb

You can make light energy in other ways, too. Obtain some wintergreen candy. In a darkened room, hit a piece of candy with a hammer. You should see sparks. The tiny molecules of the candy give off little bits of energy, which you see as light.

Look up Luke 9:28-29 in your Bible. What did Peter, James, and John see? Here is an occasion in which light is produced by Jesus Himself for His Apostles! You can read about the creation of light in Genesis, Chapter 1. In the Gospel of John, you can read about Jesus as the Light of the World, especially in Chapter 1. In Chapter 12, verse 46, we read the words of Jesus: "I am come as Light into the world, that whoever believes in Me, may not remain in darkness." Jesus meant that if we listen to Him, we will know the truth, and our minds will not remain in the "darkness" of ignorance.

Here is an interesting activity: Rub your leather shoes on carpet, then touch a metal doorknob or a person; you will get shocked from the discharge of electrical energy. The discharge spark can easily be seen in the dark. The discharge spark is **light energy**.

A similar discharge is lightning. With lightning, discharge of light is up in the air, and very bright, but it is still the same thing: a buildup of electrical charge, followed by the discharge releasing light energy.

II. Electromagnetic Spectrum

We are familiar with visible light, but what light and colors we actually see represent only a part of what is called the **electromagnetic spectrum**. The word *spectrum* means a series or range of related items, for example, from small to large, or from left to right. The **electromagnetic spectrum refers to a huge range of electromagnetic waves**, only a small portion of which are visible. Light is the visible part of the electromagnetic spectrum. Other parts include gamma rays, X-rays, ultraviolet light, infrared light, microwaves, and radio waves.

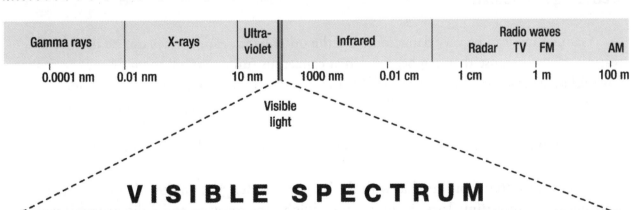

Our eyes can see only certain wavelengths, and thus only certain colors. It is believed by many that when we enter Heaven, we will see colors we never were able to see on Earth!

A. Visible Light

Visible light or white light is more than just the color white. If you hold a triangular piece of crystal known as a prism up to sunlight, you will see that the light becomes split into the colors of the rainbow. The sides of the prism split the sunlight into the different wavelengths, so we see seven different colors: red, orange, yellow, green, blue, indigo, and violet. One way to remember the order of the seven colors of the spectrum is to think of the name "Roy G. Biv." Each letter stands for one color, which corresponds to a specific group of light wavelengths. Wavelengths of visible light are measured in units called nanometers (nm), or billionths of a meter! Red has the longest wavelength, and violet has the shortest wavelength.

When the sunlight shines through raindrops, we sometimes see a rainbow of colors. The water of the raindrops breaks up the molecules of sunlight, thus producing the division of the spectrum of colors. Each raindrop acts like a little prism.

Remember in the Bible, we read that God produced a rainbow as a **covenant**, or a promise, after the great Flood (Genesis 9:13-15): "I set my bow in the clouds to serve as a sign of the covenant between me and the earth. When I bring clouds over the earth, and the bow appears in the clouds, I will recall the covenant I have made between me and you, and all living beings, so that the waters shall never again become a flood to destroy all mortal beings."

B. Invisible Electromagnetic Radiation

Waves that cannot be seen by humans are called invisible electromagnetic radiation. Short wavelengths are very high in energy; they include gamma rays, X-rays, and ultraviolet light. **Gamma rays have the shortest wavelengths and are the most powerful form of electromagnetic radiation**.

Gamma rays can be very dangerous. On the other hand, gamma rays can be useful in treating cancer, because they can be directed at cancerous tumors to kill them. X-rays are not as powerful as gamma rays, but X-rays are able to travel through thick tissues such as bone. If you have ever had a broken bone, you will recall that your doctor took a picture of it with an X-ray machine. Ultraviolet light is not as powerful as X-rays but quite capable of killing germs. For this reason, scientists in laboratories use ultraviolet light to sterilize tools or instruments.

You are probably more familiar with the **longer wavelengths** on the other end of the electromagnetic spectrum. These include infrared light, microwaves, and radio waves. If you have ever stood barefoot on a sidewalk or other pavement at the end of a hot summer day, you could feel the heat beneath your feet. This heat is infrared radiation and is invisible. It has a wavelength slightly longer than red light.

Microwaves have longer wavelengths than infrared radiation. Your microwave oven cooks food using microwave radiation. The radiation causes water molecules in the food to vibrate at a high speed. This high-speed vibration results in friction and the production of heat, which cooks the food.

Radio waves have the longest wavelengths on the electromagnetic spectrum.

III. Properties of Light

When light strikes an object, the object may reflect it, absorb it, or allow it to pass through. How light interacts with an object determines what we see. You read earlier that white light is a combination of all colors. However, what happens when you see something that has colors different from white? Typically, an object absorbs all colors except one specific color, which it reflects. For example, a red marble absorbs all colors except red; the red light is reflected to our eyes, giving the marble its red color. A blue marble absorbs all colors except blue, and so on.

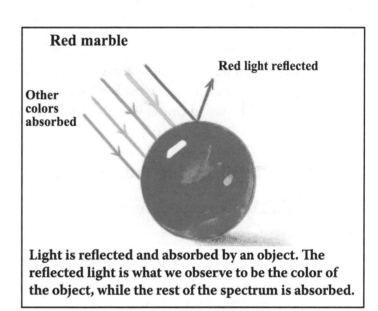

Red marble

Red light reflected

Other colors absorbed

Light is reflected and absorbed by an object. The reflected light is what we observe to be the color of the object, while the rest of the spectrum is absorbed.

Red light used for photosynthesis is absorbed by the leaf.

Green light is reflected.

Visible light is both reflected and absorbed by the leaf.

Black objects are unique; they absorb all colors and reflect none. When sunlight strikes a black object, the entire visible light spectrum is absorbed. That light energy is converted into heat energy. This is one way to "capture" some of the sun's energy. For instance, if a water tank is painted black and exposed to the sun, the water tank will absorb light energy and convert it into heat energy. This heat energy will make the water inside the tank hot! On the other hand, if we painted a jet fuel tank black, what might be the possible outcome?

White objects are the opposite: they absorb no color and reflect all colors. Objects that block the passage of light are called **opaque**. No light can pass through them. Examples of opaque objects are wood, cement, stainless steel, and lead.

A. Transparency and Translucence

Light easily passes through clear objects such as glass and cellophane or plastic wraps. We call these objects **transparent**. With other objects, **some light passes through, but it is scattered**. We call such objects **translucent**. If we look through a translucent object, such as wax paper, objects on the other side can be seen, but only indistinctly. Think of a time when you were in the woods on a spring day. The sunlight passed through the new leaves and descended toward the forest floor. Everything around you had a greenish tint. If you looked up at the leaves, you may recall that these looked like they were glowing. The translucent leaves absorbed some of the light, and some of it passed through to the forest below.

EXPERIMENT: Observing Translucence and Light Diffusion

MATERIALS: Brown paper bag, notebook paper, wax paper, butter

PROCEDURE:

1. Tear open the brown paper bag and stretch it out flat.

2. Spread butter or grease on the bag. Wipe off the excess. What happens to the bag? What does it look like?

    _____

    _____

3. Now, hold it up to a light so that the light shines through the bag. What happens to the light as it passes through the bag?

    _____

4. Try this with the notebook paper. Are there any differences between the amount of light passing through the bag and the paper?

    _____

5. In the early days on the frontier, glass windows were unusual. Instead, resourceful people used greased paper to cover the windows. These windows let in light and kept out wind. Which would be better for a window instead of glass: bag paper or notebook paper? Why?

    _____

    _____

PROCEDURE (CONTINUED):

6. Other frontier people used wax paper. Try shining light through wax paper. Is there a difference between this and the other two papers? Which is best at allowing light to pass through?

_____

_____

QUESTIONS:

1. Make a drawing showing the passage of light rays through the greased-paper window in the experiment.

```



```

2. What might be some of the practical problems associated with a greased-paper window?

_____

_____

_____

3. Why not just use water instead of grease?

_____

_____

4. Of what use is a lamp shade?

_____

_____

5. There is a white powder on the inside of most light bulbs. Compare this form of diffuser to a light bulb without powder.

_____

_____

B. Reflection

Light waves travel along straight paths known as **rays**. When light strikes an opaque object, it cannot pass through that object. The light is either absorbed by the object or bounced back (**reflected**). When light is reflected, it continues **traveling in a straight path but in a different direction**.

The best example of reflection is in an ordinary household mirror. When you look into a mirror, light bounces off you, travels to the mirror, and then reflects toward your eyes. You see your **reflection**. Your reflection is not you, but your image that is made from light. When light is reflected off a mirror, it leaves the mirror at the same angle that it hit the mirror.

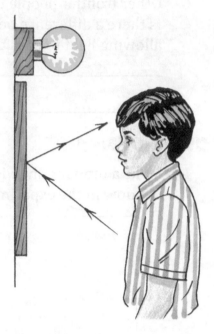

Light can reflect repeatedly. To observe this, look directly into a mirror while holding a smaller mirror in front of your face but facing the mirror. That is, the two mirrors should face each other. Try to arrange the mirrors and see how many "mirrors" or reflections you can find in the background.

This drawing illustrates the path of light as it is reflected off a mirror.

C. Refraction

As we discussed earlier, some objects are transparent, so light can pass through them. In other words, you can see through those objects. For example, you can see through a clear glass of water because both the glass and the water are transparent. However, the light does not pass *straight* through the glass of water. As the light passes through the object, the light is bent.

Have you ever looked through a glass of water with a spoon in it and noticed that the spoon looks bent or broken? (How it exactly appears will depend on the kind of glass you are using.) In reality, the spoon is not bent; rather, the *light* is bent. This is because light rays slow down as they pass from air into water. This difference in speed causes the light rays to change their path.

We refer to this characteristic as **refraction: light bends or deflects away any time it passes from one kind of medium or substance to another**. While light is passing through a transparent object, its path is bent. When a spoon sits in a glass of water, it appears to be crooked at the spot where it comes out of the water. This bending of the light wave's path is refraction.

Refraction

In a vacuum, light travels at a constant speed of 186,000 miles per second. Light travels at different speeds through different mediums. The speed of light in water is approximately 140,000 miles per second.

Refracted light rays make the spoon appear broken.

When you think of **light interacting with objects**, try to imagine a pinball machine. The pinball is pulled down the slope of the machine but interacts with levers, bumpers, and so on. The force of gravity pulls constantly, but the ball spends all of its time bouncing around. In the same way, light bounces around with molecules and slows down.

How **light interacts with objects** is best understood by the index of refraction. Objects are designated with an index number. Higher numbers indicate more refraction. Light travels unimpeded, with no refraction, in a vacuum, which has an index value of 1. Similarly, light refracts little in air and gases such as carbon dioxide and helium. Thus, carbon dioxide and helium have index values close to 1. However, water significantly bends light, so water has an index value of 1.33. Glass refracts light even more, and has a refraction index value ranging between 1.5 and 1.9. Diamonds have a very high refractive index of 2.4.

A Ray of Light Refracted in a Plastic Block

6

J.M.J.

OBSERVING AND RECORD KEEPING: Reflection and Mirrors

MATERIALS: Flashlight, mirror, protractor, posterboard, clay, scissors

INTRODUCTION:

Light rays can be reflected. Actually, they reflect off anything you can see. To increase the amount of light that is reflected, the surface of the object should be smooth and shiny. A mirror is a smooth surface, usually metallic. In the days of the Roman Empire, people had metal mirrors which were polished until they became very shiny. Today, we usually use glass mirrors which have been silvered on the back. When light rays are reflected, they are bounced back at the same angle as they arrived at the mirror. You can verify this by doing this activity.

PROCEDURE:

1. Cut out a slice of posterboard that is about a 1/2 inch thick and about 2 inches long.

2. Use the rest of the posterboard as a base and mark an arrow on one edge as shown.

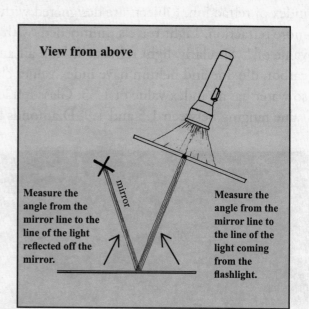

3. Stand up a mirror using a book rest or clay so that it is vertical. Place the mirror so that it touches the point of the arrow.

4. With the lights out, shine a flashlight through the slit at the mirror. Adjust the flashlight until the ray of light hits the arrow.

5. Mark the poster base with an X centered on the ray.

6. Turn on the lights.

7. Place a protractor along the mirror line and read the number of degrees from the mirror line to the light ray line coming from the flashlight.

8. Record the angle the light makes with the mirror.

9. The light should be reflected back over to the other side (the ray going to point X) at an angle equal to the angle of the light coming in. Check this angle and record.

10. Repeat steps 8 and 9 at different angles for the light shining on the mirror.

OBSERVATIONS:

Trial #	Angle in	Angle out

CONCLUSIONS:

1. What would you observe about the relationship between the angle of the light coming into the mirror and the angle of the light going away from the mirror?

    _____

    _____

    _____

2. Write your name on a sheet of paper in big letters. Hold the word up to a mirror and read it out of the mirror. What do you observe about the reflection of your name?

    _____

    _____

    _____

3. What would you hypothesize, or guess, about the reflection of your face from a mirror? Do you see yourself as others see you?

    _____

    _____

    _____

4. **Reflection:** We are given an abundance of grace from the sacraments and from the use of sacramentals. God expects us to give back to others in acts of kindness and charity.

RECORD KEEPING: A Photometer

MATERIALS: Two blocks of paraffin, aluminum foil, rubber band, candles, unknown light source, ruler

PROCEDURE:

1. Fold some aluminum foil so that it is the same size as the paraffin blocks.

2. Put the foil between the two blocks, and hold them together with the rubberband. This is your photometer.

3. Hold the photometer up toward a light source. Hold it so that one of the blocks is facing the light but not the other. Observe the light diffusing through the paraffin. In what way are the two blocks different when held in this position?

   _____

4. Place two candles about 2 feet apart. Hold your photometer between them so that the blocks are each facing a candle.

5. As you move the photometer toward one of the candles, what do you observe about the two blocks of paraffin? Which is the brightest?

   _____

6. One candle at a 1-foot distance produces 1 foot-candle of light. This is an old-fashioned measurement, but it is still useful. Choose a lamp and set up a candle at a distance of about 2 or 3 feet from it. You should dim the other lights in the room. Place the photometer between the two light sources, 1 foot from the lighted candle. Now slide the photometer and candle at the same time, keeping the 1-foot distance. Slide the pair toward or away from the lamp until the photometer shows the same intensity of light in the paraffin on both sides of the foil. At this point, the light intensity is 1 foot-candle of light. How far away from the lamp was this?

   _____

OBSERVATIONS:

1. What do you observe about the translucency of the paraffin? What did it do to the light within the block?

   _____

2. At what point was the lumination of the blocks even?

   _____

3. At what distance from the unknown light source was its light measured at 1 foot-candle?

   _____

OBSERVING: Transparency and Refraction

MATERIALS: Two glass containers, one of which fits easily inside the other; water; corn syrup, vegetable oil, pencil

PROCEDURE:

1. Place the smaller container inside the larger container and fill both with water.

2. Look into the containers. You should be able to clearly see the second glass jar, even though the water surrounds it. When a medium's index of refraction differs from another medium's index of refraction, you can see the boundary between the objects. In this experiment, you can easily see the second glass jar. This shows that the index of refraction of glass is different than the index of refraction of the water.

3. Next, place the smaller container inside the larger container and fill both with clear corn syrup.

4. Look at both containers. Can you easily see the smaller container? Do you see at least an outline of the smaller container? Record your observations.

_____

The index of refraction of syrup is nearly the same as that of glass, so the light does not bend very much as it crosses the boundary between the glass and the syrup. This means that you will not easily see the edges of the glass while it is in the syrup.

5. Another experiment to help you see the way different substances bend light differently is to pour about an inch of each of these three substances into a test tube or a spice jar. First, pour syrup, second water, finally oil. *Note: They should rest one on top of the other, since they have, in this order, decreasing densities.*

6. Place a pencil into the three substances, slowly so as to not disturb them.

7. Observe the differences in the way the pencil seems to bend as it goes through the media. You should remember that the pencil is not actually bending, but rather the light is bent as it passes through the boundaries between the media. This makes the pencil appear as if it were bent.

8. Do you notice that, in one medium, the pencil seems to disappear? Which medium is it? Remember that if a medium's index of refraction is the same as the medium it is in, the edges will not be easily seen.

_____

_____

QUESTIONS:

1. Draw a picture of the glass with water in it. Show the rays of light as they enter the water and as they pass through the glass. Show the rays of light bending as they pass through each medium.

2. What is a medium? Look up the word in a dictionary. What other media do you know through which light can pass?

   _____

   _____

3. Which medium has almost the same index of refraction as glass?

   _____

   How could you tell?

   _____

4. When you poured the three liquids onto each other in the glass, what did you observe about the liquids? Were there layers? Explain this. *Hint: Density is an important factor.*

   _____

   _____

   _____

5. What do you notice about the boundary between the syrup container and the syrup? Compare this to the jar with water in it. Compare also with the oil container and its contents.

   _____

   _____

   _____

IV. Lenses

Lenses are found in your eyes and in the eyes of nearly all animals. We also find them in microscopes, telescopes, cameras, projectors, and glasses. Some lenses are simple, and others are complex. Well, what exactly are lenses?

Lenses are objects that make use of the refractive properties of light. Lenses focus light or bend light along a certain path. There are two types of lenses: convex and concave. **Convex lenses** converge (or bring together, or focus) light rays. **Concave lenses** diverge (or scatter) light rays.

A magnifying glass is a good example of a convex lens. It gathers light rays toward one single point, known as a **focal point**. The focal point is the point in space where all light rays converge, or come together. This is the way that the lenses in your eyes work. They direct light toward a focal point on the retina.

Stand at a distance from your desk. Shine light through a magnifying glass toward your desk. At a certain distance from your desk, you will see a very strong, intense point of light on your desk. This is the focal point for that magnifying glass.

Sometimes people have difficulty seeing because the lenses in their eyes do not work properly. Light passes through the lenses, but the person sees a distorted image. As a remedy, the person is fitted with corrective lenses, either eyeglasses or contact lenses.

This 18th-century (circa 1728) microscope used the tilted mirror at the bottom to reflect light onto a specimen mounted above it on a glass slide.

When a person can easily see far-away objects, but has difficulty viewing close-up objects, we say that the person is far-sighted; the person "sights" objects far away. This person's vision will be corrected with **convex lenses**. Conversely, when someone sees close-up objects well but has difficulty seeing far-away objects, we say that this individual is near-sighted; the person "sights" objects that are near but not far away. His vision will be corrected with **concave lenses**.

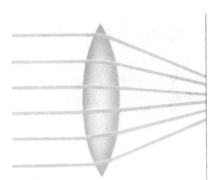

Convex Lens

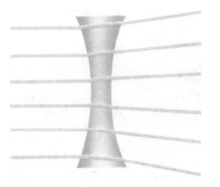

Concave Lens

OBSERVING: Transparency and Lenses

MATERIALS: Unflavored gelatin, pan, knife, flashlight, comb, posterboard

PROCEDURE:

1. Make up a stiff batch of clear, unflavored gelatin. Let it set in the refrigerator.

2. Cut out a 12 x 8 inch sheet of posterboard.

3. On one edge, cut a comb-sized notch out of the sheet of poster.

4. Tape the comb over the notch.

5. Using the patterns on the next page and a warm knife, cut lenses out of the gelatin. Move the knife slowly so as to get a smooth cut.

6. With a spatula, lift out the lenses and place on a clean surface.

7. Secure the poster sheet upright with the notch and comb on the edge resting on the table.

8. Turn out the lights in the room.

9. Shine the flashlight through the tines in the comb.

10. You should see rays of light on the tabletop opposite the flashlight.

11. Place the gelatin convex lens about 2 inches away from the comb on the side farthest from the flashlight. You should see the rays of light pass through the lens.

12. Record your observations on paper by drawing the light rays as they pass through the lens.

13. Repeat using the concave lens.

SETUP:

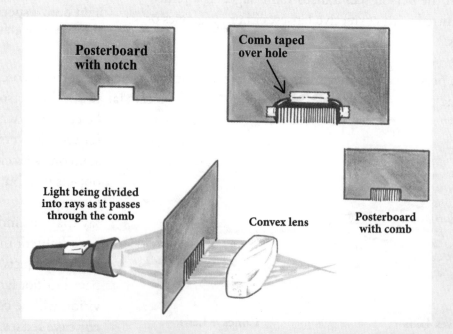

Posterboard with notch

Comb taped over hole

Light being divided into rays as it passes through the comb

Convex lens

Posterboard with comb

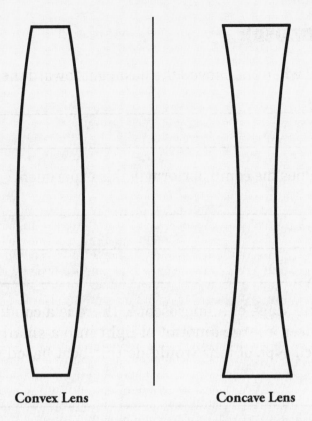

Convex Lens   Concave Lens

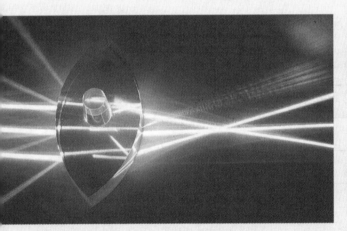 

QUESTIONS:

1. Which lens focused the light to a single point?

    _____

2. Which type of lens caused the light rays to diverge?

    _____

QUESTIONS (CONTINUED):

3. What happened when you moved the flashlight toward the comb?

_____

_____

4. What purpose does the comb perform in this experiment?

_____

_____

_____

5. Underneath the stage of a microscope, there is a condenser. This condenser focuses a large amount of light into a small area; it condenses the light. Which type of lens would do this best based upon your observations?

_____

_____

6. Optional: Look up LASER in the encyclopedia. What do the letters in the word LASER stand for?

L _____

A _____

S _____

E _____

R _____

Chapter 6 Summary

1. Light is a type of energy.

2. Light is a combination of two perpendicular waves traveling together. One is an electric field, one is a magnetic field. Light is referred to as electromagnetic energy.

3. The light bulb was invented by Thomas Alva Edison in 1879.

4. The electromagnetic spectrum refers to a huge range of electromagnetic waves, but we humans can see only a small part of them.

5. The seven colors that we can see, which are visible to our eyes, are red, orange, yellow, green, blue, indigo, and violet.

6. Electromagnetic waves that are invisible to us are short wavelengths, very high in energy, which include gamma rays, X-rays, and ultraviolet light, and long wavelengths, including infrared light, microwaves, and radio waves.

7. Visible light is both reflected and absorbed.

8. Objects that block light are opaque. Objects that light passes through are transparent. Objects that only some light passes through are called translucent.

9. When light is reflected, it continues traveling in a straight path but in a different direction. When light bends, or is deflected, away from one substance to another, we call this refraction.

10. Light travels at different speeds according to the item through which it travels. Light travels about 140,000 miles per second through water.

11. Lenses make use of the refractive property of light. Convex lenses bring together, or focus, on light rays. Concave lenses scatter light rays.

12. When people have lenses in their eyes that do not work too well, they may wear glasses or contact lenses. A person who has difficulty seeing things close up may wear convex lenses. A person who has difficulty seeing things at a distance may wear concave lenses.

Questions for Review

1. What is light? _____

    _____

2. What is the electromagnetic spectrum? _____

    _____

    _____

3. "Roy G. Biv" describes what? _____

    _____

4. What is invisible electromagnetic radiation?

    _____

5. What is the most powerful form of electromagnetic radiation?

    _____

6. Which type of waves are the longest in the electromagnetic spectrum?

    _____

7. Describe the difference between transparent and translucent.

    _____

    _____

8. What are light rays? What is difference between reflection and refraction?

    _____

    _____

9. What are lenses? _____

    _____

10. What is the difference between a convex lens and a concave lens?

    _____

    _____

~~E~~nergy: Heat, Radio, Sound

I.   **Heat**

II.   **Heat Production**

III.   **Heat Transfer**

IV.   **Radiation**

V.   **Insulation**

    A.   Conservation of Body Heat

    B.   Conservation of Indoor Heat

VI.   **Radio**

VII: **Sound**

    A.   Sound Waves

    B.   Music

Energy: Heat, Radio, Sound

Chapter 7

"His feet were like burnished bronze, refined as in a furnace, and His voice was like the sound of many waters" (Revelation 1:15).

I. Heat

Heat is a type of energy we can make and use. Heat results from molecular motion; it is produced by the motion of the molecules of a substance. We can think of **molecules** as building blocks of a substance. (We will discuss molecules in more detail in Chapter 9.) All molecules are in motion, but when we heat molecules, the molecules speed up. Removing them from the heat causes molecules to slow down and cool. When molecules are heated, they increase their motion or chemically change. When boiling water, a liquid, on the stove, not only do the molecules begin to move rapidly, but also some of the water chemically changes to steam, a gas. If a chocolate bar is heated, its molecules start moving more rapidly, and the solid chocolate becomes a liquid!

When we study motion and heat, we are studying thermodynamics. The word *thermo* refers to heat. We use a thermos to keep our drinks warm; when we go outside in cold weather, we wear thermal clothes. *Dynamics* means motion, or the study of motion. Let us recall the first two Laws of Thermodynamics that we learned about in Chapter 5.

The **First Law of Thermodynamics** states that the amount of energy in the universe always remains constant; energy can change form, but it cannot be created or destroyed.

The **Second Law of Thermodynamics** states that everything in the universe moves from higher energy levels to lower ones. Said another way, this law tells us that entropy is increasing in the universe. **Entropy** is a measure of the amount of energy in a system that is unusable for work, and thus it is a measure of the degree of disorder in the system. All systems degrade and eventually fall apart. Therefore, according to the Second Law of Thermodynamics, all motion in the universe will eventually cease, and temperature will fall to absolute zero.

One way to understand entropy is to pour water from one glass into another glass, and then into another glass. A few drops of water will remain in the previous glass; thus the amount continues to reduce with each pouring. The water still exists; it does not disappear. The same is true with energy; each time energy is transferred, the energy becomes less usable. The energy still exists; it does not disappear, but it gradually becomes less usable. We saw this in the example of a car: the car gets the energy to move from gasoline, but less than one-third of the energy from the gasoline was transformed into usable kinetic energy that could move the car. The rest of the

DID YOU KNOW?

The Second Law of Thermodynamics actually is one of the best proofs for the existence of our Creator God. Without a Creator, it would be impossible to explain the existence of a highly organized universe. Who organized the universe? If the natural tendency of things we see around us is to become disorganized, the universe must have been organized in the beginning by an Intelligent Being, Whom we call God.

In his letter to the Romans, St. Paul wrote: "For what can be known about God is plain to them, because God has shown it to them. Ever since the creation of the world His invisible nature, namely, His eternal power and deity, has been clearly perceived in the things that have been made…" (Romans 1:19-20). St. Paul meant that by seeing the beautiful design of the universe, any careful observer can see that there must be a Designer of all the laws of nature and nature itself. St. Paul also spoke of the time when all of creation will be delivered from the curse of the Second Law of Thermodynamics, saying that "the creation itself will be set free from its bondage to decay and obtain the glorious liberty of the children of God" (Romans 8:21).

QUESTIONS:

1. State the First Law of Thermodynamics:

   _____

   _____

   _____

2. State the Second Law of Thermodynamics:

   _____

   _____

   _____

3. Explain the words "bondage to decay" in Romans 8:21 (see above).

   _____

   _____

   _____

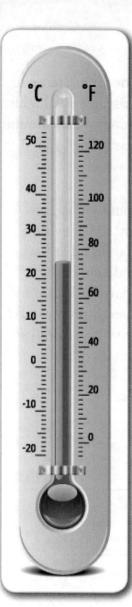

energy was "lost." That is, it was transformed into unusable forms of energy—namely, water, heat, and gas emissions, such as carbon dioxide.

These laws are important to every branch of **science** and **engineering**. They are foundational to the science of **physics**.

Heat can be produced by an energy loss during an energy transformation. An example is the use of mechanical energy to hammer a nail. The nail and the wood get hot. The heat is produced by a transfer of energy. If you were to hit a target with a baseball many times, both the target and the baseball would get hot. This is a transformation of energy. Some of the kinetic energy has been transformed into heat energy.

Heat is important to man in many ways. We use heat to cook our food, dry our clothes, and keep us warm in winter. Heat is necessary to hundreds of **industrial processes**, such as refining oil, making steel, and generating electricity.

Temperature is the measure of the amount of heat or molecular motion in an object. We measure temperature using a thermometer, a "heat meter." There are many kinds of thermometers for measuring the temperature of gases, liquids, and solids. Perhaps the two kinds of thermometers that you are most familiar with are the one that you use when you are not feeling well and the outdoor thermometer that tells what the outside air temperature is.

ACTIVITY

1. Do you think the molecules in the sun are moving slowly, moving rapidly, or not moving at all? _____
   _____

2. In the campfire, chemical energy is converted into_____ energy, but the total amount of energy present remains _____. This is because of the _____ Law of _____.

3. The _____ Law of _____ tells us that entropy is increasing in the universe.

ACTIVITY: Measuring Heat: Temperature of Water

MATERIALS: One-cup measuring cup, water, ice, pot, heat source, stirring spoon, clock or timer, thermometer

INTRODUCTION:

Heat is the energy of the molecules of a substance. In order to measure that heat, we measure the temperature of the substance. This gives us a number we can understand and use. When energy is added to the substance, the temperature of the substance goes up. When we cool a substance, we actually remove energy from the substance, and the temperature goes down.

PROCEDURE:

1. Place one cup of water in a pot and measure the temperature and record it. This is the starting temperature. Then place the pot on the stove and add energy by turning the heat on to medium for 5 minutes. After the 5 minutes, turn off the heat and record the final temperature.

2. Remove the same pot from the heat, then add five ice cubes to the water and stir the water. Take the temperature every 2 minutes for 10 minutes. Record the temperature each time.

3. Place one cup of new tap water into a pot and record the temperature.
   a) Heat the pot for 2 minutes on the lowest heat setting, and record the temperature of the water every 30 seconds.
   b) Increase the heat setting to medium and heat for 2 minutes, and record the temperature of the water every 30 seconds.
   c) Increase the heat setting to the maximum level and heat for 2 minutes, and record the temperature of the water every 30 seconds.
   d) Turn off the heat.

QUESTIONS:

1. Did the temperature of your water increase when you added energy?

2. Did the temperature of the water decrease when you subtracted energy? *Hint: You subtracted energy when you added ice.*

3. At what temperature was your water when the energy it had was the greatest? _____ At what temperature was your water when the energy it had was the lowest? _____

Time	Temperature	Time	Temperature	Time	Temperature

II. Heat Production

The production of heat is not difficult, since it is the byproduct of so many processes in nature. Heat may be produced mechanically, chemically, electrically, or radioactively. Heat may be harnessed from the sun (solar power), or from the Earth (geothermal power), such as steam.

You can produce heat by rubbing your hands together, which we do when it is very cold outside. As you rub your hands, the molecules of your hands become more "energetic," they move faster, and your hands feel warmer. You can also make heat when you hammer a nail into a board. The board and nail become hot because of friction between the wood and the nail.

When you produce light by turning on the light switch, you also produce heat from the light. When you heat water in a microwave oven, you bombard the water molecules with microwave radiation, which speeds up the motion of the molecules and makes them hot.

Perhaps the oldest method of producing heat is fire. When wood burns, it undergoes a chemical reaction which releases heat energy. The heat energy was "stored" in the tree trunk and branches, and released during the burning process. Other former plant products, such as natural gas and petroleum, also can be burned to make heat.

Today, we use stored chemical energy to produce heat in other ways. For example, sometimes athletes use *hot packs* to help their muscles or joints heal from an injury. These hot packs contain a dry chemical in a large bag, with an inner bag that is filled with water. Shaking the pack vigorously breaks the inner bag, causing the water to mix with the dry chemical. This creates a chemical reaction that gives off heat, making the pack hot for some period of time.

ACTIVITY: Measuring Heat: Using Human Sensors

MATERIALS: Three bowls, hot water, warm water, ice water, thermometer

PROCEDURE:

1. Place hot water, warm water, and ice water in separate bowls.
2. Take the temperatures of the water in the hot and cold bowls and record.
3. Put one hand into the hot water bowl (no hotter than you would use to wash your hands) and one into the cold water. Wait about 2 minutes.
4. Place both hands into the warm water bowl. Record the sensation of temperature you feel in each hand. Hypothesize as to the temperature of the warm water. Record your hypothesis.
5. Take the temperature of the warm water bowl and record.

OBSERVATIONS:

	Temperature Measured	Temperature Felt	
		Right Hand	Left Hand
Hot Water			
Warm Water			
Cold Water			

QUESTIONS:

1. Did your hands sense the same temperature in the warm water?
   _____

2. Why do you think your hands sensed a temperature difference?
   _____

3. Did you get "used" to the hot and cold water? Or did your hands feel uncomfortable in the water?
   _____

4. An **absolute measuring device** is one that will measure the same reading whenever the measurement is taken. A **relative measuring device** can tell the difference between two things. Are the sensors in your hand relative or absolute? Explain.
   _____
   _____

III. Heat Transfer

Heat is a major part of our daily lives. We produce it in a variety of ways, usually by burning wood, coal, oil, or natural gas. These natural fuels require **ignition** (the starting of a fire), whether by a match, a small flame known as a pilot light, or an electrical spark. Once the flame is ignited, oxygen helps consume the fuel in a process known as combustion. **Combustion** (or burning) is a direct method of producing heat. Three things are essential for combustion to occur: oxygen, fuel, and fire. Without all three of these, combustion is not possible.

Another way of producing heat is by using electricity. Electric ovens and water heaters contain parts known as **heating elements**. Heating elements are made from metal alloys and ceramics. Similarly, toasters, toaster ovens, space heaters, and hair dryers make use of heating elements known as **resistance wires**. Electricity flows in what is called an **electrical current**, similar to the way water flows in a garden hose. When we apply electricity to these appliances, the electrical current encounters resistance in these heating elements. Resistance is like an obstacle that impedes the flow of the current. Imagine, if a rock were stuck in your garden hose, slowing down the flow of water. In the same way, resistance hinders the flow of current. If the rock blocked the water entirely, the hose might sprout a leak, causing water to spray out the side. Likewise, the current is hindered by the resistance in these heating elements, and heat "spills out." To be more precise, when the electrical current encounters a resistance, some of the electrical energy is converted to heat energy, and the appliance gets hot.

Whenever we heat anything, we make use of a process known as **heat transfer**. We transfer heat from one material to another by convection, conduction, or radiation.

Convection is the transfer of heat from one place to another through the movement of air or liquid. Perhaps the best example of heating by convection comes from a furnace in a two-story house. When gas or air molecules have more motion, the molecules expand and rise. Heated air travels from a heating unit by one or more ducts. Heated air enters each of the rooms through registers that are located close to the floor. The warm air rises in the room and mixes with the higher, cooler air. Some of the cooler air sinks to the floor, and some of it is pulled into the intake ducts. The cooler air is pulled down to the furnace where it is heated and then recirculated throughout the house. The furnace continues to warm the air until a **thermostat** turns it off.

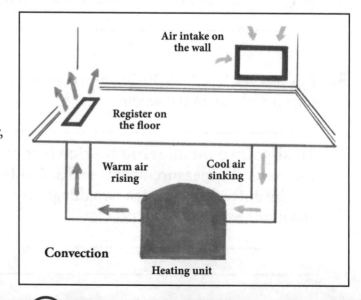

Air intake on the wall

Register on the floor

Warm air rising

Cool air sinking

Convection

Heating unit

ACTIVITY: Heat Transfer: Observing Convection

MATERIALS: Food coloring, distilled water, canning jar, ice cubes

INTRODUCTION:

Warm water rises when it is surrounded by cooler water. This movement is convection. You can demonstrate convection by showing that cool water descends. In this experiment you will observe convection and make a drawing illustrating the movement.

PROCEDURE:

Drawing of Convection Motion

1. Make some ice cubes that are colored with food coloring.
2. Fill a canning jar with hot water.
3. Place one or two of the colored ice cubes into the hot water.
4. Draw the result.

QUESTIONS:

1. Observe the cold water from the melting ice cube. In which direction did the water move as it left the ice cube?

   _____

2. Why did the cold water behave as it did? *Hint: Think density.*

   _____

   _____

3. Why does the ice float? *Hint: Think density*

   _____

   _____

4. Carefully pour cold water on top of some colored hot water. Record your results.

   _____

   _____

5. This convection motion holds true with air as well as water. How can you use this information when heating your house? *Hint: Is heating or cooling upstairs different from downstairs? Could you use fans to distribute warm or cool air more effectively?*

   _____

   _____

   _____

7

ACTIVITY: Heat Transfer: Observing Conduction and Insulation

MATERIALS: Two Styrofoam cups, thermometer, water, ice, one glass or metal cup, eight quarters, heat source, pot, tongs

INTRODUCTION:

Conduction occurs through direct contact. In this experiment, you will be observing conduction of heat through metal, which conducts heat very well. You will be observing conduction through styrofoam, which does not conduct heat well. Styrofoam is an insulator.

PROCEDURE:

1. Embed the styrofoam cups in each other and then in a pan of ice.

2. Embed the metal cup in the ice.

3. Put the same amount of cold water into each cup.

4. Put the quarters in a pot of water and boil them.

5. Take the temperature of the cold water in the cups and record.

Setup for Experiment

6. When the quarters are at boiling temperature for 2 to 3 minutes, carefully transfer them to the cups with tongs, four in each.

7. Record the temperature of the water in the cups every 2 minutes.

QUESTIONS:

1. Which cup reached the highest temperature: metal or styrofoam?

   _____

2. You added the same amount of heat in the quarters to each cup. Which cup conducted the heat away to the ice fastest?

   _____

3. Which cup was the best insulator, and which the best conductor?

   _____

4. With which material would you insulate your house?

   _____ Why?_____

5. Out of which material would you **not** make window frames?_____Why? *Hint: Think about winter time, when it is cold outside and warm inside.*

   _____

6. Which type of cup would be best for drinking hot chocolate? Why?

   _____

Temperature

Cup 1	Cup 2

Conduction is the direct transfer of heat energy to another object in physical contact with the heat source. When you place a metal spoon into a hot cup of cocoa, the heat energy quickly travels through the spoon. You will be able to feel the warmth of the spoon in your hand. Some substances, such as copper and steel, conduct heat better than others. These metals are excellent *conductors of heat* and are used in nearly all cookware.

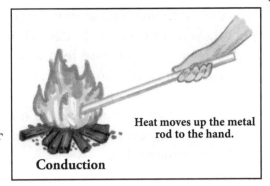

Heat moves up the metal rod to the hand.

Conduction

IV. Radiation

Convection and conduction require a medium—that is, something to carry the heat of the other object. However, there is another way to transfer heat that requires no medium, and that is radiation.

Radiation is the movement of electromagnetic waves through air or even through a vacuum. The heat energy from these waves spreads out in all directions from a source. The sun is a good example. Solar energy in the form of solar heat from the sun travels far throughout our solar system. It requires no medium, or something to carry or transfer the heat from one thing to another. Radiation, or electromagnetic waves, simply travels through space.

The space heater, found in many homes, is a good example of a household appliance that uses the principle of radiation. You experience radiated heat whenever you sit in front of a heater to warm yourself. Sitting around a campfire roasting marshmallows is another way to enjoy radiated heat.

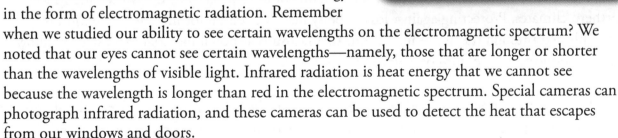

Infrared radiation is the transfer of heat energy in the form of electromagnetic radiation. Remember when we studied our ability to see certain wavelengths on the electromagnetic spectrum? We noted that our eyes cannot see certain wavelengths—namely, those that are longer or shorter than the wavelengths of visible light. Infrared radiation is heat energy that we cannot see because the wavelength is longer than red in the electromagnetic spectrum. Special cameras can photograph infrared radiation, and these cameras can be used to detect the heat that escapes from our windows and doors.

We have learned about how heat causes changes in objects. We have learned that when the molecules of a substance get more heat, they move more or move faster, but they also get farther apart and take up more space. When metal is heated, for example, it expands. When it cools off, it contracts. Have you ever noticed that when a cookie sheet is heated up or when it cools down, it makes a cracking noise? That noise is made when the metal expands or contracts unevenly. It "warps" or gets twisted out of shape as parts of it expand or contract.

Engineers are familiar with expansion caused by heat. When a concrete bridge is built, the engineers put in **expansion joints**. When the concrete becomes hot from the sun and expands, the expansion joints allow extra room for the expansion so that the concrete will not break. The next time you go over a bridge or overpass, look for the expansion joints.

Expansion Joint in a Road

ACTIVITY

You can see the action of heat expansion by doing a simple experiment. Take a screw-lid jar and screw the lid on as tightly as possible. Now unscrew it. Observe how difficult it is to unscrew. Tighten the lid again as tight as you can. BE CAREFUL not to break the glass. Now, run hot water over the lid for about 1 minute. Then unscrew the lid again. Was the lid any easier to unscrew? It should have been easier because the heat of the hot water caused the lid to expand and get larger than the glass jar it surrounded.

V. Insulation

A. Conservation of Body Heat

Conservation of heat is important for each one of us, especially in the winter and in the northern climates. Protecting against loss of body heat is essential for life. Heat retention is accomplished through the use of insulation. **Insulation** is a special material that does not allow heat (or sound) to move from one place to another.

Body heat must be conserved when you are out in the snow or the cold, especially if you are outside camping in the mountains. If a person's body temperature gets too low, a condition will set in called hypothermia. Hypothermia is dangerous and must be carefully avoided. The clothing you wear when it is cold should be chosen for its ability to keep you warm.

When traveling on long trips in the wintertime, you should take spare clothing or blankets in case of trouble on the road. An excellent blanket to store in your car is a **reflective emergency blanket.** Small and easy to pack, it has a metallic side that reflects your body heat back to you. This blanket could be used to help keep an injured person warm and thus prevent shock.

A **thermal blanket** is one that has many holes in it. You might think that such a blanket would be poor insulation for keeping warm. However, when placed under another light but tightly woven blanket, a thermal blanket is actually very warm. The many holes in the thermal blanket form air pockets with the additional blanket on top. These air pockets act as excellent insulators.

Wool is a natural fiber from sheep. When woven, it has excellent heat-conserving properties. Wool keeps a person warm even when it is wet! You can test the warmth-trapping capacity of wool by dipping a sample of wool into water, squeezing it, and observing the number of air bubbles you can force out of the material.

B. Conservation of Indoor Heat

We also use insulation to maintain a comfortable temperature in our houses. Insulation today is much better than that used by our pioneer ancestors. In the past, the logs of the cabin provided little insulation against the cold winters. Today, we put more efficient insulation in the walls and in the attics of our houses.

In the summertime, air conditioning lowers the temperature inside the house. When people do not have an air conditioner, homes can be kept cool by allowing the cool night air into the house, and then closing the windows during the day so that the air stays cool. Other efficient devices to cool the home are evaporative coolers and fans. Insulation also helps a house to stay cool.

The way that insulation in a house works is similar to a thermal blanket. They both use trapped air spaces. The **fiberglass insulation** in the walls of your house traps air and keeps the inside of the house warm in the winter and cool in the summer. In some houses, the windows have two layers of glass, called **double-paned windows**. In between the two layers of glass is trapped air, which serves as insulation.

Have you ever thought about the insulation birds have? Birds fluff up their feathers to trap air! The trapped air keeps the birds warm. When we use air insulation in our houses, we use a similar technique to that designed by God for birds!

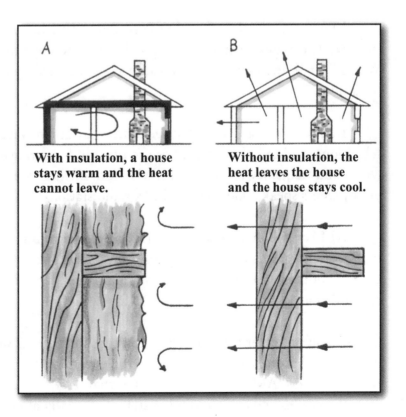

With insulation, a house stays warm and the heat cannot leave.

Without insulation, the heat leaves the house and the house stays cool.

VI. Radio

The inventor of the first practical radio transmitter was the Catholic Italian scientist Guglielmo Marconi. Marconi was born in 1874. When he was 21 years old, he began experiments with electromagnetic waves. He succeeded in establishing communication over distances just exceeding 1 mile. He went to England to obtain a British patent on a simple system of transmitting and receiving messages by wireless telegraphy. In 1899, Marconi established communication across the English Channel by wireless telegraphy. In 1909, he won the Nobel Prize for Physics.

Later, Marconi worked on the development of shortwave wireless communication, which constitutes the basis of nearly all modern long-distance radio. In 1918, he sent the first wireless messages from England to Australia.

Guglielmo Marconi

Marconi was a close friend of Pope Pius XII. Marconi set up the first Vatican radio station in 1931. This radio station made it possible for the pope to speak bravely to the world during World War II, even when the Vatican was surrounded by the brutal armies of Hitler and Mussolini.

Radio waves have longer wavelengths than microwaves. We use radio waves in radios, televisions, and cell phones. Radios use two kinds of transmission carriers, amplitude modulation (AM) and frequency modulation (FM). Both of these are commonly used today. Have you heard your parents speak about AM and FM radio stations?

AM is susceptible to atmospheric and electrical interference, called static. AM is mostly used for talk radio and news programs. FM is less affected by static and offers higher quality sound. For these reasons, FM is the standard used for listening to music, although the transmissions do not travel as far as AM.

If you have ever traveled a long distance in your car while listening to an FM station, you may recall that the signal was quick to die out, maybe after driving through just one county. On the other hand, AM signals travel farther than FM, and can sometimes be heard throughout several counties and even into other states, especially after sunset, when there is less interference from the sun's radiation.

Our civilization could not function without radio. Police, firemen, pilots, news broadcasters, opinion broadcasters, race car drivers, ham radio operators, and many others use radio signals every day.

Radio energy is able to send voice, photographs, and data great distances at the speed of light. Television is radio adapted to send video. Cellular telephones use radio waves as well.

What exactly are radio waves? Radio waves are another form of electromagnetic radiation, like visible light, infrared waves, and microwaves, but radio waves have the longest wavelengths of all electromagnetic radiation. House current alternates 60 times per second, or at a **frequency** of 60 Hertz. Sometimes you hear a raspy 60 Hertz buzz from your radio when the antenna is too close to an electric wire. It sounds much like a low note on an out-of-tune piano.

Lightning causes electric oscillations at many different frequencies. AM radios can detect lightning strikes. If you tune your AM radio to a channel with no reception, you can sometimes hear sudden, loud cracking noises, indicating lightning strikes that may be hundreds of miles away. CAUTION: electrical current from a lightning strike can travel through wiring and plumbing, so stay away from sinks, tubs, and plugged-in electronics if there is a lightning storm in your area.

VII. Sound

A. Sound Waves

Sound is the energy of **vibration**. More specifically, it is a disturbance of the molecules of a substance, which causes the molecules to vibrate. Sound waves must have a medium, something to travel through. Sound waves cannot travel in a vacuum.

When you speak, you cause the air molecules around you to vibrate back and forth. Your ears receive the message or vibration that is passed on through the air molecules.

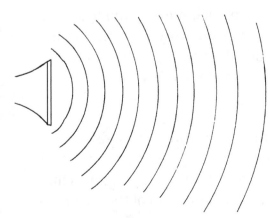

Sound travels in **longitudinal waves.** These are like the kind of waves that you see when a pebble is dropped in the middle of a pond. The water moves outward in all directions from the pebble.

Think of all the ways you can make noise. In each case, you are making something vibrate. Rattling pots, speaking, crunching on an apple—all these are examples of causing vibration.

Sound Waves

Sound is a form of kinetic energy that travels in a series of motions known as **compressions** and **rarefactions**.

Compressions are regions in the air where the air particles are compressed or pushed together. These are areas of high air pressure.

Rarefactions are regions where the air particles are spread apart. These are areas of low air pressure.

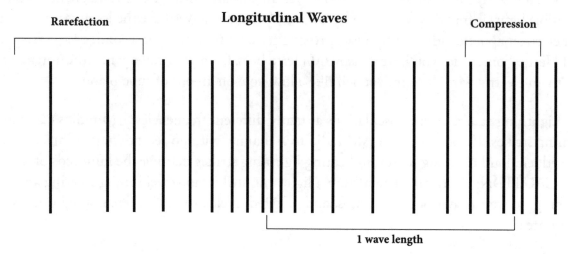

Longitudinal Waves — Rarefaction — Compression — 1 wave length

To understand this, it might be helpful for you to think of a small spring, perhaps in one of your pens. You *compress* the spring when you push both of its ends together. A *rarefaction* results when you let go of the ends or relax the spring. Besides a pen spring, you might want to experiment with a toy Slinky, to see how compressions and rarefactions travel through it.

We think of sound traveling through air, but sound also travels through solids and liquids. If you are underwater, you can hear many sounds, such as splashing and boat propellers off in the distance. In fact, sound travels four times faster through water than it does through air! The songs of whales can travel for hundreds of miles, perhaps a thousand!

ACTIVITY: You can observe sound waves moving through liquids by filling a balloon with water. Tie it off. Put the water-filled balloon against your ear, and then hold a ticking watch up to the other side of the balloon. You can hear the sound of the watch from the other side of the water balloon. Sound waves travel well through water.

ACTIVITY: You can observe the movement of sound waves through solids. Connect two cans with a string. Attach the string to the cans by putting it through a hole in the bottom of each can, tying it to a button so that it does not pull through. Pull the string tight and talk softly to your partner on the other end of the string.

ACTIVITY: Slinky Wave Production

MATERIALS: Slinky

INTRODUCTION:

Sound has waves unlike the waves of light. They are conducted through space by the molecules of the medium. The molecules move by going back and forth. In the process of moving this way, they strike other molecules and start them moving back and forth, and so on. This continues until the wave front meets something. The longitudinal waves of sound are demonstrated with a Slinky. **Note: The sound wave does not travel in straight-line rays like light. We are using the Slinky in a straight line because that will illustrate the motion, but the sound wave travels outward from the source of sound in all directions like waves spreading from a disturbance in a pond.**

PROCEDURE:

1. Have your partner hold one end of the Slinky while you hold the other. If you have no partner, attach one end to a table leg or something else immovable.
2. Lay the Slinky along the tabletop in a straight line.
3. Quickly push the Slinky end you have toward the other end. What do you observe?
4. Observe the effect of repeating the action every second.
5. Observe the wave as it hits the other end.
6. Stretch the Slinky out to several meters. Now, repeat your actions.
7. Start a wave from both ends at the same time. Observe the response.

QUESTIONS:

1. When the Slinky longitudinal wave hit the unmoving hand, what was the response?

   _____

2. Name a few instances when the reflection of sound was noticeable to you. What happened?

   _____

   _____

3. Did the reflected wave look similar to the first wave?

   _____

   _____

The speed of sound varies with temperature. When temperatures are warm, the air molecules vibrate faster and can quickly transmit sound. Conversely, when temperatures are cold, the air molecules vibrate more slowly, which slows the transmission of sound. The speed of sound is not the same at all times, even in the same medium of air or water. In air, sound waves move slowly at high altitudes because the air is colder at high altitudes. The speed of sound at room temperature or 68 °F (20 °C) is 1126 feet per second, or 768 miles per hour. That's pretty fast!

The speed of sound is slower than the speed of light. You have noticed that thunder can be heard *after* a lightning flash! The light traveled to your eyes first, and then the noise from the lightning reached your ears.

ACTIVITY

You and a partner can experiment with the speed of sound. Take a hammer and a board, and walk away from your partner, who should have a stop watch. Hit the board with the hammer, and ask your partner to record the time to the millisecond between seeing the hitting of the board and the sound of the hitting of the board. Did seeing the hammer hitting the board come before the hearing of the hitting of the board?

Sound waves can be reflected. We call this reflection an **echo**. Have you ever heard of **sonar**? Sonar is an acronym for SOund Navigation And Ranging; it is a navigation technique that involves emitting sound and then using the echo to determine the location of nearby objects. Men in submarines use sonar to determine how far they are from the bottom of the sea. Bats can fly in total darkness because they use echolocation, a natural form of sonar. By emitting a constant stream of high-pitched squeaks and hearing the echoes, bats are actually able to locate prey, even fast-moving insects!

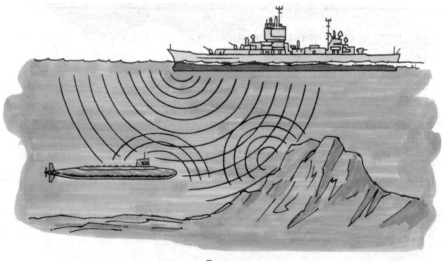

Sonar

This reflection of sound has an interesting effect. If you stand in a stairwell, maybe in an office building, and sing a set of notes, you will notice that as the notes change in pitch, one of them will sound especially loud. This effect is called **constructive interference**. The sound waves bounce off the walls (which are at a short distance from each other) and match, resulting in a louder sound!

B. Music

Musical instruments produce sound by a variety of techniques. Pianos, violins, and guitars use vibrating strings. Throughout the centuries, people have learned a few basic principles about string instruments. Shorter strings produce higher notes, and tighter strings increase the frequency of the vibrations, which is referred to as the "pitch." These instruments make use of a sound box to amplify the sound.

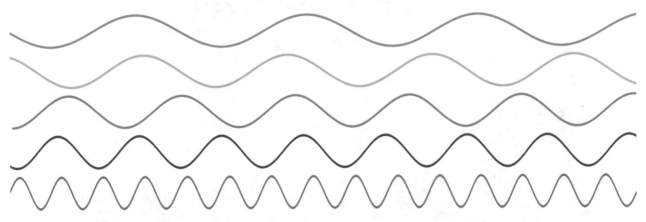

Waves Showing Different Frequencies of Sound

Clarinets and other instruments that use wood employ a thin reed clamped to a mouthpiece. Air is blown across the reed, which causes the reed to vibrate. In oboes, two reeds vibrate together to produce sound. In both cases, the wooden pipes that are attached to the mouthpieces amplify the sound. The shorter the wooden pipe, the higher the note.

In brass instruments such as a trumpet, trombone, and tuba, the vibrations are produced by the blowing across tightened lips. The vibrating air from the lips is amplified by the metal tube attached to the mouthpiece. The tighter the lips, the higher the note!

The pipes of an organ are specially designed to enhance constructive interference. A pipe organ does not need electronic amplification to make a very loud sound. The constructive interference of the pipes can make a huge cathedral reverberate with sound.

Music is the arrangement of sound to form complete and emotionally expressive compositions. David learned to play the harp before he became king. He composed many of the Psalms that we know from the Old Testament. When he was very young, David played music to help King Saul relax. You can see that music is a blessing to us in many ways. It can be relaxing as it was for Saul. It can be stirring like the marches of John Philip Sousa. It can be inspirational like Handel's *Messiah* and Beethoven's *Missa Solemnis* (Solemn Mass). Both of these composers sought a closer relationship with God through their music.

David Playing the Psalms

Chapter 7 Summary

1. **Heat** is a product of excited (or "sped-up") molecules.

2. **The First Law of Thermodynamics** states that the amount of energy in the universe always remains constant; it can change form, but cannot be destroyed or created.

3. **The Second Law of Thermodynamics** states that everything in the universe moves from higher energy levels to lower ones. Said another way, this law tells us that entropy is increasing in the universe. **Entropy** is a measure of the amount of energy in a system that is unusable for work, and thus it is a measure of the degree of disorder in the system.

4. The Second Law of Thermodynamics indicates the existence of God insofar as the universe has great order, despite the natural tendency of things to be disordered.

5. The Laws of Thermodynamics are fundamental principles for applied sciences, such as engineering, or medical biochemistry.

6. **Temperature** is the measurement of heat, or molecular motion in an object.

7. Many natural and artificial processes produce heat: mechanical, chemical, electrical, radioactive, solar, and geothermal.

8. **Combustion** is the burning of a fuel (any flammable material). There are three essential components for any combustion: oxygen, fuel, and fire.

9. Any artificial (or man-made) means of producing and conducting heat is called **heat transfer**. The three most common are convection, conduction, and radiation.

10. An artificial means of generating heat is by conducting electricity with **"heating elements."**

11. **Radiation** is an electromagnetic energy whose movement does not require a medium. Solar energy is radiation.

12. **Infrared radiation** is the transfer of heat energy in the form of electromagnetic radiation.

13. **Insulation** is any material that traps or retains heat, such as fiberglass or even air.

14. **Radio waves** are a form of electromagnetic radiation.

15. **Sound** is the vibration of disturbed or moving molecules through a medium.

16. Materially, sound behaves in longitudinal waves.

17. Sound is a form of kinetic energy that moves in a series of motions known as **compressions** and **rarefactions**.

Questions for Review

1. What is Thermodynamics?

   _____

   _____

2. What are the first two Laws of Thermodynamics?

   _____

   _____

3. What are the three essentials for combustion?

   _____

   _____

4. What is the difference between heat production and heat transfer?

   _____

   _____

5. What is radiation?

   _____

   _____

6. What is an indispensable condition for the production of sound?

   _____

   _____

7. The motion of sound through a medium has two distinct parts. What are they?

   _____

   _____

Electricity

I.   **Introduction**

II.   **Electric Current**

III.   **Production of Electric Current**

       A.   Mechanical Energy

       B.   Chemical Energy

       C.   Light Energy

IV.   **Electrical Energy**

V.   **Elements of a Circuit**

       A. Series Circuits

       B. Parallel Circuits

Electricity

"And now the third day was come, and the morning appeared: and behold thunders began to be heard, and lightning to flash, and a very thick cloud to cover the mount ..." (Exodus 19:16).

I. Introduction

We have come to the last section on types of energy: **electricity**, or **electrical energy**. Electricity is part of our everyday lives, and we could not maintain our way of life without it. From the time you woke up this morning until the time you started your work, you used electricity at least ten ways. The electric alarm clock probably woke you up. Perhaps you listened to the radio to hear the weather report. Can you name some more ways you used electricity this morning?

It has taken us years to develop our understanding of electricity. We know how to make it, store it, and use it, and yet we do not fully understand how it works. Notice that we use the word *understand*. We can know that something exists without fully understanding how it works. For this reason, much of what we know is cloaked in mystery. This is true not only for the natural world but also for the supernatural world. For example, we know about the Holy Trinity. We know that there is only one God but three Persons in God, but we do not fully understand how this is possible. The Holy Trinity remains a mystery.

The discovery of electricity has been a long and winding path. The ancient Greeks discovered that if a piece of **amber** was rubbed with wool, it gave off sparks and also attracted small bits of paper. The Greek word for amber is *elektron*. Over the centuries, people continued investigating sparks and electricity. A big breakthrough came in the 19th century when **Hans Oersted** of Denmark discovered that an electric current flowing through a wire created a magnetic field. A few years later, in England, **Michael Faraday** found that the reverse was also true: a magnet moving near a wire produced an electric current. During that time, scientists learned that electricity and magnetism were closely related. We now know that both of these are the same force: the **electromagnetic force**, or **electromagnetism**.

It is very easy to produce electrical charges, or sparks. Have you ever combed your hair and made tiny sparks crackle from your comb? Have you ever pulled clothes out of the dryer and found them sticking together? Perhaps you have rubbed a balloon on the carpet and then made it stick to the wall. In all of these examples, you produced static charges, or **static electricity**. Electrons were rubbed from the surface of one material and transferred to another. They will remain stationary (or static) on the new material for some time.

Static electricity results from a buildup of charges. These charges are known as **electrons**. This term comes from the Greek word for amber, elektron, which we discussed above. Electrons are part of an **atom**. An atom consists of three parts: **protons**, **neutrons**, and **electrons**.

Electrons have a negative electrical charge. Protons have a positive electrical charge. Neutrons have no electrical charge. The protons and neutrons combine to form the nucleus of the atom. The electrons are part of the atom and spend their time orbiting the nucleus. Like charges repel each other, and opposite charges attract each other. Thus, **positive charges repel other positive charges, and negative charges repel other negative charges**. However, positive charges are attracted to negative charges. When you pulled the clothes out of a dryer, the reason some of them stuck together is that they had opposite electrical charges.

II. Electric Current

Imagine a drinking straw that has been filled with peas. Now imagine taking one more pea and pushing it into the end of the straw. The first pea pushes the second pea, which pushes the third pea, and so on. All this pushing causes the last pea in the straw to pop out at the other end. Now, suppose we had a wire and could push an electron into one end. The first electron would push the second electron, which would push the third electron, and so forth. The last electron would pop out of the wire. This can give you an idea of how electrons flow through a wire to produce **electric current**.

The unit of measurement for electric current is an **ampere**, or **amp** for short. One amp of electric current means that 6.24 quintillion (6.24×10^{18}) electrons flow past a given point each second! Electric current is a flowing stream of electrons just like a stream of flowing water. We typically think of electricity flowing through metal wires made from copper. Although electricity can easily travel through other metals, copper is an excellent **conductor** of electricity. This means that it has low **resistance** to the flow of electrons; thus, electrons travel through the wires very quickly.

Resistance is measured in units called **ohms**. Electricity flowing through a wire is like water flowing through a garden hose. Resistance slows down the flow of electricity, just like the shut-off valve in the hose slows down the flow of water. When you open the valve slightly (high resistance), the water comes out as a trickle. When you open the valve fully (low resistance), the water comes out with full force. In electrical circuits, small components called **resistors** provide the resistance.

Electric current can flow only when it is in a **circuit**. This means that there must be a complete pathway for electrons to flow from a source, through an electrical device, and finally to an electrical ground. An **electrical ground** is a wire that is connected directly to the earth (so that large spikes in electricity will be diverted to the ground). For example, consider an ordinary household flashlight. When you close the switch (turn the flashlight on), current flows from one end (or terminal) of the battery to the tiny wire filament in the light bulb. It then flows back to the other end (terminal) of the battery. The current will continue to flow in this circuit until you open the switch (turn the flashlight off) or until the battery is exhausted.

ACTIVITY: Making an Electrostatic Charge

MATERIALS: Balloon, hair, TV screen, running water from a faucet

PROCEDURE I:

1. Blow up your balloon and tie it off.
2. Rub the balloon on your hair for a few minutes. This sends electrons from your hair to the balloon.
3. Hold the balloon away from the hair and observe the result.
4. Draw your observations.
5. Turn on the TV, computer, or video monitor.
6. Hold the back of your hand up to the front of the TV screen. This sends electrons from your hand to the TV screen.
7. What do you observe about the hair on the back of your hand?

_____

QUESTIONS:

1. When you rub your hair with the balloon, what is the charge on the balloon: negative, positive, or no charge?

_____

2. After rubbing your hair with the balloon, what is the charge on your hair?

_____

3. When you hold the back of your hand up to the TV screen, what is the charge on your hand hair?

_____

4. What is the charge on the TV screen when you hold the back of your hand up to it?

_____

PROCEDURE II:

1. Turn on the water faucet in the kitchen.
2. Hold the balloon next to the running water.
3. What happens to the stream of water?

_____

QUESTIONS:

1. Since you know that the balloon has been charged by rubbing it on your hair, what can you say about the water?

_____

2. Water is made up of molecules. What can you say about the molecules of the water?

_____

III. Production of Electric Current

There are several ways to make electric current. The power company converts **mechanical energy** into electrical energy. A battery converts **chemical energy** into electric current, and a solar cell converts **light energy** into electrical energy.

A. Mechanical Energy

When a magnet is swept along a wire, it causes an electric current. A magnet is like a broom that can sweep electrons. The power company uses this principle to make electricity. At the generating station are **dynamos**. A dynamo uses mechanical energy to spin large coils of wire next to large **magnets**. You may have seen a smaller version of a dynamo. Cars use **alternators** to make electricity. Your bicycle may have a small **generator** to power a headlight. The generator, the alternator, and the dynamo all work in a similar fashion. Small generators usually have permanent magnets inside; alternators and dynamos often use **electromagnets**. All three devices make electric currents.

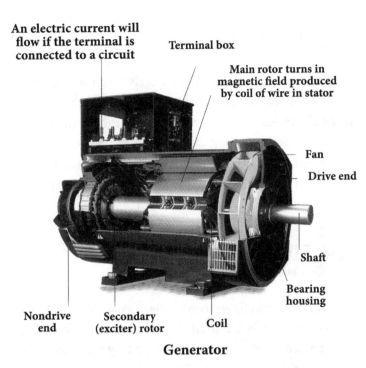

An electric current will flow if the terminal is connected to a circuit

Terminal box

Main rotor turns in magnetic field produced by coil of wire in stator

Fan

Drive end

Shaft

Bearing housing

Coil

Secondary (exciter) rotor

Nondrive end

Generator

B. Chemical Energy

Certain chemical reactions release large amounts of electrical energy. A battery is a container for this type of chemical reaction to take place. Inside a car battery, sulfuric acid reacts with lead, producing a strong electric potential. Inside a transistor radio battery, other chemicals also produce electricity. You may have heard the terms **alkaline battery**, **nickel-cadmium battery**, or **lead-acid battery**. These are all types of chemicals used in different batteries.

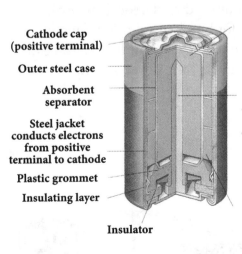

Cathode cap (positive terminal)

Outer steel case

Absorbent separator

Steel jacket conducts electrons from positive terminal to cathode

Plastic grommet

Insulating layer

Insulator

Mixture of ammonium chloride electrolyte and powdered zinc anode

Steel nail collects electrons from anode and conducts them to negative terminal

Mixture of alkaline manganese (IV) oxide cathode and graphite conductor

Dry Cell Battery

A **battery** is made of two or more electrical **cells**. Each cell is an individual electricity source. Your flashlight may use two D cells. A tape player may use four AA cells. The two D cells or four AA cells together are a battery. A 9-volt radio battery contains several cells joined together inside a small metal case. A 12-volt car battery contains six cells joined together.

The cells in a car battery are called **wet cells** because the acid is a liquid. The cells in a small flashlight are called **dry cells** because the chemical inside is only a moist paste, called an **electrolyte**.

C. Light Energy

Electricity can be made directly from sunlight. When light shines on specially prepared materials, the light energy causes electrons to be given off. If enough of these solar-electric cells are joined together, a large amount of electrical power can be generated, and useful work can be done. Often, highly refined **silicon** is the special material used to make solar cells.

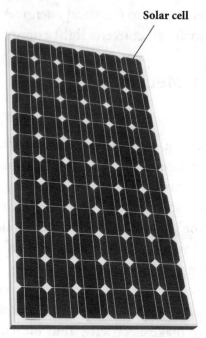

Solar cell

Solar Panel

IV. Electrical Energy

Perhaps you have seen a solar-powered calculator or maybe an array of solar cells powering a radio. Solar cells are used to provide electricity where it is not convenient or economical to run electric wires. Solar cells can charge large batteries to provide electricity at night or during cloudy weather. Some people have built solar-powered cars, solar-powered homes, and solar-powered radio stations.

One of the most useful features of electricity is the convenient way it may be used for the transportation of energy. For example, water power may be converted to electrical energy by a dynamo. The electrical energy is transmitted through wires for hundreds of miles. Finally, the electrical energy is converted to many other useful forms of energy at your house. You can convert electricity to sound energy in your stereo, or heat energy in your stove, or light energy from your lamps, or mechanical energy in your washing machine.

When an apple falls from a tree, its movement is a result of gravitational force. When an electron flows through a wire, an **electromotive force** causes it to move. The unit of electromotive force is called a **volt**. If we compare the flow of electricity with the flow of water-filled pipes, we can say that differences in **voltage** are like differences in water pressure.

Materials such as glass, wood, and plastic do not conduct electricity. These materials are called insulators. Materials that do not conduct heat very well are also called insulators. The same materials that make good heat **insulators** usually make good electrical insulators.

Many electrical devices use a current with the electrons all flowing continuously in one direction. This type of electricity is referred to as **direct current** (**DC**), and it is the type of energy provided by batteries in a flashlight or in a car.

Some electrical devices use electricity that changes direction many times each second. This type of electricity is called **alternating current** (**AC**) and is the type supplied to your house by the power company. Alternating current can be transmitted many miles using smaller wires than the equivalent amount of direct current. It is much more economical to use smaller wires, especially when you consider how many miles of wire a power company needs.

V. Elements of a Circuit

An **electrical circuit** is a path along which electrical current can flow. In order for electricity to flow in a circuit, the path must begin and end at the same point. Common elements of a circuit are wire, fuses, switches, batteries, and light bulbs. There are many other electrical components as well. When an engineer draws a circuit on paper, he does not draw tiny light bulbs and switches and so forth. Instead, he draws symbols that represent electrical devices. The drawing is called a **schematic diagram** because it shows the scheme (illustration) of how a circuit is laid out.

Wire comes in many sizes and types. The schematic symbol for wire is a line. Where two wires are connected, a dot is used to show it. Where two wires cross but do not connect, a schematic drawing just shows two lines that cross.

Switches are for opening and closing electrical circuits. There are several symbols for switches, just as there are several kinds of switches. When you close a switch, the electrical device is on. Opening a switch turns the circuit off.

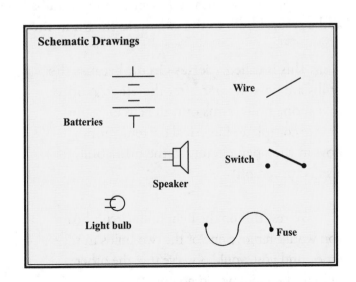

To protect against fires caused by electrical overloads, circuits have **fuses** or **circuit breakers**. The schematic symbol for a fuse is a small S-curved line between two dots. A circuit breaker's symbol looks like a pushbutton. These two safety devices break an electrical connection if too much current flows in a circuit. This situation might develop from a frayed wire allowing electricity to flow where it should not. This is known as a **short circuit**. A short circuit can damage the devices on the circuit or can cause a fire.

God has made us with fuses, too. When we are under too much stress, we experience symptoms, like headaches, which tell us to kneel before God and pray. If we ignore the symptoms, our stress will increase. Stress can cause illness or make an illness worse.

A. Series Circuits

Inside an incandescent light bulb is a tiny wire filament. The schematic symbol for an incandescent light resembles a coiled filament inside a glass bulb. When electricity passes through the filament, it gets white hot and produces light. Most of the air was removed from the light bulb when it was manufactured; otherwise, the filament would burn out.

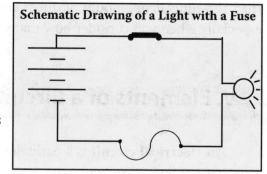

Schematic Drawing of a Light with a Fuse

Batteries are a convenient source of electrical power. The symbol for a battery looks like the lead plates in a lead-acid battery. Radios, **flashlights**, hearing aids, and watches are just a few devices that rely on batteries.

Look at the schematic diagram above. Can you tell what it means? Follow the wiring. Current flows from the battery (see the symbol), through the switch, and then through the light bulb. The current leaves the bulb, and returns to the battery through the fuse.

Suppose you wish to power two light bulbs from the battery at the same time. You might add a second bulb to the circuit, as shown in the schematic drawing below.

This is called a **series circuit** because the bulbs are lined up one after the other. Notice that if one bulb burns out, the circuit is no longer complete. Electrical current cannot flow in the open circuit, so the other bulb also is turned off.

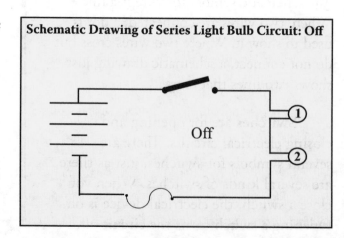

Schematic Drawing of Series Light Bulb Circuit: Off

Off

① ②

To test this on the light bulb circuit board, you would remove one of the two bulbs in the series, and you would observe that the other bulb in the series would go out.

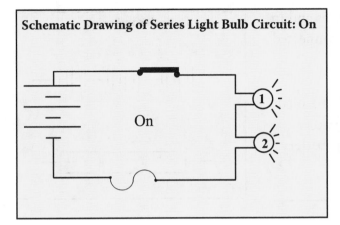

Schematic Drawing of Series Light Bulb Circuit: On

On

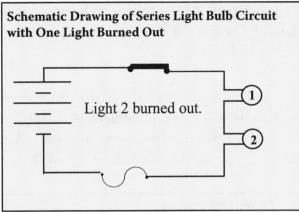

Schematic Drawing of Series Light Bulb Circuit with One Light Burned Out

Light 2 burned out.

B. Parallel Circuits

Another way to power two bulbs is to connect them as shown in the schematic drawing on the right.

This is called a parallel circuit. The wires connecting each light bulb in the schematic drawing actually resemble parallel lines.

If one bulb burns out in a parallel circuit, there is still a complete circuit for the other bulb, and it remains on, as shown in the schematic drawing below.

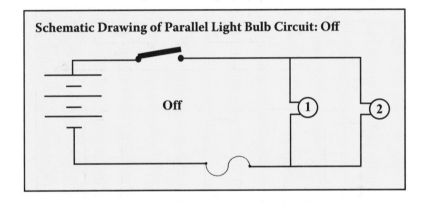

Schematic Drawing of Parallel Light Bulb Circuit: Off

Off

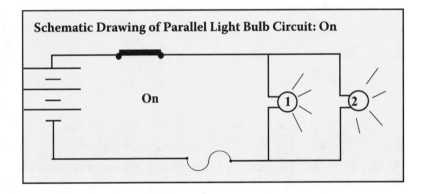

Schematic Drawing of Parallel Light Bulb Circuit: On

On

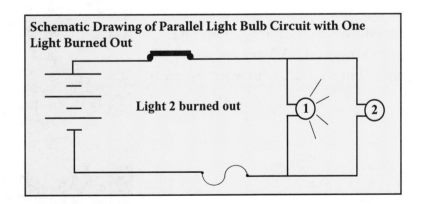

Schematic Drawing of Parallel Light Bulb Circuit with One Light Burned Out

Light 2 burned out

Batteries and cells may also be wired in series and in parallel. Look at the diagram. The dry cells are connected end to end in a series.

When cells are wired in series, the voltage obtained is the sum of all the **cell voltages**. A flashlight battery using two 1.5-volt cells operates at 3 volts. A car battery has six 2-volt cells, so it produces 12 volts.

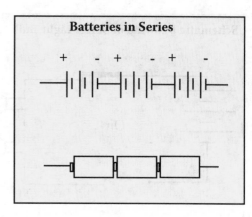

Batteries in Series

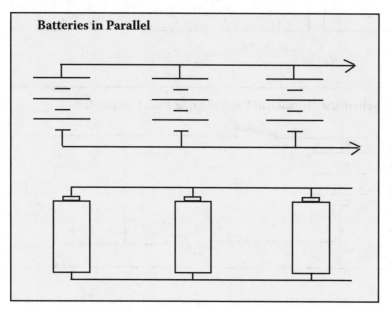

Batteries in Parallel

When cells are wired in parallel, the voltage obtained is equal to just one cell. Look at the parallel-wired cells in the diagram at the left. If one cell is removed, you can see that the circuit is still powered. Two parallel cells will power a circuit twice as long as only one cell.

The story of electricity is short. We have not had electrical power very long. The amazing thing about electricity is that God created this power source thousands of years before we figured out how to use it. He knew at the creation that we would need electricity, and He provided it then. The lightning and thunder present in a rain storm show the evidence that electrical power has existed since God created this world. We use electricity all the time. It is dangerous, but we are careful when we use it.

ACTIVITY: Making an Electromagnet

MATERIALS: Two nails, C-cell battery, bell wire 22 to 30 gauge, needle-nose pliers with wire cutter built in

DIRECTIONS:

1. Cut a 12-inch length of wire with pliers. Strip plastic off both ends of the wire.
2. Attach a piece of wire to one terminal of the battery with tape.
3. Wrap a nail with wire. Attach the end of wire to the other terminal of the battery.
4. Test the electromagnet with the other, unused nail to see if the wrapped nail is magnetic.

QUESTIONS:

1. Draw a diagram for the circuit in the box below.

1. When one of the wires is not connected, what happens to the magnetism?

2. A switch is a device used to deliberately disconnect the circuit. How is a switch useful?

3. What is traveling around your circuit?

ACTIVITY: Directions for Making a Light Bulb Circuit Board

MATERIALS: Light bulb (from a flashlight), light bulb socket, bell wire (can ask for this at hardware store), electrical tape, board (approximately 6" × 10"), thumb tacks, 1-inch nails, 9V battery

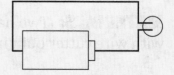

Circuit of Light, Battery, and Wire

TO MAKE THE CIRCUIT BOARD:

1. Secure the light socket in place on the board using nails, tacks, or screws, in positions 4 and 5 in the picture below.

2. Secure the battery to the board using a rubber band around the three nails in positions A, B, and C, as shown in the diagram.

3. Position nails 2 and 3, and tacks 6 and 7, as shown in the diagram. Measure and cut a piece of wire about 1 inch longer than the distance from 1 and 3. Strip 1/2 inch of the insulation (outer covering of the wire) from both ends of the wire using a pocket knife. Twist one end into nail 1.

4. Pull the wire tightly to nail 2, and mark on the wire where it touches the nail. Remove enough insulation around the mark on the wire so that it can be securely twisted around nail 2. Do not attach the free end at this time, as it will act as a switch later.

5. Cut four pieces of wire, no less than 4 inches each. Strip insulation from the ends and connect wires:
   a. Between nail 3 and the light socket at 4
   b. Between socket at 5 and tack at 6
   c. Between tacks at 6 and 7
   d. Between tack 7 and nail 8

6. Be sure the wires at 1 and 8 are making contact with the battery. You may want to wrap a piece of tape around the battery holding nails 1 and 8 tight to the battery.

7. Put the bulb in the socket. Touch the loose end of the wire from nail 2 to nail 3. This will complete the circuit and cause the light bulb to glow.

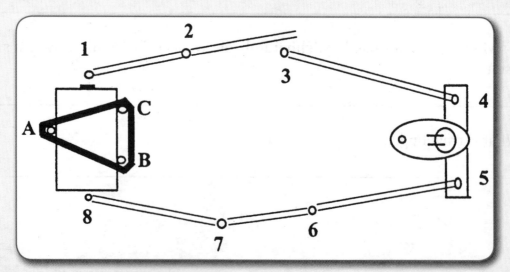

ACTIVITY: Making a Fuse in a Light Bulb Circuit

MATERIALS: Light bulb circuit board (see previous page), foil from gum wrapper (paper carefully removed) or very thin aluminum foil

DIRECTIONS:

1. Make the light bulb circuit board discussed on the previous page.
2. Cut a rectangular piece of foil long enough to reach between the two tacks. Cut the rectangular foil into the shape of an hour glass by carefully trimming away metal near the center.
3. Remove the wire between the two tacks on the board and replace it with the foil. **This foil acts as a fuse in the circuit.** (Note: The foil is very delicate. You may find it easier to trim the foil to an hourglass shape after it is tacked to the circuit board.)

QUESTIONS:

1. When the wires are connected, what happens to the light?

   _____

   What does the fuse do?

   _____

2. A fuse is a device that deliberately disconnects the circuit when it is overloaded. How is a fuse useful?

   _____

3. Draw a diagram of the circuit in the box below.

8

ACTIVITY: Making a Flashlight

MATERIALS: Flashlight bulb, C or D cell battery, wire, tape, pliers, or scissors

TO MAKE THE FLASHLIGHT:

If you have built the light bulb circuit board on the previous page, you may use it to perform this experiment. If you have not built the light circuit board, proceed as follows:

1. Cut two 6-inch lengths of wire with the pliers and strip the insulation off each end of both wires.

2. Securely tape the wires to the battery. Tape one wire at each end.

3. Touch one wire to the metal side of the light bulb, and touch the other wire to the bottom tip of the light bulb. The bulb should glow.

PROCEDURE:

1. Set up your apparatus and complete the circuit so that the light comes on.

2. Answer the questions and record.

QUESTIONS:

1. When one of the wires is not connected, what happens to the light?

   _____

2. A switch is a device used to deliberately disconnect the circuit. How is a switch useful?

   _____

3. What is traveling around your circuit?

   _____

4. Draw a diagram of the circuit in the box below.

Chapter 8 Summary

1. **Electricity** has two forms: static and current. **Static electricity** is made up of standing electrons. **Current** is a flow of **electrons**. Current is measured in **amperes**, or amps.

2. Electricity travels in a **circuit**, a complete pathway for the flow of electrons. They travel from a **voltage source** through the electrical device and on to an **electrical ground**. If all the electrons are flowing in the same direction all the time, the current is called **DC**, or **direct current**. If the electrons switch directions rapidly back and forth, the current is called **AC**, or **alternating current**. Alternating current can be carried over wires for many miles; this is the type of current used in our homes.

3. A **conductor** allows electrons to flow easily through it, whereas a non-conductor resists the flow of electrons. Materials that do not pass electrons are called **insulators**. The measure of the **resistance** to the flow of electrons is in units called **ohms**.

4. There are three types of energy that can be converted into electricity: mechanical, chemical, and light.

5. **Dynamos** make electrical current using mechanical energy. Cars use an alternator, and your bicycle may have a generator to produce electrical current for a light. These work by sweeping electrons along a wire. This is done with a set of magnets.

6. **Batteries** use chemical means to produce electricity. Each **cell** of a battery is an electron source. A car battery is a **wet cell** because the acid in it is a liquid. A **dry cell** uses a moist paste instead of a liquid. **Solar energy** can be used to generate electricity using **solar cells**.

7. **Electromotive force** is the force moving the electrons along the wire. It is measured in **volts**.

8. Some **elements in an electrical circuit** are: wires, fuses, switches, batteries, and light bulbs. We draw these and others in a diagram called a **schematic diagram**. You should review the symbols used for these elements.

9. A **short circuit** occurs when electricity is flowing where it should not. Too much current may damage electrical devices or cause fires.

10. A **series circuit** is a set of devices wired into a line so that the current flows through each device to get to the next one. **Parallel circuits** have the devices hooked into the circuit so that they are parallel to one another. The current goes through all the devices, but not one after the other.

11. We must make sure that we always follow the safety rules for electricity.

8

Questions for Review

1. What are the two forms of electricity? How are they different from one another?

   _____

   _____

2. What is an electric current?

   _____

   _____

3. What are the three energies that can undergo electrical conversion?

   _____

   _____

4. Give three examples of machines that convert mechanical energy into electricity.

   _____

   _____

5. Cars use an _____ to produce alternating electrical current.

6. Large magnets are used to make electrical current in a _____.

7. We must make sure that we always follow the _____ _____ for electricity.

8. Current that changes direction: _____, or _____.

9. Current that does not change direction: _____, or _____.

Chemistry, Part I

I. **Matter**
   - A. Mass and Weight
   - B. Volume
   - C. Density

II. **Observing and Reporting**
   - A. Observing
   - B. Reporting

III. **Properties of Matter**

IV. **Atoms: Protons, Neutrons, Electrons**
   - A. Atomic Number
   - B. Physical and Chemical Characteristics of Elements
   - C. Atomic Mass

V. **Isotopes**

Chemistry, Part I

"In the beginning, God created Heaven and Earth. And the Earth was void and empty, and darkness was upon the face of the deep; and the Spirit of God moved over the waters" (Genesis 1:1-2).

I. Matter

The science of chemistry is all about investigating and characterizing matter. What exactly is matter? All the things you see around you, all the things you use, and even your own body are made of matter. **Matter** is anything that has mass and takes up space. An object's **mass** is how much matter that object has. Matter is the physical material that makes up our entire world, including all the stars in the heavens.

God is the Creator of Heaven and Earth. In the beginning of time, God created matter out of nothing. God is a Spirit; although He created matter, He Himself is not made of matter.

When Jesus became Man, He became fully human, yet He remained fully God. Jesus is both God and Man. His Body, like ours, was made subject to physical laws. However, as God, He possessed the power to overcome death and the physical laws He had created. By His suffering and death on the Cross, Jesus redeemed us. His Resurrection from the dead reveals a Divine Power greater than the physical laws of matter, energy, time, and space. Of course, God not only created everything in the universe; He also is the author of all the physical laws of matter.

Physical entities, therefore, must obey the laws that God has set up for them. One of these laws is known as the **Law of Gravitation**. This law states that different masses attract one another. The weight of an object (like your baseball) is the measure of the pull of the Earth's mass upon the object's mass. This is called the pull of **gravity**. The greater the mass of an object (the more matter that object has), the heavier it will be on Earth.

**A Balance-Type Weighing Scale
(Photo by Jean Poussin)**

We measure mass in the chemistry laboratory with a type of scale known as a **balance**. Mass is measured in units known as **grams** (in the metric system). A sample of material is placed in a small pan on one side of the balance scale, and metal weights of known mass are added to the pan on the other side. Weights are added or removed until the pans are brought to the same height. Today, most laboratory balances are completely automated.

A. Mass and Weight

Sometimes people confuse the terms mass and weight. What is the difference between the two? Gravity determines weight. Weight changes with gravity, but mass does not. For example, an object that has a mass of 1 kilogram (kg), which is 2.2 lbs. on Earth, will have the same mass on the moon, but the weight would be 1/6 of your weight on Earth because the forces of gravity on the moon are less than on Earth. If you weigh 100 lbs. on Earth, then your mass is 45 kg (100 lbs. ÷ 2.2 lb./kg = 45 kg). Your mass would be no different on the moon or anywhere else. However, your weight on the moon would be only 16 lbs. We can summarize the above as follows. **Mass** is the amount of matter in something. **Weight** is the measurement of how hard gravity is pulling on something.

Changing locations does not change the mass of an object, but the location may change an object's weight. Out in space, an object is farther away from our planet Earth, and the pull of gravity of the Earth is less. However, the mass of an object remains the same. On the planet Jupiter, an object weighs more than on Earth, even though the mass, the matter contained in the object, remains the same.

B. Volume

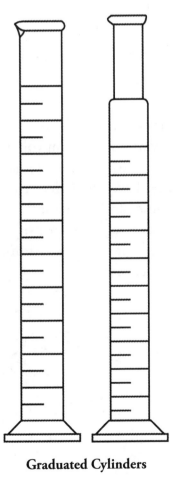

Graduated Cylinders

The **volume** of a substance is the amount of space that substance takes up. In other words, volume is the three-dimensional space the substance occupies. In your previous math classes, you learned to calculate volume for three-dimensional objects. For example, the volume of a rectangular object is length times width times height ($l \times w \times h$). The volume of a cylinder is π [pi] times the square of the radius (the radius times itself), times the height ($\pi \times r^2 \times h$, which can be written as $\pi r^2 h$). Chemists measure the volume of fluids using devices such as marked or measured (**graduated**) cylinders, **volumetric** flasks, or beakers. This glassware is precisely **calibrated** (measured on the sides with numbers and lines that indicate volume).

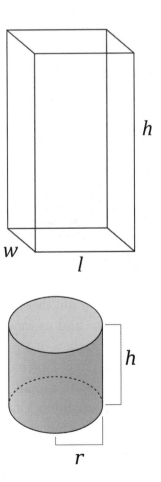

How much volume of milk or juice does your favorite cup or glass hold? How much volume of hot chocolate does it hold? When your mother follows a recipe, she measures the volume with a measuring cup.

You can calculate the volume of an object according to the rules you have studied in math class. You must use a formula to determine the volume according to the shape of the container. A formula for the volume of a cube is width times length times height. A formula for a prism is $\frac{1}{2}(l \times w \times h)$. A prism has a triangular shape, and two prisms put together make a box, so the volume of a prism is $\frac{1}{2}$ the volume of a box.

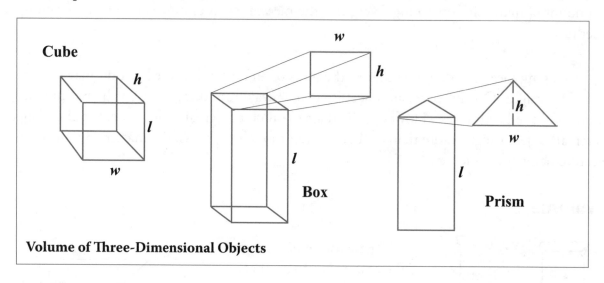

Volume of Three-Dimensional Objects

C. Density

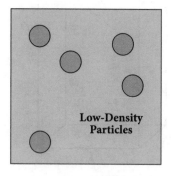

Density is another characteristic of matter. The **density** of a substance is the amount of matter it contains within a certain volume of space. In other words, density indicates how closely the matter is packed inside that substance. Some substances have a high density, and others have a low density. The particles in high-density substances are closely packed together. Conversely, the particles in low-density substances are spaced farther apart. For example, the particles within sandstone are packed closer together than in Styrofoam.

To help put this in perspective, consider an old trick question that used to find its way into science classes. Which weighs more: a pound of feathers or a pound of lead? The answer is that they both weigh the same. Gotcha! Lead is denser than feathers, so a pound of lead occupies a smaller volume than a pound of feathers. You can easily fit a small block of lead in the palm of your hand. However, you cannot fit a pound of feathers in your hand; the density is so loosely packed, you would need a large bag to hold just one pound of feathers!

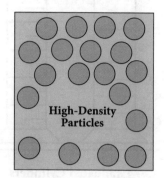

Density, mass, and volume are related to one another as follows. We calculate the density of a substance by dividing its mass by the volume of space the object occupies:

Density = Mass ÷ Volume

Likewise, chemists determine the mass of a substance by that substance's density by its volume, thus rearranging the above formula as follows:

Mass = Density × Volume

Chemists express density using the International System of Units and report it in grams per cubic centimeter (g/cm^3). For example, water has a density of $1.00 \ g/cm^3$. An object that has a density far lighter than water would more easily float on water than one that does not. If an object has a density greater than water, it won't float at all.

Earth is the densest of the nine planets.

Chemists calculate the volume of an object by measuring its shape. They may also calculate the volume by adding the object to fluid and measuring fluid displacement (how much fluid is pushed out of the way by the object). Legend has it that Archimedes discovered this principle when a king suspected that his crown was not made of pure gold. Archimedes took two pieces of pure gold and pure silver that weighed the same as the crown. He successively immersed the gold, the silver, and the crown in a container, which had a measured volume of water. The crown displaced more water than gold but less than the silver. This proved that the king was correct. The crown contained some metal other than gold.

Archimedes Thoughtful, by Domencio Fetti

Table 1 shows the density of various substances, listed from lowest to highest. Use this table to answer the questions on the following page.

Table 1. Comparative densities of various substances.	
Substance	**Density (g/cm³)**
Helium	0.00018
Nitrogen	0.00125
Air	0.0012
Carbon dioxide	0.0018
Balsa wood	0.16
Ash wood	0.65
Oak wood	0.75
African teak	0.98
Water	1.00
Honey	1.36
Glass	2.60
Pyrite (fool's gold)	5.02
Silver	10.49
Lead	11.36
Gold	19.32

QUESTIONS: Examine Table 1 and answer the following.

1. Which wood would float best in water?

    _____

2. Which wood has a density greater than balsa but not as great as oak?

    _____

3. Which wood would be a poor choice for constructing a raft, because it almost sinks or floats poorly in water?

    _____

4. Why is balsa wood used for constructing model airplanes?

    _____

5. Which gas is the lightest? What is one of its uses?

    _____

6. Which type of substance has the least density?

    _____

7. Which type of substance has the greatest density?

    _____

8. How can you determine whether an object is lighter or heavier?

    _____

9. Calculate the density of a type of matter that has a mass of 15 grams and a volume of 10 cubic centimeters (10 cm^3).

    _____

PROBLEMS: Volume

The Holy Bible is full of fascinating and detailed descriptions of material things. In the book of Genesis, for example, God has given us the exact dimensions of Noah's Ark.

According to Genesis 6:15, God told Noah: "the length of the Ark shall be 300 cubits, its width 50 cubits, and its height 30 cubits."

Note: The measurements of the Ark show that it was perfectly designed to carry a vast cargo in rough waters for a long period of time. According to Bernard Ramm, on page 230 of *The Christian View*, "a model was made by Peter Jansen of Holland, and Danish barges called 'fleuten' were modeled after the Ark. These models proved that the Ark had a greater capacity than curved or shaped vessels. They were very seaworthy and almost impossible to capsize." The ark was about the size of ocean-going vessels of today.

At the time of the building of the Ark, the cubit was used as the standard unit of measurement instead of feet or meters. A cubit is the distance of a man's arm from fingertip to elbow. This was between 1.5 and 2 feet, or 18 to 24 inches. In these problems, we will be using 2 feet as our standard cubit. *For extra credit, measure your father's cubit length and use that measurement for the following problems.*

1. Using these figures, what was the total volume in cubic cubits? **Hint:** The Ark was 300 cubits (C.) long, 50 C. wide, and 30 C. high.

   _____

2. Assuming a measurement of 2 feet per cubit, what was the total volume of Noah's Ark in cubic feet?

   _____

3. To appreciate the size of Noah's Ark, find the volume of a boxcar 30 feet long, 10 feet wide, and 10 feet high.

   _____

4. Using your answers to questions 2 and 3, roughly how many boxcars could the Ark have carried?

   _____

5. God told Moses: "You shall make an ark of acacia wood, two and a half cubits long, one and a half cubits wide, and one and a half cubits high...In the Ark you are to put the Commandments which I will give you." (Exodus 25:10 and 16) What was the volume of the Ark of the Covenant in cubic cubits?

_____

6. Using the measure of 2 feet per cubit, what was the volume of the Ark of the Covenant in cubic feet?

_____

7. In Exodus 27, God told Moses to design a court for the sanctuary. He told him to surround the courtyard with columns 5 cubits high. The width of the courtyard was to be 50 cubits, and the length was to be 100 cubits. What was the volume of the Court for the Dwelling Place?

_____

8. **Challenge:** If you like measuring things, why not read Exodus 25-27, and try to make a scaled drawing of the sacred sanctuary, including the courtyard? You will find all of the measurements you need in these three chapters.

THINKING ABOUT DENSITY

1. A ball weighing 12 grams lands in a swimming pool and floats on top of the water. The volume of the ball is about 20 cubic centimeters. How dense is the ball?

   _____

2. The density of water is 1.00 grams per cubic centimeter. Is the ball more or less dense than the water?

   _____

3. If the ball floats on the water, then it is less dense than the water. If it sinks, then the ball is more dense than the water. This means that you can compare densities without doing any math at all. Your helium balloon floats in the air. Is the balloon heavier or lighter than a balloon of regular air that is the same size as the helium balloon? Is it more or less dense than the air?

   _____

   _____

4. What would you guess about the densities of a life raft and the ocean? Which is greater? How can you tell?

   _____

   _____

5. Which of these objects do you hypothesize is the most dense: a spoon, a dishwater, or bubbles? Explain your reasoning.

   _____

   _____

   _____

ACTIVITY

You are at a festival in the "Gold Rush" part of California. You approach a booth where a man dressed as an old-time prospector is selling gold, silver, and semiprecious gemstones. He offers to sell you a "gold nugget" at a very good price. You and your parents are suspicious that it might not be a real nugget, but pyrite (or fool's gold). However, it is very pretty, and you'd like to buy it. How can you tell whether the nugget is real? You have a ruler in your backpack, and the prospector has a balance.

Table 1. Comparative densities of various substances.	
Substance	Density (g/cm³)
Helium	0.00018
Nitrogen	0.00125
Air	0.0012
Carbon dioxide	0.0018
Balsa wood	0.16
Ash wood	0.65
Oak wood	0.75
African teak	0.98
Water	1.00
Honey	1.36
Glass	2.60
Pyrite (fool's gold)	5.02
Silver	10.49
Lead	11.36
Gold	19.32

Step 1: You measure the nugget and find that it is almost a perfect cube. Each side is 1 centimeter in length. You quickly calculate its volume by multiplying $1 \times 1 \times 1 = 1 \text{ cm}^3$.

Step 2: Your dad does a quick search on his smart phone and finds that gold has a density of 19.32 g/cm^3, and pyrite has a density of 5.02 g/cm^3 (see Table 1).

Step 3: You multiply Density times Volume to *estimate the mass* for each of these two substances. Pyrite: $5.02 \times 1.0 \text{ (cm}^3) = 5 \text{ g/cm}^3$; Gold: $19.32 \times 1.0 \text{ (cm}^3) = 19.32 \text{ g/cm}^3$

Step 4: Next, you ask to borrow the prospector's balance (scale). You weigh the sample and find that its mass is about 5 grams, not the 19 grams that you calculated. You ask him if he would accept $10 for his perfect sample of fool's gold. He smiles at you and walks over to his next customer.

Problem: Next, the dishonest prospector tries to sell a small ingot of silver to a brother and sister who are about your age. You suspect that the price is too affordable. Perhaps it is some other metal that is silver plated. The ingot is shaped like a rectangle, with dimensions of 10 cm × 5 cm × 1 cm, and weighs 1.25 lbs. (568 grams). Using Table 1, can you help out this brother and sister, and find out whether they really are buying silver? Is the ingot made of silver or some other metal?

Answer: The volume is 50 cm³, and the mass is 568 grams. When you divide mass by volume, you obtain the density, 11.36 g/cm³. The metal is lead, not silver!

II. Observing and Reporting

Density, mass, weight, and volume are only a few of the many characteristics we use to classify, identify, and discuss matter or material things. Everyone, not only scientists, uses these characteristics to describe matter. **Observing matter accurately** is an important skill. Our Catholic Faith is reasonable precisely because it is supported by so many reliable witnesses who described material things with great care.

In the first letter of St. John, the "Beloved Apostle" emphasized the importance of careful observation to the Gospel message when he wrote: "That which was from the beginning, which we have heard, which we have seen with our eyes, which we have looked upon and touched with our hands, concerning the Word of Life…" (1 John 1:1).

St. Luke, a doctor and a scientist, began his Gospel by stressing the care he had taken to obtain accurate observations of the Life, Passion, and Resurrection of Jesus.

"Since many have undertaken to compile a narrative of the events that have been fulfilled among us, just as those who were eye-witnesses from the beginning, and ministers of the Word have handed them down to us, I too have decided, after investigating everything accurately anew, to write it down in an orderly sequence" (Luke 1:1-3).

Our faith in Jesus Christ and His Church is supported by many facts that were carefully described and handed down to us by the Apostles of Jesus, and their successors. The importance of a faithful and accurate record of these facts helped to make Christians careful observers and describers of the physical world. Many Christian scientists paved the way for the great scientific discoveries of the past two thousand years. Many were priests and monks, and usually the Church itself financially and otherwise supported the scientific work of Catholics.

Let us always strive to practice accurate observation in science, and practice accurate reporting of our observations.

A. Observing

In observations, we must use as many different senses as possible to be aware of the characteristics of matter we are studying. In the first activity, you will try to discover as many different attributes of a candle as you can. The first few things you write down will be the most obvious characteristics about the candle, such as its color, its length, and its width. Then you should start thinking about other things, such as how it smells or feels to your fingers. Then you need to advance to deeper thinking and analysis: How much water will the candle displace if put in a container with water? How high is the wick? What other characteristics do you find? Use all of the senses God gave you for observing the material things around you.

B. Reporting

Reporting what is seen and done is an important skill of the scientist. Doing your own observation and testing is often easier than doing reporting. Scientists are usually excited about their observations and testing, but many are careless about their reporting.

Alexander Graham Bell was so poor that he could not even afford paper on which to record his testing of various materials to produce the telephone. When he finally was successful, a big company claimed that they had invented the telephone. Alexander Graham Bell had to go to court to try to prove he was the inventor, but no one believed him because he had no notes or evidence. Finally, his wife found an old bill from years before on the back of which he had written her a note about his work on inventing the telephone. Because of that piece of paper, the court ruled that Alexander Graham Bell was the inventor of the telephone and was due the money being made by the sales of the telephone.

Jesus Himself performed miracles when others were around to observe. Remember the times when Jesus healed someone and asked the person to go to a priest to report and show an authority the miracle. Remember the ten men cured of leprosy who were told to go to a priest. Remember when the young girl was reported dead, and the weeping women were in her room; they observed that she was dead. However, after the miracle, when Jesus brought her back to life, that group of mourning women were observers and reporters of the miracle.

Observing and reporting (or record keeping) are essential for accuracy, reliability, and accountability.

ACTIVITY: Observing Characteristics about a Physical Object

DIRECTIONS:

Get a candle. Feel, smell, and see the candle. Observe the candle in as many different ways as you can imagine. Record the characteristics of your candle. The more characteristics you have, the more observant you have been.

_____

_____

_____

_____

_____

_____

_____

CONCLUSIONS:

Did you have more than twenty-five different characteristics? Write two or three sentences using the characteristics you found to describe your candle.

_____

_____

_____

_____

_____

ACTIVITY: Recording How to Make a Peanut Butter Sandwich

DIRECTIONS:

Write down all of the steps that you would use in making a peanut butter sandwich. Include everything you would do, without leaving anything out. Take your record to your parents or to a lab partner and let them try to make a sandwich based only upon your record. Tell them not to do anything that is not actually written down in your record.

_____

_____

_____

_____

_____

_____

_____

_____

RESULT:

What did your parents do? How did their sandwich turn out?

_____

_____

_____

CONCLUSIONS:

What do you think about the form of communication which you used to tell your parents what to do? Was it accurate? Did you make a complete record? If not, how could you improve the record? What would make it easier to do correctly and completely?

_____

_____

_____

_____

SOME PROPERTIES OF MATTER

1. **Mass:** The measure of the matter contained in the object.

2. **Weight:** The measure of the pull of Earth's gravity on the mass of an object.

3. **Volume:** The amount of space the object takes up.

4. **Density:** The amount of mass in a volume of substance.

5. **Color:** Matter will reflect some types of light.

6. **Luster:** Matter may have a distinctive sheen.

7. **Porosity (how porous it is):** The amount of space between its particles.

8. **Buoyancy:** How well does it float?

9. **Smell:** The matter may be volatile and have an odor.

10. **State of matter:** Is it a solid, liquid, gas, or plasma?
    (You will learn about plasma in the next chapter. Plasma as a state of matter is not the same as the part of blood that is called plasma.)

III. Properties of Matter

All matter is made up of atoms, the basic building block of matter. Each kind of atom has unique characteristics that distinguish it from other kinds of atoms. There are many different kinds of atoms. Each kind is called an element. Gold is an element; silver is an element. If something is pure gold, all of the atoms are alike; they are all gold atoms. If someone has a pure silver medal, every atom in that medal is pure silver.

Imagine taking some table salt, which is also known as sodium chloride. You take one of the small grains and then divide it in half. Next, you take one of those pieces, and divide it in half, and so on. If it were possible for you to keep dividing, you would eventually end up with molecules of sodium chloride. **Molecules** are the building blocks for compounds or complex substances, meaning they are composed of more than one atom. If you took just one of those molecules and then divided it in half, you would have one atom of sodium and one atom of chlorine, not salt. **Atoms** are the building blocks for molecules.

Now, instead of table salt, let's imagine dividing a piece of copper wire into very small pieces. You will still end up with copper, regardless of how tiny the pieces are. You cannot break up a tiny molecule of copper into its atoms, because it has only one kind of atom. Materials that cannot be broken down into different atoms are known as elements. An **element** is a substance that cannot be broken down into simpler substances. All the pieces, no matter how tiny, will always have the same properties.

It actually is difficult to find a metal in nature that is purely one kind of atom. If you find gold, to purify it of other substances, such as dirt, it must be heated until the gold melts. Then the impurities of dust and dirt are revealed, floating on the top of the melted gold. A goldsmith scoops out the impurities of dust and dirt, and removes them from the gold. The heating and cleaning process takes time and many repetitions to obtain the pure gold.

ACTIVITY

There are elements all around you. List a few elements you can observe in your house, such as a copper penny, a gold ring, or a lead fishing weight. Refer to the periodic table in Chapter 10 for a list of elements.

_____

_____

_____

IV. Atoms: Protons, Neutrons, Electrons

Atoms consist of several tiny parts (or particles): protons, neutrons, and electrons. With these three types of particles, God created close to a hundred elements, each with different properties.

The **proton** has a mass equal to that of a hydrogen atom and has a **positive electrical charge**. It is found in the nucleus, or center, of the atom. Also in the nucleus of the atom are neutrons. The **neutron** has a mass that is approximately equal to that of a proton, but it has **no electrical charge**. Protons and neutrons combine to form the **nucleus** of an atom.

A **strong nuclear force** keeps the nucleus together. Strange as it may seem, we do not yet fully understand this force.

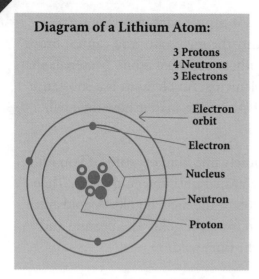

Diagram of a Lithium Atom:

3 Protons
4 Neutrons
3 Electrons

Electron orbit

Electron

Nucleus

Neutron

Proton

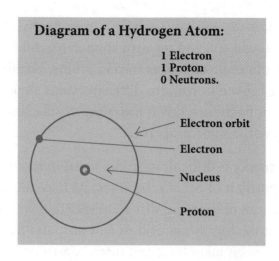

Diagram of a Hydrogen Atom:

1 Electron
1 Proton
0 Neutrons.

Electron orbit

Electron

Nucleus

Proton

Atoms also contain **negatively charged** particles called **electrons**. The electrons travel in orbits around the nucleus. Electrons have a great amount of kinetic energy, the energy of motion. The electrons are moving fast. Electrons have a negative electrical charge.

Electrons are always moving.

These three particles are not packed closely together like sardines in a can. The distance between the electrons and the nucleus of an atom is far greater than the size of the nucleus itself. As a comparison, if the nucleus were the size of a golf ball, the nearest electron would be more than ½ mile away! This means that there is a good deal of space within all atoms. We often don't give this much thought, but it is an important point: **matter cannot exist without space, and space would not exist without matter!**

The nucleus of every atom contains some number of protons. **In the natural state of every atom, the number of protons is equal to the number of electrons**. Certain chemical processes can sometimes cause an atom to gain or lose electrons, causing the number of protons and electrons to be unequal. In this case, the atom has a positive or negative electrical charge and is called an **ion**. This term was introduced by English physicist and chemist Michael Faraday in 1834.

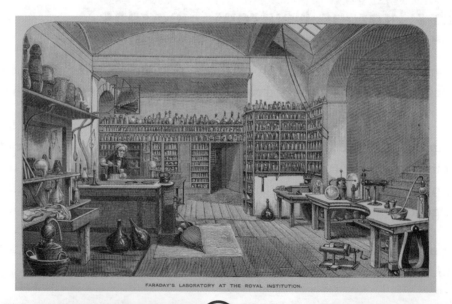

FARADAY'S LABORATORY AT THE ROYAL INSTITUTION.

A. Atomic Number

The number of protons in the nucleus determines the kind of element the atom is. Normal hydrogen atoms have one proton and one electron. Normal oxygen atoms have eight protons and eight electrons. The number of protons is always equal to the **atomic number** of an atom. For example, hydrogen has an atomic number of 1 because it has one proton, oxygen has an atomic number of 8 because it has eight protons, and copper has an atomic number of 29 because it has twenty-nine protons.

If the nucleus of an element has six protons, that element is carbon. The element with seventy-nine protons is gold; the element with eight protons is oxygen.

B. Physical and Chemical Characteristics of Elements

The **physical** characteristics of the elements depend upon their protons and their neutrons. These are characteristics such as weight, color, crystal shape, surface luster, and ability to conduct electricity. Scientists must be observant and diligent to record the characteristics of the objects they study.

The **chemical** characteristics of the elements depend on the electrons. When elements react with other elements, the electrons are either shared or traded. The protons and the neutrons are not affected at all.

C. Atomic Mass

The atomic mass is equal to the number of protons and neutrons in the atom's nucleus. The total mass or matter of an atom is nearly equal or about equal to the sum of the protons and neutrons. Electrons have very little mass, even though they have great energy and move fast.

Mass number; this is the number of neutrons and protons

Neutrons:

Electrons:

4

2

He

Helium

Protons:
This number lets us know how many protons there are. In a neutral atom this is also the same as the number of electrons.

V. Isotopes

Sometimes atoms of the same element have different numbers of neutrons in their nucleus. Hydrogen will always have one proton, but if it appears in different forms, hydrogen may have 0, 1, or 2 neutrons. These different forms of elements are known as **isotopes**. Isotopes will always have the same number of protons of the element but will have a different number of neutrons.

Note that, for isotopes, a hyphen follows the name of the element. We list the isotopes of hydrogen and uranium below as examples. The number after the hyphen indicates what is called the mass number. The **mass number** is the sum of the protons and neutrons in the nucleus.

mass number = number of protons + number of neutrons

Thus, the three isotopes of hydrogen have mass numbers of 1, 2, and 3, respectively:

Hydrogen-1 = 1 proton + 0 neutrons

Hydrogen-2 = 1 proton + 1 neutron

Hydrogen-3 = 1 proton + 2 neutrons

Uranium-235 and uranium-238 are other examples of isotopes. They have mass numbers of 235 and 238. Both contain 92 protons but differ in their numbers of neutrons, 143 and 146.

Uranium-235 = 92 protons + 143 neutrons

Uranium-238 = 92 protons + 146 neutrons

In Chapter 10, we will continue our discussion on matter, beginning with a special chart that lists all the elements known to man. This chart is called the Periodic Table.

Chapter 9 Summary

Chemistry

1. **Matter** is anything that has mass and occupies space. **Mass** is the amount of matter in something.

2. The **Law of Gravitation** states that different masses attract one another. The greater the mass, the greater its gravitational exertion. Mass is measured in terms of **grams**.

3. **Weight** is a measurement of how much gravity is pulling on an object. **Volume** is the amount of three-dimensional space an object occupies.

4. **Density** is the amount of matter a given body contains within a certain volume.

5. The formula for density is mass divided by volume.

6. The formula for mass is density times volume.

Observing and Reporting

7. Observations naturally proceed from the most obvious features of something to the less obvious. In the scientific method, one uses tools for measuring weight, size, and motion.

8. Observing and reporting (or record keeping) are necessary habits for accuracy, reliability, and accountability.

Physical and Chemical Characteristics of Elements

9. All matter is made of **atoms**. Atoms are divided into kinds by their unique characteristics. Each kind is called an **element**: a substance that cannot be reduced to something simpler.

10. Atoms are constituted by three principal particles: protons, neutrons, and electrons. Protons and neutrons combine to form the **nucleus** of the atom. In the normal state of the atom, the number of protons is equal to the number of electrons. If either particle exceeds the other in number, the atom becomes an **ion**.

11. When elements interact and react with one another, the electrons are either shared or traded, while the protons and neutrons remain unchanged.

12. **Isotopes** are elements of the same atomic kind that have different numbers of neutrons in their nuclei.

Questions for Review

1. What is matter?

   _____

   _____

2. What is mass?

   _____

3. What is the unit for measuring mass?

   _____

4. What is weight?

   _____

5. What is density?

   _____

6. What is all matter composed of?

   _____

7. What is an element?

   _____

   _____

8. What is a nucleus?

   _____

   _____

9. What is an ion?

   _____

   _____

10. What is an isotope?

   _____

   _____

Chemistry, Part II

I. **The Periodic Table**
II. **Chemical Compounds**
III. **Reactants and Products**
IV. **Radioactive Elements**
V. **The Four States of Matter**
   A. Solid, Liquid, or Gas
   B. Plasma – The Fourth State of Matter
VI. **Matter and Change: Change of State**
   A. Physical Change
   B. Chemical Change
   C. Transubstantiation
VII. **Chemical Reactions**
   A. Analysis Reactions
   B. Synthesis Reactions
   C. Substitution Reactions
   D. Metathesis Reactions
VIII. **God's World**

Chemistry, Part II

Chapter
10

> "How great are Thy works, O Lord! Thou hast made all things in wisdom: the Earth is filled with Thy riches" (Psalm 103:24).

I. The Periodic Table

The **Periodic Table** lists all known elements by their chemical symbols. **Chemical symbols** are groupings of up to three letters that represent each element. Examine the Periodic Table on the following page. The symbol for hydrogen is "H," oxygen "O," copper "Cu," and uranium "U." You might be wondering why the symbol for copper is not "Co" instead of "Cu." Many of our elements have their origins with Latin or Greek terms. In the case of "copper," it comes from the Latin word *cuprum*.

The elements are the simplest bits of matter in our universe. God created all elements found in nature. God used these *building blocks* to construct the entire universe. Iron (Fe) is found on both the Earth and Mars. Silicon (Si) is abundant on the Earth and on the moon. Helium (He) is found in our atmosphere and accounts for 27% of the sun's mass. There are many other examples of elements found on Earth and in other parts of the universe.

The Periodic Table also arranges the elements by atomic number (number of protons in each element). Look closely at this table, and you will see the atomic numbers in lower left-hand corner. The mass number for each element is also found in the Periodic Table. You can find these above the chemical symbols.

Scientists currently recognize 118 elements. You read in the above paragraph that 98 elements are found in nature. What's going on here? The reason for this difference is that twenty of these elements have been made in the laboratory by scientists! The number will probably grow in the coming years. These *synthetic* laboratory elements are radioactive and have a short existence. Their lifespans range from a fraction of a second to about 1 year. Some of the natural 98 elements are radioactive as well, but last longer than synthetic ones.

ACTIVITY

Memorize the following ten chemical names and their symbols:

Oxygen (**O**)	Nitrogen (**N**)	Chlorine (**Cl**)	Sodium (**Na**)	Calcium (**Ca**)
Hydrogen (**H**)	Carbon (**C**)	Helium (**He**)	Sulfur (**S**)	Gold (**Au**)

Periodic Table

Key

Those numbers appearing within brackets are the mass numbers of common isotopes

Those elements underlined are radioactive

N element is a gas

Hg element is a liquid   at room temperature and pressure

Li element is a solid

Relative atomic mass — Symbol — Atomic number

1																	18
1.0 **H** Hydrogen 1	2											13	14	15	16	17	4.0 **He** Helium 2
6.9 **Li** Lithium 3	9.0 **Be** Beryllium 4											10.8 **B** Boron 5	12.0 **C** Carbon 6	14.0 **N** Nitrogen 7	16.0 **O** Oxygen 8	19.0 **F** Fluorine 9	20.2 **Ne** Neon 10
23.0 **Na** Sodium 11	24.3 **Mg** Magnesium 12	3	4	5	6	7	8	9	10	11	12	27.0 **Al** Aluminium 13	28.1 **Si** Silicon 14	31.0 **P** Phosphorus 15	32.1 **S** Sulphur 16	35.5 **Cl** Chlorine 17	39.9 **Ar** Argon 18
39.1 **K** Potassium 19	40.1 **Ca** Calcium 20	45.0 **Sc** Scandium 21	47.9 **Ti** Titanium 22	50.9 **V** Vanadium 23	52.0 **Cr** Chromium 24	54.9 **Mn** Manganese 25	55.8 **Fe** Iron 26	58.9 **Co** Cobalt 27	58.7 **Ni** Nickel 28	63.5 **Cu** Copper 29	65.4 **Zn** Zinc 30	69.7 **Ga** Gallium 31	72.6 **Ge** Germanium 32	74.9 **As** Arsenic 33	79.0 **Se** Selenium 34	79.9 **Br** Bromine 35	83.8 **Kr** Krypton 36
85.5 **Rb** Rubidium 37	87.6 **Sr** Strontium 38	88.9 **Y** Yttrium 39	91.2 **Zr** Zirconium 40	92.9 **Nb** Niobium 41	95.9 **Mo** Molybdenum 42	(99) **Tc** Technetium 43	101.1 **Ru** Ruthenium 44	102.9 **Rh** Rhodium 45	106.4 **Pd** Palladium 46	107.9 **Ag** Silver 47	112.4 **Cd** Cadmium 48	114.8 **In** Indium 49	118.7 **Sn** Tin 50	121.8 **Sb** Antimony 51	127.6 **Te** Tellurium 52	126.9 **I** Iodine 53	131.3 **Xe** Xenon 54
132.9 **Cs** Caesium 55	137.3 **Ba** Barium 56	138.9 **La*** Lanthanum 57	178.5 **Hf** Hafnium 72	181.0 **Ta** Tantalum 73	183.9 **W** Tungsten 74	186.2 **Re** Rhenium 75	190.2 **Os** Osmium 76	192.2 **Ir** Iridium 77	195.1 **Pt** Platinum 78	197.0 **Au** Gold 79	200.6 **Hg** Mercury 80	204.4 **Tl** Thallium 81	207.2 **Pb** Lead 82	209.0 **Bi** Bismuth 83	(210) **Po** Polonium 84	(210) **At** Astatine 85	(222) **Rn** Radon 86
(223) **Fr** Francium 87	(226) **Ra** Radium 88	(227) **Ac†** Actinium 89	(261) **Rf** Rutherfordium 104	(262) **Db** Dubnium 105	(263) **Sg** Seaborgium 106	(262) **Bh** Bohrium 107	(265) **Hs** Hassium 108	(266) **Mt** Meitnerium 109									

* 58-71 Lanthanide series

140.1 **Ce** Cerium 58	140.9 **Pr** Praseodymium 59	144.2 **Nd** Neodymium 60	(147) **Pm** Promethium 61	150.4 **Sm** Samarium 62	152.0 **Eu** Europium 63	157.3 **Gd** Gadolinium 64	158.9 **Tb** Terbium 65	162.5 **Dy** Dysprosium 66	164.9 **Ho** Holmium 67	167.3 **Er** Erbium 68	168.9 **Tm** Thulium 69	173.0 **Yb** Ytterbium 70	175.0 **Lu** Lutetium 71

† 90-103 Actinide series

232.0 **Th** Thorium 90	(231) **Pa** Protactinium 91	238.1 **U** Uranium 92	(237) **Np** Neptunium 93	(244) **Pu** Plutonium 94	(243) **Am** Americium 95	(247) **Cm** Curium 96	(247) **Bk** Berkelium 97	(251) **Cf** Californium 98	(252) **Es** Einsteinium 99	(257) **Fm** Fermium 100	(258) **Md** Mendelevium 101	(259) **No** Nobelium 102	(260) **Lr** Lawrencium 103

Published by
ICIEducational Liaison

ACTIVITY

Look at the Periodic Table and write the symbols for these elements:

Oxygen _____   Silver _____   Iodine _____

Hydrogen _____   Iron _____   Tin _____

Nitrogen _____   Mercury _____   Fluorine _____

Carbon _____   Lead _____   Krypton _____

Chlorine _____   Aluminum_____   Nickel _____

Helium _____   Silicon _____   Radon _____

Sodium _____   Uranium _____   Copper _____

Sulfur _____   Potassium_____   Phosphorus _____

Calcium_____   Neon _____   Zinc _____

Gold _____   Magnesium_____   Platinum _____

II. Chemical Compounds

When two or more elements are bonded together, we call it a **chemical compound**. When we make waffles, we take several simple ingredients, combine them, mix them, then bake them on a waffle iron, and we have a new product. There exist many chemical compounds, which combine elements to form another product or chemical.

Most of the things we use every day are not plain elements, but a combination of chemicals. A water molecule is a chemical compound because it is composed of two atoms of hydrogen and one atom of oxygen. All water molecules are the same. Another chemical compound we use every day is table salt.

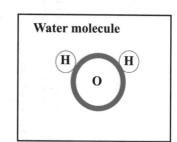

Water molecule

Two Atoms of Hydrogen

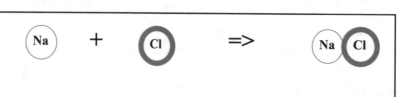

Sodium and chlorine bond to form sodium chloride (table salt).

When chemicals combine by chemicals bonding, the process is called a chemical reaction or chemical change. The new chemical might not look like any of the elements that were combined to make it.

ACTIVITY

Make a chemical compound by combining oxygen and copper in a penny. Holding a penny with tongs or pliers, heat it over a candle for a few minutes. Cool it and wipe off the black carbon build-up on the penny. The surface of the penny will have an iridescent sheen instead of the copper color. The iridescent sheen is copper oxide, a chemical compound.

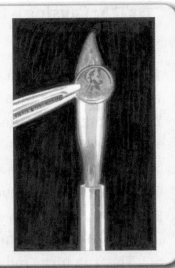

Burning a copper penny forms a compound of oxygen and copper.

When we write the names for compounds, or elements bonded together, we use chemical symbols. An example is sodium chloride, common table salt. You would write sodium chloride as NaCl. This ingredient that we put on our food to make it more tasty is made up of the bonding of two dangerous chemicals: sodium and chlorine. Sodium is explosive in the presence of water vapor, and chlorine is a deadly gas. Sodium (Na) is a silvery-colored metal, and chlorine (Cl) is a green gas. Yet, in God's plan, we can safely eat the combination of the two (NaCl)!

Investigate your house! Try to find some compounds made up of elements bonded together. For instance, sugar is a compound of carbon, oxygen, and hydrogen atoms. It is one of the compounds called carbohydrates.

Another type of compound we find in our houses is oxide. An **oxide** is a compound of a metal and oxygen. When something combines with oxygen, we say that it is oxidized. The chemical symbol for iron is Fe. Iron is what makes up steel wool. If we burned a steel wool pad, we would be forming an oxide of iron (Fe_3O_4). This means that three atoms of iron are bonded together with four atoms of oxygen. We can write a chemical sentence for this chemical reaction as follows:

$$3Fe + 2O_2 => Fe_3O_4$$

Another type of iron oxide compound is **rust**. Look outside for unpainted iron that has been damp. This compound is reddish, crumbly, and non-magnetic. The chemical name for rust is Fe_2O_3. Here is the chemical sentence for this chemical reaction:

$$4Fe + 3O_2 => 2Fe_2O_3$$

Burning a Steel Wool Pad

ACTIVITY: Causing a Chemical Change to Make Iron Oxide

PROCEDURE:

1. Gently fluff up a steel wool pad (not a soap pad) by stretching it into a big, fuzzy ball.
2. Stick the ball of steel wool to the bottom of a jar with clay.
3. Invert the jar into a pan with water in it.
4. Mark the water level with a crayon.
5. After several days you will notice at least two changes. The iron of the steel wool will have turned rusty, and the water level should have increased.
6. The iron turns red as it bonds with the oxygen of the air in the jar. This is iron oxide. Also, the air in the jar loses some of its oxygen as it bonds with the iron. So, the water level rises to take the place of the missing oxygen atoms.

OBSERVATIONS: What do you observe about the product?

_____
_____
_____

CONCLUSIONS: What do you conclude about the nature of the product?

_____
_____
_____

QUESTIONS:

1. Did the product, iron oxide, appear like the original iron?

_____
_____

2. Did the product, iron oxide, appear like the original oxygen?

_____
_____

3. Why did the water level go up?

_____
_____
_____

There are other oxides you can make or find around your house. If you have a box of old crayons, look for a metallic one, such as copper. The outside of the crayon will be greenish, not the true color of the inside. The outside of the crayon is copper oxide. Oxides form on the outside of the metal where it comes into contact with the oxygen in the air.

We are like the tarnished metal when we sin. Through the graces of the sacraments, we can return our souls to an untarnished condition.

III. Reactants and Products

Many things rust easily. Bridges, antennas, ships, barrels for oil, and steel building support structures are made of steel, which can and will rust. To protect steel from rusting, we paint the steel. The extra coating of paint keeps oxygen in the air away from the iron in the steel. By separating them, we keep them from bonding into rust.

The metal furniture some people have outside in their yards is painted to protect the iron from the oxygen in the air. If the paint gets chipped, the iron underneath will begin to rust. This is true for any iron and some other metals on the outside of a car! Today, many cars are built with a type of plastic on the outside!

ACTIVITY

You can test ungalvanized nails for rust prevention. Get several nails. Leave one alone. Paint one, cover another with petroleum jelly, and another with hand cream. You can think of other ways you might coat the nails to prevent rust. Label the nails according to the treatment you gave them. Place them in a jar with a damp sponge or paper towel. (You may stick them into a piece of foam first.) Seal the lid. In a few days, the untreated nail may be rusting, and some of the others may be also. Record the result of this experiment. Which treatment was best for preventing rust? Why?

_____

_____

_____

_____

Chemical Symbols and Their Names

1. Hydrogen **H**
2. Helium **He**
3. Lithium **Li**
4. Beryllium **Be**
5. Boron **B**
6. Carbon **C**
7. Nitrogen **N**
8. Oxygen **O**
9. Fluorine **F**
10. Neon **Ne**
11. Sodium **Na**
12. Magnesium **Mg**
13. Aluminum **Al**
14. Silicon **Si**
15. Phosphorus **P**
16. Sulfur **S**
17. Chlorine **Cl**
18. Argon **Ar**
19. Potassium **K**
20. Calcium **Ca**
21. Scandium **Sc**
22. Titanium **Ti**
23. Vanadium **V**
24. Chromium **Cr**
25. Manganese **Mn**
26. Iron **Fe**
27. Cobalt **Co**
28. Nickel **Ni**
29. Copper **Cu**
30. Zinc **Zn**
31. Gallium **Ga**
32. Germanium **Ge**
33. Arsenic **As**
34. Selenium **Se**
35. Bromine **Br**
36. Krypton **Kr**
37. Rubidium **Rb**
38. Strontium **Sr**
39. Yttrium **Y**
40. Zirconium **Zr**
41. Nobium **Nb**
42. Molybdenum **Mo**
43. Technetium **Tc**
44. Ruthenium **Ru**
45. Rhodium **Rh**
46. Palladium **Pd**
47. Silver **Ag**
48. Cadmium **Cd**
49. Indium **In**
50. Tin **Sn**
51. Antimony **Sb**
52. Tellurium **Te**
53. Iodine **I**
54. Xenon **Xe**
55. Cesium **Cs**
56. Barium **Ba**
57. Lanthanum **La**
58. Cerium **Ce**
59. Praseodymium **Pr**
60. Neodymium **Nd**
61. Promethium **Pm**
62. Samarium **Sm**
63. Europium **Eu**
64. Gadolinium **Gd**
65. Terbium **Tb**
66. Dysprosium **Dy**
67. Holmium **Ho**
68. Erbium **Er**
69. Thulium **Tm**
70. Ytterbium **Yb**
71. Lutetium **Lu**
72. Hafnium **Hf**
73. Tantalum **Ta**
74. Tungsten **W**
75. Rhenium **Re**
76. Osmium **Os**
77. Iridium **Ir**
78. Platinum **Pt**
79. Gold **Au**
80. Mercury **Hg**
81. Thallium **Tl**
82. Lead **Pb**
83. Bismuth **Bi**
84. Polonium **Po**
85. Astatine **At**
86. Radon **Rn**
87. Francium **Fr**
88. Radium **Ra**
89. Actinium **Ac**
90. Thorium **Th**
91. Protactinium **Pa**
92. Uranium **U**
93. Neptunium **Np**
94. Plutonium **Pu**
95. Americanium **Am**
96. Curium **Cm**
97. Berkelium **Bk**
98. Californium **Cf**
99. Einsteinium **Es**
100. Fermium **Fm**
101. Mendelevium **Md**
102. Nobelium **No**
103. Lawrencium **Lr**
104. Unnilquadium **Unq**
105. Unnilpentium **Unp**
106. Unnilhexium **Unh**
107. Unnilseptium **Uns**
108. Unniloctium **Uno**
109. Unnilennium **Une**

ACTIVITY: Making a Chart of Elements

DIRECTIONS:

Look at the Periodic Table presented earlier in this chapter. Find the elements listed and record the atomic characteristics of them.

Element	Symbol	# Protons	# Neutrons	# Electrons
Oxygen				
Sulfur				
Hydrogen				
Nitrogen				
Radon				
Neon				
Helium				
Chlorine				
Iron				
Gold				
Silver				
Carbon				
Mercury				

IV. Radioactive Elements

Some elements are radioactive. What do we mean by the term **radioactive**? Radioactive elements, such as uranium, are isotopes that have an excess number of neutrons in their atoms. Recall that **isotopes** are different forms of the same element that have different numbers of neutrons in their nucleus. The nuclear force that holds these atoms together is not strong enough to keep them from losing parts of their nuclei. These atoms are unstable—that is, they constantly lose particles.

This natural process of losing particles is known as **radioactive decay**. When an atom decays, it gives up a great amount of energy. As it loses the energy, the atom gains some stability. The atom keeps losing particles and energy, but keeps gaining stability. Eventually, it decays into a new, lighter element. For example, uranium eventually decays into lead (Pb).

There are three ways by which radioactive elements decay. The first way occurs when an element loses two neutrons and two protons. The nucleus literally ejects these two neutrons and two protons out at a high speed in the form of an **alpha particle**. This particle has the same mass as an atom of helium. The second way involves a neutron changing into a proton! The extra energy that is given off as it changes is used to make a **beta particle**. A beta particle has the same mass as an electron.

The third way that elements decay but become more stable is by a proton changing into a neutron. The atom of the element ejects two small particles, which then collide with an electron. The end result is the release of high-energy protons known as **gamma rays**.

Radioactive elements are an important part of our life on Earth. We use these radioactive elements in medicines and for producing electrical power in nuclear reactors. However, all particles emitted from radioactive elements are potentially harmful to us. They travel at high velocities, have a great deal of energy, and can damage the cells within our bodies. For this reason, we have a number of safeguards to protect everyone from the *dangers of radiation*. When you receive X-rays at the dentist or hospital, you may be fitted with a heavy vest made from lead. It shields the rest of your body from unnecessary exposure to radiation. Despite the hazards from radiation, people around the world work with radioactive materials every day. However, they must work with special equipment and protective clothing.

DID YOU KNOW?

Gamma rays and heat are the primary types of energy produced by what is called nuclear fission. **Nuclear fission** is a reaction in an atom that causes its nucleus to split in half. The decay of just one atom of uranium produces 200 million electron volts. The energy produced in one pound of uranium would equal the energy produced from one million gallons of gasoline!

ROSARY MIRACLE

Priests Survive Near Center of Nuclear Attack on Hiroshima!

There was a Jesuit rectory and church in Hiroshima, Japan, during World War II. Because Germany was an ally of Japan in the war, the German Jesuits were not forced to leave Japan during the war. Fr. Hubert Schiffer was the head of the contingent of eight German Jesuits in the mission.

The mission was only about a half mile from "ground zero," where the atomic bomb exploded. The city buildings were flattened to the ground all around the mission complex. Even their church building was destroyed, but the parish house where the priests lived was left standing after the explosion. All eight Jesuit missionaries survived both the blast and the subsequent effects of radioactivity.

Allied doctors entered the city and found the Jesuits alive. The doctors told these priests to expect to die soon from radioactive poisoning. However, all eight of these priests survived without any ill effects for many years. In the subsequent years, they were questioned and medically examined more than 250 times since that fateful day, but they never showed the expected fatal results.

Fr. Schiffer was asked many times, "How do you account for your survival?" He always answered that these Jesuits formed a "Fatima House." They prayed the rosary together every day, as requested by Our Lady of Fatima. Fr. Schiffer stated: "We believe that we survived because we were living the message of Fatima. We lived and prayed the rosary daily in that home."

More than 55 years after that day, most of the Jesuits were still alive, and scientists still could not provide a natural explanation for this.

God has shown His mercy and His power over nature, even over nuclear power and radiation, by saving these priests from this nuclear attack. Praise God for His goodness!

V. The Four States of Matter

Matter can exist in different ways. These different forms of matter are called **states**, or states of matter or forms of matter. Matter can exist in four different states: solid, liquid, gas, and plasma. Most things on Earth exist as one or more of the first three; the state of plasma is not common on our planet, but is plentiful in the rest of the universe.

WHAT ARE THE FOUR STATES OF MATTER?

GAS: A gas is the state of matter in which the particles of the substance have neither a definite volume nor a definite shape. A gas is an air-like fluid substance that expands freely to fill any space available, regardless of that space's size.

LIQUID: A liquid is the state of matter in which the particles of the substance have a definite volume but not a definite shape. In a liquid, the particles are free to flow, so the liquid takes up the shape of the container that holds it.

SOLID: A solid is the state of matter in which the particles of the substance are arranged such that their shape and volume are relatively stable. The particles of a solid tend to be packed together much more closely than the particles in a gas or liquid.

PLASMA: Plasma is the state of matter consisting of gas-like ions and free electrons in equal proportions, resulting in a more or less neutral overall electric charge. The charged particles in plasma react collectively and strongly to electromagnetic fields. The sun and the stars and most of the universe outside the Earth are made of plasma.

A. Solid, Liquid, or Gas

Whether matter exists as a solid, a liquid, or a gas depends on temperature and the measure or speed of molecular motion—that is, the motion of the molecules of the matter. This means that temperature can change the state of matter. Here, once again we see kinetic energy at work. **Kinetic energy** is energy that is in motion. Examples of kinetic energy include moving or rushing water and wind. Electricity is kinetic energy because, even though you can't see it happen, electricity involves electrons moving in conductors.

A substance that is a solid can be a liquid and still be the same substance, just in a different form. The substance has not changed. Water may be a liquid, a solid (ice), or gas (steam) but the chemical is still H_2O, hydrogen and oxygen, in any of these three forms.

Gold is normally a solid, just as your bike, your table, and your pencil are all solids. These solid objects have a definite size and shape. Matter is in the **solid** state when it has a definite shape and a definite volume.

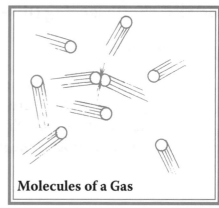

Molecules of a Gas

The ocean is a good example of a liquid that must take the shape of its container. A **liquid** exists when it has no definite shape but has a definite volume.

Water is commonly in the liquid state. If you pour water into a container, it takes on the shape of the container, but the volume stays the same content; the volume of water takes the "shape" of the container. When you pour your drink into a glass, the liquid has the shape of the bottle you purchased until you pour it into your glass.

Think about a gas. Helium is normally a gas. If you put helium into a container, it takes on the shape and volume of the container. A **gas** exists when it has no definite shape and no definite volume. Therefore, a gas will expand until it fills up the container in which it exists.

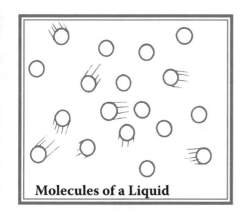

Molecules of a Liquid

You have already learned that when you *raise* the temperature of a substance, you cause the molecules to *speed up* and *spread farther apart*. Conversely, when you *lower* heat, the molecules in a substance *slow down*. Matter is capable of existing in one or more states—solid, liquid, or gas—when you change the amount of kinetic energy by increasing or decreasing the temperature to make the molecules speed up or slow down.

The explanation for the differences between the states of matter is in the energy of the molecules. Let's use water to describe the state changes in matter. Water is absolutely necessary for life. Water is an important part of our sacraments, and we use water every day. For one moment, make a mental list of how many things for which you use water in your daily life. Don't forget that water is necessary for the production of all the food that you eat!

Water consists of hydrogen and oxygen atoms in a ratio of two to one, or H_2O, two hydrogen atoms to one oxygen atom. Between the temperatures of 32 °F (0° C) and 212 °F (100 °C), water exists as a liquid. *Liquids have no definite shape but have a definite volume.* Water and other liquids take the shape of the container in which they are poured, for example, cups, vases, bathtubs, sinks.

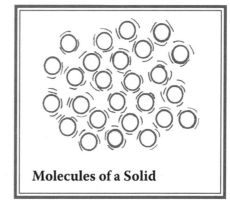

Molecules of a Solid

ACTIVITY: Observing Different States of Matter in a Chocolate Sundae

DIRECTIONS:

Observe this chocolate sundae. The sundae in the picture at the bottom has hot fudge on top. There are all three states of matter present. Identify which parts of the picture are in which of the three states of matter: *Hint: Do not forget the atmosphere around the sundae.*

Gas:

_____

_____

Liquid:

_____

_____

Solid:

_____

_____

Now, observe more closely and try to point out three places in the sundae which are boundaries between the states of matter. For example, one is the spot where the hot fudge (a liquid) meets the ice cream (a solid).

_____

_____

_____

_____

_____

_____

_____

_____

_____

ACTIVITY: Recording Characteristics of the Three States of Matter

DIRECTIONS:

Define the three states of matter (gas, liquid, and solid) according to their characteristics by filling in the chart below.

State of Matter	Shape	Volume	Molecular Motion
Gas			
Liquid			
Solid			

When the temperature of water falls to 32 °F (0 °C), water becomes a solid known as ice. *Solids have both a stable shape and a stable volume.* When you place an ice cube tray in the freezer, the water begins to cool, and the molecules slow down. Before freezing, it conforms to the shape and volume of the container. Water that freezes in clouds results in tiny crystals of snow. These too have a stable shape and volume.

Water begins to boil when its temperature rises to 212 °F (100 °C). The molecules speed up, and this action causes the formation of vapor or gas, known as steam. *A gas has neither a definite shape nor a definite volume.* Steam will remain a gas until it cools off and then condenses to form a liquid.

A gas has very energetic molecules, which bounce all around the area they occupy. Liquid molecules do not have as much energy, and they roll around each other without flying off as the gas molecules do. Solid molecules have the least amount of energy. Solid molecules just stay in one location and vibrate. The solid molecules have much less movement than the motions of the other two states of matter. Since the molecules of a solid stay in the same location, the solid has a definite shape.

Glass is an unusual phenomenon. Glass is between a solid and a liquid, which is called the amorphous state. Glass is not a true solid nor a true liquid. Over several centuries, hundreds of years, the glass in a piece of window will slightly "flow" downward, so that the glass at the bottom of a window is thicker than the glass at the top of a window. This has been noticed in some of the oldest Catholic cathedrals of Europe. Some of their glass windows are much thicker at the bottom than they were in the past.

B. Plasma – The Fourth State of Matter

We think of matter in one of its three states. However, there is a fourth state of matter called plasma. If you have never heard of plasma, then you might be surprised to learn that the sun and the stars, as well as 99 percent of the visible matter in the universe outside the Earth, are actually made of plasma! Here on Earth, lightning and the northern lights are examples of naturally occurring plasmas. You may have plasma in your home too. Every time you flip a switch on a fluorescent or neon light, the resulting light is plasma.

What precisely is plasma? **Plasma**, like gas, has no definite shape or volume. Unlike gas, which is composed of molecules, plasma consists of particles, both positively charged ions and free-roaming electrons (which are negatively charged). (An **ion** is a charged particle of a substance.)

All the states of matter are related to temperature. At extremely low temperatures, everything is solid. As temperature rises, some things become liquid. At still higher temperatures, liquids change into gas. An example is water, which is solid ice below 32 °F, but has the form of liquid water above 32 °F. At 212 °F, it becomes a gas, which we call steam. Plasma is the next state of matter beyond gas (steam in our example). At extremely high temperatures, the hydrogen and oxygen atoms of water would lose their electrons and become hydrogen and oxygen ions. The electrons become totally free roaming, as if not connected to any atom, yet still related to the entire mass of ionized particles. For this reason, plasma is sometimes referred to as **ionized gas**. Plasma is a highly electrified collection of nuclei and free electrons. The sun and all stars and nebulae are in the plasma state. The northern lights on Earth are caused when plasma streams ejected from the sun strike the upper atmosphere. Fluorescent lights glow when the electric current causes the gas in the tubes to heat up to a plasma state.

Perhaps the best way to understand plasma is with a plasma ball or plasma globe. These are popular items in science centers and museums. Plasma balls are inexpensive and can be purchased in some department stores. A plasma ball is a clear glass sphere that contains two electrodes and a gas, such as neon or argon. When electricity flows from the electrodes, it causes the formation of colored **plasma filaments**. These filaments look like miniature lightning displays and bounce around the inside of the sphere. When you touch the outside of the sphere with your finger, the filament continues to move around but one end of it stays "connected" to your finger. Increasing the electricity to the electrodes causes an increase in the number of plasma filaments.

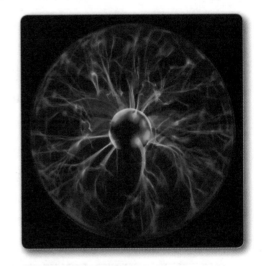

Plasma Lamp (Image by Luc Viatour)

So where does the plasma come from? It all starts with electricity or electrons. These gain energy upon exiting the electrode. They speed up and collide with the gas. In turn, this causes the molecules of gas to split up into atoms that become stripped of their electrons, turning them into positively charged ions. These form an **ion trail**, which serves as a pathway for the other electrons and creates a plasma streamer. Within the **plasma streamer**, the charged particles combine with the electrons. This gives them too much energy and they need to return to a lower energy level. They do so by giving off a burst of photons known as plasma filaments or plasma light.

The northern and southern lights over our planet work using the same principle found in the plasma ball. In this case, the sun emits a high-energy plasma stream consisting of protons and electrons. These travel toward the north and south poles along the Earth's magnetic field. The particles then collide with gases in the upper atmosphere. These collisions raise the energy levels within the gases.

To return to a normal state, the gas molecules release light (photons) in the process. Oxygen produces red and green light. Nitrogen results in dull red, blue, and purple light. The northern and southern lights in our atmosphere are some of the most beautiful events in nature—and they are the result of plasma! Unfortunately for those of us who live in the United States, these light shows occur only in latitudes fairly close to the North and South Poles, such as Canada and New Zealand.

ACTIVITY: Recording Temperature for Changes of State

PROCEDURE:

1. Make a little boat from aluminum foil. Unwrap a solid chocolate bar and put it in the foil boat.

2. Take its temperature and record.

3. Fill a pan with HOT water. The pan must be larger than the little boat with the bar of chocolate. Ask a parent to make sure you are doing this safely.

4. Float the boat inside the pan of hot water.

5. Take the temperature of the chocolate bar every minute. Try to get the tip of the thermometer into the chocolate. Observe the characteristics of the melted chocolate. Include such things as taste, texture, and appearance.

6. After the chocolate is totally melted, place the little boat into another pan containing a bed of ice.

7. Again record the temperatures of the chocolate, this time as it is refreezing. **Remember freezing does not mean it is very cold, but only that it is becoming solid.**

8. After the bar has refrozen, record the characteristics of the chocolate again.

Time	Temperature	Time	Temperature
0		0	
1		1	
2		2	
3		3	
4		4	
5		5	
6		6	
7		7	
8		8	
9		9	
10		10	

QUESTIONS:

1. Write your observations about the shape and molecular motion of the liquid chocolate. Does the chocolate have a definite volume? A definite shape?

   _____

   _____

   _____

2. What about the shape and molecular motion of the solid chocolate? Does it have a definite volume? A definite shape?

   _____

   _____

   _____

Beggar Girls **by Murillo**

Melting and Freezing Points
of a
Chocolate Bar

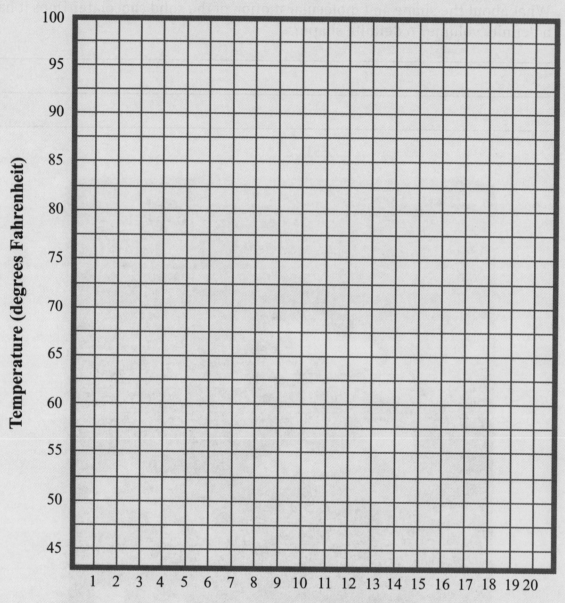

Temperature (degrees Fahrenheit)

Time (minutes)

VI. Matter and Change: Change of State

When matter changes from one state to another, we say that matter has undergone a **change of state**. Matter may change in either of two ways: physically or chemically.

A. Physical Change

Physical changes alter the appearance or form of a substance, but the substance itself does not change. In previous examples with state changes of matter, you learned that changes in temperature cause water to turn into ice or steam. **The molecules of water never change, however; only the speed of motion of the molecules change**. Likewise, if you took a rock and broke it into small pieces, you would change the appearance of the rock, but not its composition. There are many examples like this, such as leaving a candy bar out in the hot sun. The molecules of the chocolate gain energy from the sun and start moving around. It becomes a gooey candy bar, but it does not change into something else.

Another example of physical change is cutting a piece of pie. The pieces of pie may get smaller and smaller, but the pieces are still pie, no matter how tiny the pieces are. Ice cream is still ice cream, even when it melts. The substance is still the same. The nature of the substance has not changed. Only the physical appearance has changed.

B. Chemical Change

Chemical changes, however, completely change a substance into something new and different. If electricity is applied to water (electrolysis), the water splits into two gases, hydrogen and oxygen. The water no longer exists. Burning wood in the fireplace produces heat, carbon dioxide, and water, and leaves behind a pile of ash, different from the original wood logs. The wood has been changed into something different. Some chemical changes break a substance down into its parts. Sugar changes when it is burned, and becomes another substance.

Other examples of chemical change include what happens to food after you have eaten. The food is broken down into molecules through the process of digestion. Your body takes these tiny molecules and turns them into new substances in your body.

Chemical changes affect the nature of the substance. After a chemical change, the substance is a different substance.

> **WARNING**
>
> **Mixing together certain chemicals (including cleaning fluids)—or even just opening them in close proximity to each other—can be very dangerous. In some cases, doing so can even be fatal! Therefore, it is extremely important to read all labels very carefully. Do *not* perform any experiments without first asking your parents.**

ACTIVITY: Observation of Physical and Chemical Changes in Matter

PROCEDURE:

1. Take a sugar cube and hit it with a hammer.
2. Observe its characteristics: appearance, taste, and feel.
3. Will the powder still dissolve in water like the original sugar cube? Test this.
4. Would you say that this powder is still sugar?
5. Now take another sugar cube and place it in an old spoon.
6. Heat it over a candle. After a while, it will begin to burn and turn first brown, then black. When the sugar has turned black, go on to step 7.
7. Again, observe its characteristics: appearance, taste, and feel. Will the black substance dissolve in water?
8. Is this still sugar?

Characteristics			
	Color	**Feel**	**Taste**
Powder			
Residue			

OBSERVATIONS:

_____

_____

_____

CONCLUSIONS:

Explain your observations of the physical and chemical changes you witnessed. Which change was physical? Which was chemical?

_____

_____

_____

_____

_____

_____

ACTIVITY: Identifying Changes in Matter: Physical or Chemical

PROCEDURE:

1. Identify the types of changes these objects are undergoing.
2. Record your answers and your reasons.

Change	Physical	Chemical
Cheese melting		
Toast cooking		
Candle melting		
Ice cream freezing		
Candle burning		
Wood being chopped		
Iron rusting		
Steel being magnetized		
Lemonade being poured		
Salt dissolving in water		
Rock ground to powder		
Clay drying		
Food being digested		
Pencil being sharpened		
Glass breaking		
Wood burning		

QUESTIONS:

1. When you are roasting a marshmallow, are you making a physical change or a chemical one? Upon what do you base your answer?

   _____

   _____

   _____

   _____

   _____

2. When is a change chemical, and when is it physical?

_____

_____

_____

_____

3. When can a little heat produce a physical change, and great heat produce a chemical change? Explain.

_____

_____

_____

_____

C. Transubstantiation

Transubstantiation is another kind of change that affects matter. A divine mystery unfolds when a Catholic priest consecrates bread and wine: they are miraculously changed into the Body and Blood of Jesus Christ. We refer to this spiritual change as Transubstantiation, which is neither a physical nor a chemical change. **In Transubstantiation, the entire substance of bread and wine are changed into the substance of the Body and Blood of Jesus Christ. The appearances of bread and wine remain, but the substance has changed entirely.**

The Holy Eucharist is a sacred and precious gift, which we receive during Holy Communion. It is the Body, Blood, Soul, and Divinity of Jesus Christ! Transubstantiation is a reminder that God created the physical laws of the universe, and He is not bound by them.

VII. Chemical Reactions

Our entire world runs on chemical reactions. Chemical reactions are going on around us all the time. Even as you read this, your body is providing glucose to all of your cells. Miniature power plants within the cells of your body transfer electrons from glucose to other compounds. In turn, these compounds drive other chemical reactions.

When we take substances, such as flour, sugar, salt, baking powder, eggs, and water, and make a cake with these ingredients, we are combining elements to form a new compound with heat when we put it in the oven. Think about the alphabet: there are only twenty-six letters, but we can write an almost endless number of words by combining those letters in different ways.

The same is true of all the elements. There are a limited number of elements in the Periodic Table, but when they are combined in different ways and in different amounts, and with the influence of heat or cold, they produce a chemical reaction and often a different substance.

Another example of chemical reactions comes from lightning. Somewhere at this very moment, lightning is striking the Earth. The static electricity from lightning converts nitrogen into ammonia, which then dissolves in rainwater and forms nitrates. These chemicals, nitrates, find their way into the roots of the soil and help plants grow! God has planned for a nitrates fertilizer for our food that is made from a gas within our atmosphere!

Some chemical reactions are much simpler. Suppose you are cleaning a tool shed and find an old iron nail on the floor. Every day that the nail has been sitting there, molecules of oxygen in the air have bombarded it. No longer does the nail look new; it is wearing a fine coating of rust. The rust is the result of a chemical reaction from the oxygen molecules.

All chemical reactions involve **reactants** and **products**. In the above example of the rusty nail, iron and oxygen are the reactants. The reaction begins when atoms of iron and oxygen form a chemical bond.

A **chemical bond** results when two or more atoms come together and share or transfer their electrons. The combined atoms form rust, or iron oxide, the product. The rust (iron oxide) is a new substance, but it uses the same protons and neutrons that are found in the reactants of iron and oxygen.

Chemical reactions are the changes among atoms or molecules when they form or break bonds. There are four types of chemical reactions: **analysis**, **synthesis**, **substitution**, and **metathesis**.

A. Analysis Reactions

An **analysis reaction** is also called a **decomposition reaction** or a breakdown reaction. In an analysis reaction, a compound is broken down into smaller pieces, often for scientists to analyze the elements in the compound. The compound is decomposed, or broken down. The electrolysis of water is a good example. Molecules of water (H_2O) are broken down into its elements of hydrogen (H_2) and oxygen (O).

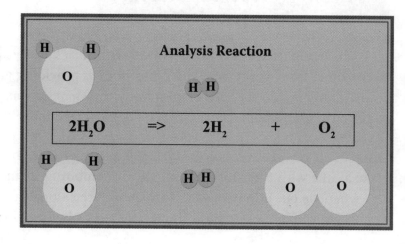

The purification of lead is another good example of decomposition. Lead has many uses in our society: car batteries, wheel balances, fishing sinkers, and radioactive shields.

You will notice that the symbol for lead is Pb, which stands for the Latin word *plumbum*. Lead had its earliest practical use in the **plumbing** (water pipes) of ancient Rome, and in past years in our country.

Lead occurs as a beautiful shiny mineral known as galena or lead sulfide (PbS), found in rocks. The lead atoms are bound to sulfur atoms in a ratio of 1:1. Lead purification involves heating the lead to a high temperature. This causes the sulfur (S) in the galena (PbS) to react with oxygen (O_2) in the air. The sulfur is driven from the galena as sulfur dioxide (SO_2) that escapes into the air. Molten metallic lead is the product.

B. Synthesis Reactions

Synthesis (or **synthetic**) **reactions** involve making a complex substance from two or more simple substances. Iron combining with oxygen to form iron oxide (rust) is an example of a synthetic reaction. The iron oxide ($2Fe_2O_3$) is more complex than the reactants of iron (4Fe) and oxygen ($3O_2$).

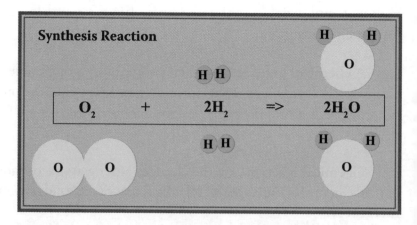

Another example of a synthetic reaction is combining hydrogen with oxygen to make water. Yet another example is the synthetic fiber in our clothes; different substances are combined to make a new fiber.

C. Substitution Reactions

Substitution reactions occur when only *one part* of a compound leaves to form a bond with another substance. When a piece of metallic zinc (Zn) is placed in hydrochloric acid (HCl), atoms of chlorine break away from the hydrogen to react with the zinc. Zinc substitutes for the hydrogen and forms a new product: zinc chloride ($ZnCl_2$).

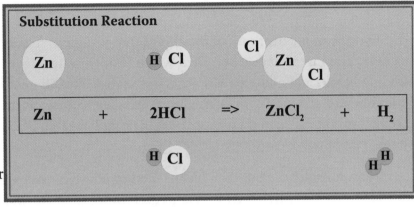

Substitution Reaction

$$Zn + 2HCl \Rightarrow ZnCl_2 + H_2$$

The hydrogen gas simply escapes as bubbles. The formula is as follows:

$$Zn + 2HCl \Rightarrow ZnCl_2 + H_2$$

A good way to make hydrogen is with a new penny. (Old pennies used to be made of bronze. In 1982, the US Treasury changed the composition of pennies. They are now 97.5% zinc and copper plated.) Just like M&Ms are candy-coated chocolate, modern pennies are copper-coated zinc. Find a creative way to scrape off or remove the copper plating. (For example, heating the penny until the copper turns black works well. Allow it to cool before handling. It might be easier to use a galvanized roofing tack.)

Next, allow the penny to soak in vinegar (acetic acid). The zinc liberates hydrogen gas upon reacting with the vinegar, thus forming copper acetate. The bubbles of hydrogen are not produced as fast as with hydrochloric acid, but you can still see them. ***Never light matches around hydrogen gas!***

D. Metathesis Reactions

A **metathesis reaction** is a substitution reaction in which both substances trade parts. For example, if a solution of potassium chloride (KCl) is mixed with a solution of silver nitrate ($AgNO_3$), the products formed will be silver chloride (AgCl) and potassium nitrate (KNO_3). Here is the molecular equation for this metathesis (or double-displacement) reaction:

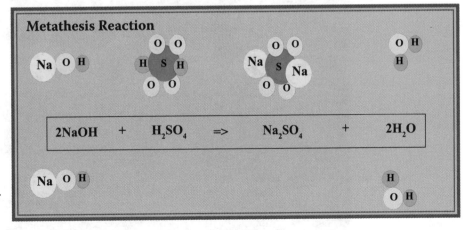

Metathesis Reaction

$$2NaOH + H_2SO_4 \Rightarrow Na_2SO_4 + 2H_2O$$

$$KCl + AgNO_3 \Rightarrow AgCl + KNO_3$$

VIII. God's World

For one moment, think of the things that we use to make something. Take bread for example. The ingredients are crushed wheat (flour), water, yeast, salt, and sugar. Using these building blocks and adding a few others, we can make different kinds of bread, biscuits, pancakes, and all kinds of desserts and pastries. Of course, we must mix these reactants in specific proportions and then apply heat. Baking is a series of complex chemical reactions caused by the heat of the oven.

Now consider the building blocks used to construct our entire universe: protons, neutrons, and electrons. Every living creature and everything (that we know of) in the solar system is made from these particles. The entire creation of God, along with the forces that govern it, are too tremendous to comprehend. The more we study and learn about our universe, the more we should stand in wonder and awe at the power of our Creator God.

Miracle of the Loaves and Fishes

Chapter 10 Summary

1. **The Periodic Table** is a catalog of all the known elements according to their chemical symbols. It is also organized on the basis of an element's given protons (or atomic number).

2. A **chemical symbol** is an arrangement of up to three letters that represent an element.

3. One hundred and eighteen elements are currently known; only 98 were discovered in nature. The remaining 20 were manufactured. These are called **synthetic chemicals**.

4. If two elements bind together (covalent bond), then scientists call it a **chemical compound**.

5. **Radioactive elements** are isotopes in which the strong nuclear force has been compromised, resulting in a fragmentation of nuclei. This natural process of losing particles is called **radioactive decay**. Eventually, the element will decay into some other simpler element.

6. Radioactive decay happens in three ways. The first occurs when the nucleus loses two protons and neutrons. This entity of particles is called an **alpha particle**. The second is the transformation of a neutron into a proton. The excess energy of the transformation is called a **beta particle**. The third way elements decay is when a proton becomes a neutron. The atom of the element ejects two small particles, which then collide with an electron. The product of this process is called a **gamma ray**.

7. There are four states of matter: **solid**, **liquid**, **gas**, and **plasma**.

8. What determines these material states is temperature and molecular motion.

9. **Kinetic** energy is simply energy in motion.

10. **Plasma** consists of positively charged ions and free-roaming electrons (which are negatively charged). The production of plasma is initiated when electrons escape the electrode and collide with gas. Consequently, the gas atoms are stripped of their electrons, rendering them positively charged ions. These form a **plasma streamer**.

11. **Physical change** alters the appearance of a given substance, but the substance itself remains the same. **Chemical change** transforms a substance into another by breaking down its constituents into simpler substances.

12. **Chemical reactions** are the changes among atoms or molecules that form or break bonds. All chemical reactions involve **reactants** and **products**. A **chemical bond** is when two or more atoms come together and share electrons. There are four kinds of chemical reactions: **analysis**, **synthesis**, **substitution**, and **metathesis**.

13. An **analysis reaction** (also called a **decomposition reaction**) is when compounds are broken down into simpler ones. A **synthesis reaction** is when simple elements coalesce to form a more complex compound. A **substitution reaction** occurs when one part of a compound leaves to form a bond with another substance. A **metathesis reaction** is a type of **substitution reaction** in which both compounds exchange parts.

Questions for Review

1. What is the Periodic Table?

_____

_____

2. If two elements bind together, what is produced?

_____

_____

3. What is a radioactive element?

_____

_____

4. List the three ways an element can decay.

_____

_____

5. What are the four states of matter?

_____

_____

6. What is the difference between physical changes and chemical changes?

_____

_____

7. What occurs with a chemical reaction?

_____

_____

8. How are chemical bonds formed?

_____

_____

9. List the four kinds of chemical reactions.

_____

_____

The Five Senses

I. **The Gift of Sight**

    A. Parts of the Eye

    B. Taking Care of Your Eyes

II. **The Gift of Hearing**

    A. Parts of the Ear

    B. The Gift of Balance

    C. Caring for Your Ears and Hearing

III. **The Gift of Smell**

IV. **The Gift of Taste**

    A. The Tongue

    B. Taking Care of the Mouth

V. **The Gift of Touch**

    A. Layers of the Skin

    B. Taking Care of Your Skin

The Five Senses

Chapter 11

"That which was from the beginning, which we have heard, which we have seen with our eyes, which we have looked upon and touched with our hands, concerning the Word of Life..." (1 John 1:1).

God created our world using a combination of invisible forces, matter, and energy. He gave His creation natural laws to maintain it and keep it running. No one on Earth can comprehend how He did this. We also believe that God made our wonderful world with us in mind. He gave us our bodies and souls so that we might come to know His glory, goodness, and love for us. We experience His creation with our minds and five senses.

Our senses are important for a number of reasons. They help us enjoy the beauty of this world and tell us about the environment in which we live. Our senses help us make decisions and avoid danger. We see the senses at work in all animals, especially with our pets. Every so often, you will read about a household pet that alerts a homeowner to danger, such as smoke from a fire.

We hardly think about what our senses do for us. They work quietly in the background, and we usually take them for granted. Some people lack the use of one or more senses. Some may not be able to see or to hear. Some people have lost their sense of taste or smell. We need to thank God for our healthy senses.

I. The Gift of Sight

"He answered, 'Whether he is a sinner, I do not know; one thing I know, that though I was blind, I now see'" (John 9:25).

From the time that we wake up in the morning until the time we go to sleep at night, we need light to do everything. Most of us cannot imagine spending our lives without vision and living in darkness. Perhaps that is why Jesus' cures of the blind were so astounding to the people who witnessed those cures. Jesus' cures of the blind, lame, and people with diseases often resulted in spiritual conversions for the afflicted, who sometimes became his followers. All of Jesus' cures occurred in a time when people knew very little about the human body. Today we know more about the human body than ever before. However, Jesus continues to cure people in ways that science cannot explain.

One of the most wonderful senses that God has blessed us with is the gift of sight. It is the most important of our five senses and the one that we use the most often. More than three-fourths of learning occurs through our eyes.

The eye is a sense organ designed to capture light. We can compare the eye with a camera, but the human eye is far more complex. Both convert patterns of light into images. **The eye sends the image to the brain**; the camera records an image only on film or a sensor. No one quite understands how the brain actually processes what we see. With our eyes, **we are able to determine colors and color contrasts, shades, shapes, patterns, and depth**. A camera simply records what comes through the lens. Vision is a wonderful, amazing, beautiful, and unique gift from God.

A. Parts of the Eye

Look at your eyes in the mirror. Your eyes sit slightly below your forehead and on either side of your nasal bridge. You see only a fraction of the eye, which is about the size of a ping-pong ball. About 5/6 of the eye sits in **a bony socket, or in an orbit in the skull**. Take the time to gently feel the hard bony orbit around your eye. It was designed to protect your eyes against serious injuries.

The eye orbit is lined with **fat tissue**, which surrounds the eyeball and its muscles. The fat has two purposes. It **allows for smooth movements of the eyeball and provides cushioning against injuries**.

There are two types of eye muscles: **extrinsic** and **intrinsic**. **Six extrinsic eye muscles** attach the eyeball to the bones of the orbit. These muscles can move the eyeball in any direction and are **voluntary**. That means that you can control them.

There are **two intrinsic eye muscles** in your eyes. These muscles are **involuntary**, which means you cannot control them. One of these attaches to your iris and **regulates the size of the pupil of the eye**. The other involuntary muscle **adjusts the shape of your lens** so that your eye can quickly adjust to viewing near and far objects. The **eye is the only organ in the body that has both voluntary and involuntary muscles**.

The **eyebrow** is made up of thick hairs that lie above your eyes. Along with your **eyelashes**, these give your eyes their appearance and **help protect them from foreign objects, dust**, and other debris. Small **glands located at the base of the eyelashes keep your eyes moist by secreting lubricating fluids**. An **infection** in these glands results in a swelling known as a **sty**.

Your **eyelids also protect your eyes**. Sometime in your life, someone has probably acted like they were going to tap you on the face and then pulled their hand away at the last second. You probably flinched, moved your head away from their hand, and closed your eyelids. It happened very quickly. The **closing of your eyes was an instinct or instant reflex that prevented your eyes from suffering injury**. Your eyelids also respond to bright light. When you go for a walk on a bright sunny day, you squint, or attempt to reduce the amount of light coming into your eyes.

Lacrimal (tear) glands are found above the eyes, underneath the eyelids. They secrete tears through small openings known as **lacrimal excretory ducts**. We typically think of crying when we hear the word tears; however, tears have other important roles. Each time we blink, the **blinking action spreads tears across the surface of the eye.** Blinking **helps lubricate our eyes,** keeps them moist, and **wipes away surface debris.**

Sometimes foreign materials such as smoke, chemicals, and debris find their way into our eyes. These produce an immediate sense of irritation. However, God gave us a few ways for our eyes **to remove irritants.** If an eyelash falls into the corner of your eye and becomes stuck, you experience some discomfort and find yourself blinking in an attempt to remove it from your eye. If blinking does not remove the eyelash, then your eyes instantly respond by producing **reflex tears.** These are produced **involuntarily,** which means that you have no control over their release.

After the **tears** have circulated through your eyes, they **drain into little tubes** known as **lacrimal ducts.** The tears **pass through the nasolacrimal duct and then into the nasal passages.** Once the tears enter the nasal passage, they are swallowed or blown out with other nasal secretions. You may recall that the last time you cried, you also had a runny nose or the sniffles. The flow of tears takes the following pathway:

Tears flow into lacrimal gland → lacrimal excretory duct → bathe, lubricate, and moisten → drain through lacrimal duct → nasolacrimal duct → nasal passages → expelled

The Lacrimal Apparatus

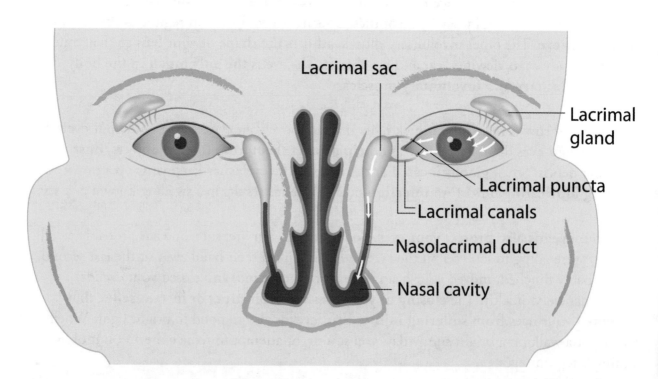

The **sclera is the white part of your eye**. It is a thick fibrous tissue that surrounds the entire eye. Look closely at your sclera, and you will see tiny red lines. These **are blood vessels** that deliver blood to the sclera. The **conjunctiva is a thin membrane that covers the sclera** and **lines the inside of your eyelids**. The conjuctiva **secretes oils and mucus that moisten and lubricate the eye**. Whenever you have a bad cold or an allergic reaction to something in the air, the conjunctiva may appear reddish and puffy. You may feel like there are grains of sand in your eyes, and they will become teary.

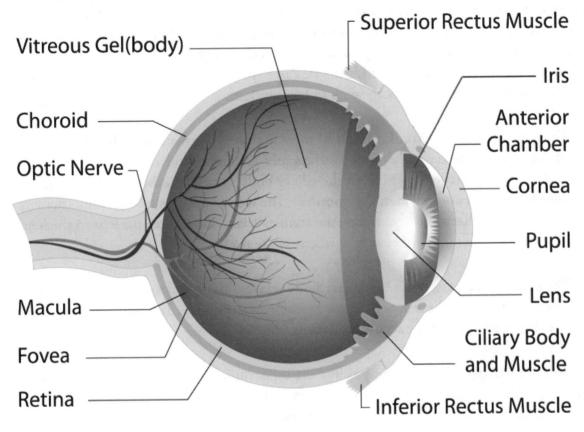

The **cornea is located in the center of your eye** and bulges outward. It is the **window** through which we see. The **corneal epithelium** is a fine layer of tissue that covers the cornea and is about 6 cells thick. Although the cornea is small, it is rich with nerves. There are more **nerve endings in the cornea** than anywhere else in the human body.

The cornea is clear because it contains no blood vessels. With no direct blood flow to its tissues, how does it obtain oxygen and nutrients? The oxygen comes from the air, which diffuses into the tear film. In turn, the cornea absorbs the oxygen from the tear film along with dissolved nutrients.

The **iris is the colored part of the eye**. It has another purpose besides giving us eye color. The iris **regulates the amount of light that passes through to the lens**. In this respect, we can compare the iris to the aperture or opening of a camera. When you take a photograph, the aperture opens up and allows light to pass to the lens. Likewise, when you look at something, the iris changes the size of the **pupil or the round black opening in the center of your eye**.

The size of the **pupil changes with light. When your eye is exposed to bright light** on a **sunny day, the iris reduces the size of the pupil**. This action reduces the amount of light coming into the eye. The opposite happens in darkness. When you sit in a darkened room, the iris increases the size of the pupils. As a consequence, more light is allowed to enter your eye. You can think of the iris as a type of valve, which decreases or increases the passage of light.

The **aqueous humor is a fluid that sits between the cornea and iris. It provides nutrients to the cornea and lens, and gives the eye its rounded shape**. In addition, the aqueous humor helps maintain pressure in the eye and allows focusing of the crystalline lens. The **lens sits near the front of the eye and lies directly behind the iris and pupil**. Its job is **to focus light** and form an image. Here again we can make the comparison between the lens of an eye with that of a camera. They both work to form images.

The **ciliary body is a circular band of muscle that is connected to the lens directly behind the iris**. The ciliary body produces the aqueous humor fluid and has two other important roles. The first of these is that the ciliary body suspends or **holds the lens in place** by tiny fibers known as **zonular fibers** (or **zonules**). The second role has to do with its activity as a muscle. When the ciliary body contracts, the zonules relax. This causes the lens to thicken, and allows for close-up focusing, for example, when we are reading.

The opposite happens when the ciliary body relaxes. The zonules shorten, which causes the lens to become thinner. These actions allow focusing at a distance. This **process of changing the shape of the lens is known as accommodation**.

You can see that the ciliary body is like the other muscle groups in the body. It undergoes cycles of contraction and relaxation. This one small part of the eye is a testament to our Creator. Our highest quality cameras have lenses consisting of multiple elements or pieces of glass. These lenses cannot match the abilities of our God-given single lens and the ciliary body that controls it. Keep in mind that we are only talking about one part of the eye!

The **vitreous humor** (or **vitreous**) **is found behind the lens. It is composed mainly of water and accounts for 2/3 of the eye's volume**. The vitreous humor gives form and shape to the eye, and allows the eye to return to its normal shape if compressed. The consistency of the vitreous humor is neither like water nor like jelly. Rather, it is a lot like fresh egg white. The light passes through this substance and reaches the retina, its final destination in the eye.

The **retina is a multi-layered tissue that lines the back of the eye**. It contains millions of tiny structures known as **photoreceptors. Photoreceptors capture light and convert it into electrical impulses, or electrical energy**. There are two types of photoreceptors: **rods and cones**. The shape determines their names. **Rods are shaped liked rods**; **cones are shaped like cones**.

There are about **120 million rods in the retina**. **Rods allow us to see black and white, and work best in dim light or partial darkness**. In addition, rods are responsible for both peripheral and night vision. **Peripheral vision** is what you see **out of the corner of your eye**. For example, you may be reading at a table, and a family member walks past you. **Peripheral vision** allows you to see them without looking directly at them. **Night vision** is the ability to see in low light conditions. It takes several minutes or more before our eyes adjust to the dark. Our nighttime vision is poor when we compare it with that of nocturnal creatures. For example, the eyes of owls are about 100 times more sensitive to light than our own!

There are about **six million cones in the retina**. **Cones help us see color and objects in great detail**. They work best in bright light. Cones are sensitive to one of three different colors: red, green, or blue. Some people do not have certain cones or possess cones that are weak. We call these people **color vision deficient** or **color blind**. They cannot experience color like everyone else. Imagine what it would be like to not see color. It would prove especially difficult when shopping for clothes. You would need help with matching colors. At one time, color-blind people had useful roles in the U.S. Armed Forces. They were able to spot camouflage colors that went unseen by people with normal vision.

The Ishihara test is given to people who have indications of color vision deficiency. The test consists of viewing plates that are filled with colored dots. The dots are colored in different shades, and a hidden number is shaded with a different color. If persons are color-blind, they will not be able to identify the number(s) in the plates.

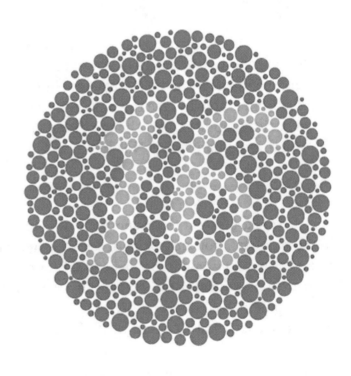

The image to the right is an example of one of these plates. This image is taken from the Ishihara color vision test provided by Dr. Terrace L. Waggoner at TestingColorVision. com. Look at this image and see if you can identify the number that is in the circle. You have 3 seconds to decide. (Note: The correct answer is provided at the end of the "Taking Care of Your Eyes" section of this chapter.)

The **choroid** lies between the retina and sclera. It attaches to the ciliary body at the front of the eye, and extends to the edge of the optic nerve at the back of the eye. The choroid is not a membrane but **consists of several layers of blood vessels that provide oxygen and nourishment** to the eye.

So far, we have discussed the parts of the eye and their different jobs. Now let's put it all together to understand how we see. Imagine you are looking at waterfall that is cascading down a mountainside. Reflected light from the waterfall, trees, hills, and sky strikes your cornea and iris. Your iris detects the brightness of the scene and adjusts the size of the pupil. The light passes through the aqueous humor and enters the lens. The ciliary muscles work together to adjust or flatten the shape of the lens. The light passes through the lens and vitreous humor; the lens focuses the light rays on the retina. The rods, but mostly the cones, of the retina absorb the light and form an image. Again, this is like the film or sensor behind the lens of a camera. What happens to the image once it strikes the retina?

ACTIVITY

Here's a twist that science cannot explain. Use a magnifying glass to look at something close up—for example, a prayer card. Everything on the card is magnified and looks fine, right? Now take the magnifying glass and hold it at arm's length in front of your face. Look around the room or outside a window. Everything is upside down, right? This is no different from how our eyes work. When light passes through the lens in our eye and strikes the retina, it forms an upside-down image, which has two dimensions (length × width).

The images from each eye are sent to the brain via the optic nerve. Get ready for another twist. The image from the right eye is sent to the left side of the brain, and the image from the left eye is sent to the right side of the brain. Somehow, the brain is able to take the upside-down, two-dimensional images, in the form of electrical impulses, and change them. The image or picture becomes right side up and three-dimensional. No one knows how this is done—except God, of course!

Let's take a look at vision another way, in terms of **matter** and **energy**. As you read the words in this paragraph, you are looking at reflected light that enters your eyes at 186,000 miles per second. Most of us cannot comprehend this speed. The light or photons bounce off the molecules of matter (ink and paper). We can take it a step further and break the molecules down into atoms, or their protons, neutrons, and electrons. The photons (or light energy) travel to the retina and are converted to electrical impulses. This *information* is sent to the brain, and it forms an **image**.

B. Taking Care of Your Eyes

God made eyes with protective safeguards, including: eyebrows, eyelashes, reflex tears, and blinking. We find protective safeguards in many other creatures too. For example, camels have very long eyelashes that help keep sand out of their eyes. They also have thick eyebrows that shield their eyes from the bright desert sun. **Nictitating membranes** are found in birds, fish, amphibians, reptiles, and many mammals. These membranes are either transparent or translucent, and can be drawn across the eyes to protect them from injuries. In birds of prey, the

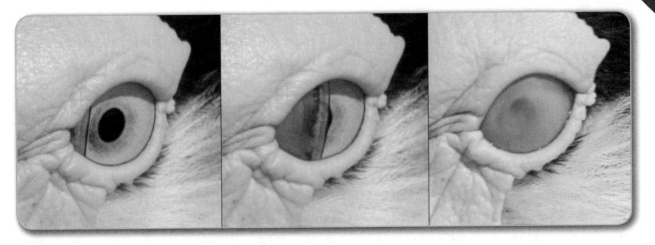

Nictitating Membrane (Photos by Toby Hudson)

nictitating membrane protects the eyes of the parents from the beaks of their chicks when they are feeding them. Sharks close these membranes when striking prey. A captured and thrashing fish could easily puncture the eyes of a shark with its fins. Humans lack these protective features that we find in other creatures.

We must take certain precautions to protect and take care of our eyes. Let's review some examples.

Goggles are protective eyewear to keep foreign objects and chemicals away from our eyes. You should always wear safety goggles when working with machines and tools that produce small pieces of debris and dust. These machines include lathes, electric drills, sanders, saws, and hammers.

Many of us have **allergies to pollen, dust, and other foreign materials**. Allergies can seem unbearable at times and may cause sneezing, a runny nose, and itchy eyes. These responses are an **overreaction to a substance known as an allergen**. If you have allergies, you may find that your eyes itch severely. Your family doctor may recommend **eye drops that contain compounds known as antihistamines**. These help alleviate the itching and provide comfort. It is never a good idea to scratch your eyes, no matter how much they itch. The scratching may feel good in the short term, but you most likely will make the symptoms worse. If your allergies are severe, your doctor may refer you to a specialist known as an allergist.

Occasionally, you will read or hear about an eclipse in the news. During a solar eclipse, the moon passes between the sun and the Earth. Although the moon blocks much of the sun's visible light, a significant amount of ultraviolet light passes through to the Earth. ***You should never look directly at an eclipse***, just as you should never look directly at the sun. The ultraviolet light can easily burn your retina and cause permanent damage—even blindness! There are no pain receptors in the retina to warn you of burning and damage. In a matter of seconds, you can severely injure your retina. Every time there is an eclipse, a small number of people view it with their eyes and receive serious injuries. There is no safe way to look at an eclipse except on a television or computer monitor.

While we are covering the sun, it's a good idea to wear sunglasses when you are outside on a bright sunny day. **Sunglasses reduce glare and help shield your eyes from the damaging effects of ultraviolet light**. Polarized sunglasses are slightly more effective than regular sunglasses. They work by blocking light traveling in a horizontal plane. Only light that travels in a vertical plane is allowed passage to your eyes. Polarized sunglasses block glare and are soothing to wear on bright sunny days. In addition, they are helpful for certain activities, such as fishing. Wearing polarized sunglasses, you may be able to see patterns of current flow and even fish below the surface of the water that others cannot see.

Most everyone enjoys playing some kind of sport or participating in an outdoor activity. All activities involve risks to our health; some activities are more risky than others. Beware of activities that expose the head and eyes to tremendous forces. President Teddy Roosevelt enjoyed boxing even when he served in the White House. One day he received a blow to the head that caused a detached retina in his left eye, which resulted in partial blindness. He switched to a safer activity. His partial blindness wasn't made public until after he completed his presidency.

Finally, there used to be an old joke that went like this: Q - Did you know that carrots are good for your eyes? A – No, why? Q – Well, you never saw a rabbit with glasses, did you? Well, it turns out that **carrots are an excellent source of Vitamin A, an important nutrient for your eyes. Other sources of Vitamin A are found in milk, eggs, liver, fortified cereals, and darkly colored orange or green vegetables, such as pumpkins, sweet potatoes, and kale**. Another very good source of Vitamins A (and D) is cod liver oil. Even if we eat a balanced diet, minor vitamin supplements can be helpful for promoting good health.

Note: The answer to the color vision test in the previous section is 16. If you did not correctly identify this number, your parents should consider giving you a more complete color vision test, such as the one at http://colorvisiontesting.com/ishihara.htm.

II. The Gift of Hearing

God gave us two ears and one tongue so that we could listen twice as much as we speak. This is a common quote to remind us all about the importance of listening to others before we speak.

The ability to hear is another remarkable gift from our Creator. Many things come to mind when we hear the word "hearing." We think of conversation, music, sirens on emergency vehicles, train horns, songs. In addition to these, there are many other wondrous sounds: crickets chirping, birds singing, kittens purring, and waves on the beach.

There is a beauty in silence, too, and these days there is not enough silence in the world. We need quiet for our prayer life, but sometimes it can be hard to find. It is in silence that God speaks to us. When we spend time in front of the Blessed Sacrament, we find that we pray more fervently. This is the time when the Holy Spirit speaks to our hearts.

Your ears are sense organs. As with the eye, much of what goes on in the ear is inside your head. There are three parts or sections of the ear: outer ear, middle ear, and inner ear. All three parts work together to collect sound—or, more precisely, to collect vibrations in the air. You will recall that sound is the energy of vibration.

A. Parts of the Ear

The outer ear is the part that is visible to us. It has two **other names, the auricle** or **pinna**. Its primary job is to **collect, amplify, and funnel sound waves to the other parts of the ear**. Sound is collected by the auricle and **travels to the ear canal**. The ear canal is a tube that is about 1 1/4 inches long. It is not straight but travels forward and downward. The **ear canal is lined with glands** that **secrete or make cerumen, which we call earwax**. Earwax lubricates the skin of the ear canal and **helps keep it clean**. Earwax **also serves to protect the ear from harmful germs, insects, and water**.

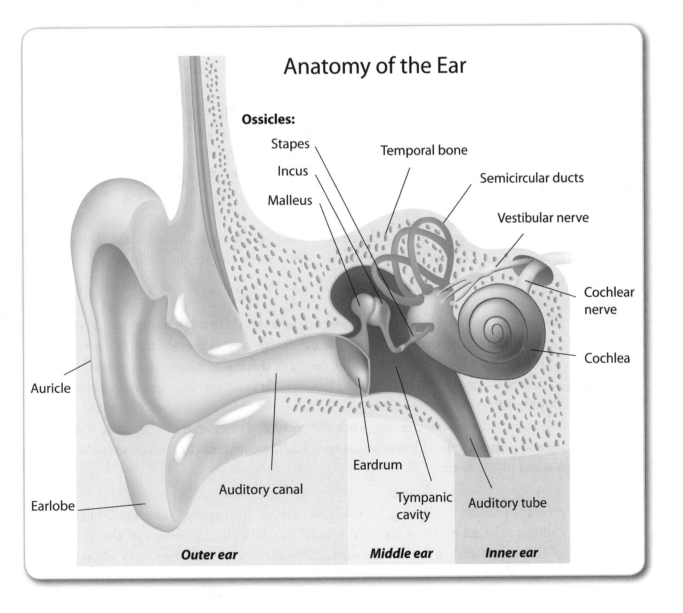

Anatomy of the Ear

The **tympanic membrane (or eardrum) lies at the end of the ear canal**. It is a piece of skin that is tightly stretched and serves as the border between the outer ear and middle ear. **Sound waves journey through the ear canal and cause the eardrum to vibrate. The vibrations pass on to three bones that are connected to each other. These tiny bones are known as ossicles**. The first **bone that vibrates is the malleus (or hammer)**. The *handle* of the hammer attaches directly to the eardrum. In turn, the *head* of the hammer passes these vibrations on to the **incus** (or anvil). Next, the vibrations **are passed on to the stapes (or stirrup)**.

The **auditory (eustachian) tube is part of the middle ear**. The **auditory tube** helps **maintain air pressure between the outer and inner surfaces of the tympanic membrane**. Whenever you travel to high altitudes, the air becomes thinner. This causes an imbalance of air pressures on both sides of your eardrum. The air pressure becomes higher on the inside of your eardrum. It continues to buildup until you yawn or swallow. Either of these actions normally causes the air pressures to balance. You hear a popping noise in your ear and no longer feel pressure on your eardrum.

When you travel to high altitudes with a cold, mucus in the auditory tube may prevent the balancing of air pressure. This imbalance causes pain on the eardrum. Yawning, swallowing, and even chewing gum may not reduce the pressure. One possible remedy is to close your mouth, pinch both nostrils, and blow very gently (it is important that you do not blow hard, especially if you feel pain). Your cheeks will fill up with air and hopefully you can hear a slight popping sound in your ears. This causes the pressure on the outside of your eardrum to balance with the pressure on the inside.

The **inner ear** is also known as the **labyrinth** because of its complicated shape. It consists of membranes and bones. The two main structures of the inner ear are the cochlea and the semicircular canals.

Sound vibrations pass from the stapes (or **stirrup**) and **travel through a tiny membrane known as the oval window. The cochlea lies on the other side of this membrane. It resembles a snail's shell** and is filled with fluid. Throughout the center of this coiled tube is the final destination for the *energy of vibration*—the **organ of Corti (KORT-eye). It is a tiny structure with between 15,000 and 20,000 tiny hairs**. Each of these hairs is connected to its own nerve. Vibrations pass through the fluid and cause pressure changes inside the cochlea. The **changes in pressure move these tiny hairs and cause electrical impulses to travel to the cochlear (or auditory) nerve. These impulses then travel to the brain**.

Let's review the process of hearing for one moment. Sound energy (energy of vibration) is amplified and transmitted by the outer and middle ear. Within the inner ear, the vibrations cause pressure differences within a fluid. In turn, these activate nerves that carry electrical impulses to the brain.

B. The Gift of Balance

Our sense of balance comes from sense organs of the inner ear known as the semicircular canals. They are three fluid-filled tubes that are lined with fine hairs. The hairs attach to nerves and send information about position to the brain. The fluid and the hairs work together. When you move your head around, the fluid sloshes and puts pressure on the hairs. This pressure activates nerves that send messages to the brain. The brain interprets this information as balance.

When you sit upright in a chair, your head is straight and level. The fluid in your ears does not move. The nerves collect and send information to your brain. In turn, your brain tells you that all is well. Now, what happens when you try to stand on your head or do a somersault? As soon as your head is upside-down, the fluid sloshes around and activates a different set of nerves. You see an upside-down world and feel differently than when you sat in the chair. You might enjoy this sensation for a little bit, but you will certainly be more comfortable when your head returns to the normal, upright position.

Another example of imbalance is the feeling you have after spinning around in a circle. You feel dizzy and may have difficulty walking for several seconds. The dizziness results from the fluid continuing to slosh around, even though you stopped spinning. This also happens after you finish riding a roller coaster or various spinning rides at an amusement park. You continue to have the sensation that you are moving; you have lost your sense of balance!

C. Caring for Your Ears and Hearing

Taking care of our ears and hearing requires two things, cleaning and avoiding loud sounds. Most of the time, cleaning our ears involves gently washing the outside surfaces. The inside of our ears pretty much takes care of itself. You could even say that the ear is self-cleaning. Earwax is constantly secreted, and the new earwax pushes out the old. It either falls out on its own, or you remove it when you wash.

Never stick anything inside your ear smaller than your elbow. This old saying holds true even today. Some people use cotton swabs to clean the inside of their ears, but you should not do this. When you put any object inside your ear canal, it pushes the earwax inward, and it may become stuck. The earwax may even build up and push against your eardrum. If this happens, it can cause irritation and infection. If the infection is severe, it could result in the partial loss of hearing. Partial hearing loss is not temporary, but permanent!

Hearing loss today is more common than ever before. This is due to a variety of factors, including infections, poor nutrition, and loud music. Yes, you read that correctly: loud music! Perhaps you didn't realize that **listening to music through headphones can damage your hearing**. When you listen to loud music or any loud sounds for a long period of time, you overwork the hair cells of the inner ear. These become exhausted and begin to lose their function. This is a serious problem in our society. At the moment, about 12.5 percent of young people between the ages of 6 and 19 suffer from partial hearing loss.

Have you ever heard someone's music playing through their earphones as they walk by? These people are damaging their hearing. If you listen to music through earphones, make sure you set the volume no higher than 60 percent. If a friend is trying to speak to you and you cannot hear what he or she is saying, you have the volume set too high. Remember, **once you lose your hearing, you can't get it back**. Complicating this problem is the fact that most people do not know when they have suffered partial hearing loss. It requires testing by an audiologist.

If you find yourself working in a noisy environment, then you should be wearing earplugs or sound attenuators. The latter look like an old-fashioned pair of headphones or earmuffs. They consist of two hard plastic cups that are connected by a band, which slips over the top of your head. The cups are filled with foam rubber. When these are worn properly, they absorb all loud sounds.

How do you know if you work in a noisy environment? If the sounds or noise around you begin to make you uncomfortable, then that is a sign that you are in a noisy environment. For example, years ago, Dr. Stein worked in one of the noisiest environments in the world: the flight deck of an aircraft carrier. It was so noisy that he had to wear sound attenuators over a set of earplugs. If he wore just the former, the noise was unbearable; it made him feel like he wanted to crawl out of his skin.

Swimmer's ear is an infection that results when water and bacteria invade the inside of your ear. To prevent swimmer's ear, shake the excess water from your ears when you finish swimming. If shaking doesn't remove it, turn your head downward and press a towel gently to your ear. Gently shake your head once again. If that doesn't work, try using special eardrops that help dry out moisture.

III. The Gift of Smell

The nose sits in the front and center of the face. It consists of two openings (or **nostrils**) that are separated by a structure known as the **septum**. Directly behind the nose is a space known as the **nasal cavity**. It sits above the hard palate of the mouth and connects with the back of your throat.

The nasal cavity has several jobs, including filtering and warming the air that we breathe. It also contains the **olfactory** (ole-FACK-tore-ee) **sense organs**. There is one for each nostril, and we use them for our sense of smell. They are small and measure one square centimeter.

The olfactory sense organ consists of a fine layer of tissue known as the **olfactory epithelium**. It is a mucous membrane that contains millions of odor receptors and cilia, or fine hairs. Whenever we breathe, special **olfactory glands** secrete substances that work to dissolve odors or compounds into the mucus of the epithelium. These dissolved odors or chemicals bind to specific receptors, and send messages to the brain via the nerves.

People have the ability to distinguish about 10,000 different odor molecules. We develop memories for many odors. For example, we know the aroma of our favorite foods, whether it is pizza, watermelon, or a grilled hamburger. We know the odor of many other things, too. Some of these are pleasant, such as the fragrance of flowers. Others are very unpleasant, like a skunk or a dead animal lying on a highway in the summer.

IV. The Gift of Taste

Your **tongue** is another sensory organ of the body and has several important jobs. It makes **speech possible**, **allows us to taste food**, and **helps keep food between the upper and lower teeth** until it has been chewed well. The **tongue also positions chewed food for swallowing**. **Swallowing** is the passage of food toward the digestive tract by a series of coordinated movements.

A. The Tongue

The tongue is bathed in saliva that is secreted from three major **salivary glands**. The **submandibular** and **sublingual glands** are located under the tongue. The **parotid glands** are found in front of and below the ears. They discharge saliva through ducts that empty into the mouth near the second molars. In addition, the tongue has its own salivary glands.

The Salivary Glands

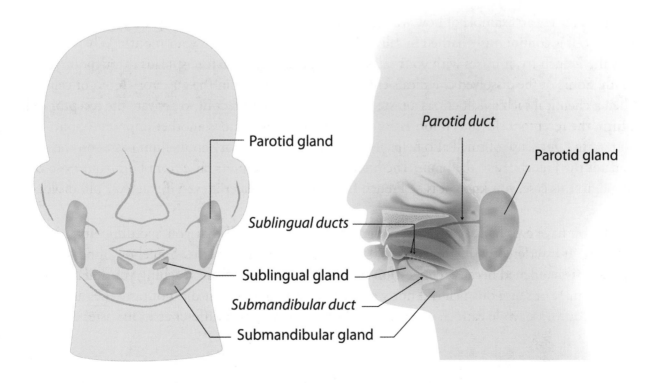

11

Saliva works to moisten and lubricate food. It also contains digestive enzymes such as amylase and lipase. These are mixed in with your food when you begin chewing. **Amylase** (AM-uh-lace) begins breaking down starches into sugars before they enter your digestive tract. **Lipase** (LIE-pace) breaks down fats after they enter the digestive tract.

Walk over to the nearest mirror. Open your mouth and stick out your tongue. What do you see? The tongue is covered with little bumps known as **papillae**. These help create friction between the tongue and the food inside your mouth. This means that they help the tongue grip the food and move it around while you chew.

The **taste buds** are much smaller in size than the papillae. They are tucked away in folds among the papillae. Each taste bud contains about 50 **gustatory** (or **taste**) **receptor cells**. These specialized cells contain **taste pores** (or tiny openings) that respond to the chemicals of foods. When food molecules enter the taste pores, they cause the receptor cells to send electrical impulses to the **gustatory region** of the brain. This is the region of the brain where we interpret information about food.

Think of the taste pores as a lock and key fit for each of the tastes. Or you can consider them as two pieces of an interlocking puzzle. Sweet chemicals can only fit in a sweet pore, salt molecules can only enter a salty pore, and so on. At one time, we recognized four kinds of taste buds. However, in 2002, scientists discovered a fifth taste bud that they named **umami** (oo-MAH-mee), which is Japanese for "savory." Umami or savory taste buds respond to a compound known as **glutamic acid**. We find it in foods that are produced by natural fermentation, for example, cheese and soy sauce.

Let's review an example of how we taste food, say with a salty French fry. Each gustatory receptor cell is continuously bathed in saliva – with or without food in your mouth. When you chew the French fry, it mixes with your saliva. This entire soupy mixture spreads throughout your mouth. Some of the dissolved chemicals enter the taste pores within the gustatory receptor cells. When a chemical such as salt enters a taste pore, it must be a perfect fit to activate the receptor cell. In turn, the receptor cell sends information to the brain. Now, here is another important point about taste. Our sense of smell also helps us taste food. The olfactory epithelium passes on the aroma of the French fry to the brain. The brain, therefore, interprets taste from both your nose and tongue. In this case, you know it is a "French fry" and could detect it even if you were blindfolded.

If you have ever had severe nasal congestion, you may recall that you had difficulty breathing. It interfered with your sense of smell and even your appetite. Somehow, food lost its appeal. This happened because congestion blocked food aromas from reaching your olfactory epithelium. Your sense of smell did not work properly, and food just did not taste the same. Try holding your nose while eating something and see if you notice a difference in its taste.

B. Taking Care of the Mouth

There are all kinds of germs or microbes in your mouth. These are ever present, even after you brush your teeth and rinse out your mouth. When we eat something and do not brush and rinse, these microbes build up and can cause cavities. Likewise, a buildup of debris, microbes, and dead cells on the tongue can cause bad breath. For this reason, cleaning our tongues makes sense as well.

When you finish brushing your teeth, you should also brush your tongue. You can do this easily with gentle pressure. The brushing cleans the tongue surface of debris and toxins, resulting in fresher breath.

V. The Gift of Touch

We mostly think of the skin as a tissue, but it really is the largest sensory organ of the body. The average skin of an adult weighs about 8-10 lbs. and covers an area of about 22 square feet; that's a lot of skin! The skin protects us against microbes and prevents water loss. Its other functions include insulation, temperature regulation, and providing information about the environment and objects that we touch. Finally, the skin manufactures Vitamin D whenever it is exposed to sunlight. Vitamin D is necessary for good health, but don't spend too much time in the sun.

A. Layers of the Skin

The skin consists of three layers: the epidermis, dermis, and subcutaneous (sub-cue-TANE-ee-us) layer. The **epidermis** is the outermost layer and the one that is visible to you. It contains the cells that make **melanin**, the pigment that gives our skin its color. Our bodies produce additional melanin whenever we spend time in the sun. This extra melanin is what gives us a suntan. A suntan may look nice, but its primary job is to protect the skin from solar or ultraviolet radiation.

The cells of the epidermis grow, divide, and die. These processes are continuous, and your epidermis produces many new cells each day. Many of these die, about 30,000-40,000 every hour. That's a lot of dead cells! This is the primary reason we bathe: to prevent the buildup of dead cells and help keep our bodies clean.

The **dermis** lies right below the epidermis. It contains blood vessels, oil glands, sweat glands, and many **nerve endings** and **skin receptors**. There are four major classes of skin receptors: mechanoreceptors, thermoreceptors, pain receptors, and proprioceptors. These allow us to feel touch, pressure, warmth, cold, and pain.

The skin uses **mechanoreceptors** to detect vibrations, pressure, and texture. Merkel's disks and Meissner's corpuscles are two kinds of mechanoreceptors that we use when touching objects. Although these are found throughout the body, they are especially concentrated in the ridges of our fingertips. They work together by letting you know when you are touching something and the texture of the thing. These sensations are interpreted by your brain, which processes this information in the background.

Thermoreceptors, or cold and hot receptors, are found throughout the body with the highest concentrations on your face and ears. For this reason, your nose and ears seem to feel colder faster than the rest of your body on cold winter days.

Cold receptors sense cold when the surface of the skin drops a few degrees below normal body temperature (98.6 °F). They remain stimulated until the surface temperature of the skin drops below 41 °F. At this temperature, the hands and feet start to go numb. If the body does not heed these warnings, especially numbness, then frostbite is a possibility. Frostbite is a medical condition in which freezing causes damage to the skin and other tissues.

Hot receptors begin to perceive warmth when the surface temperature of the skin rises above 86 °F. Rising skin temperatures results in more nerve stimulation. When the surface temperature of the skin rises above 113 °F, pain receptors become stimulated and take over. It is the body's way of telling you that the skin and other tissues will soon suffer damage.

There are more than three million **pain receptors** in the human body. Besides the skin, they are found in muscles, bones, blood vessels, and many of our organs, for example, the eyes, ears, nose, and tongue. You know when you experience pain compared to other sensations. Pain is sharp! Think of a time when you experienced sharp pain. Maybe it was the sting of a bee or wasp, or maybe you touched something on the stove when you didn't realize that it was still hot. Pain receptors were given to us to help avoid severe injuries.

Every so often, you may read about someone who was born without pain receptors or is indifferent to pain. The parents were the first people to notice that something with their child wasn't quite right. Their child may have had a broken bone, yet showed no signs of experiencing pain. We may not like pain, but it is one of our gifts that help protect us. Now, think of what Jesus had to go through during His Passion and Crucifixion!

Proprioceptors sense the position of the different parts of the body in relation to one another and the surrounding environment. They are found in our muscles, tendons, and joints. Proprioceptors send messages to the brain about changes in muscle length and muscles tension. They help us with coordinated movements, such as eating or putting on clothing. We can only imagine how much we depend on proprioceptors when playing a musical instrument or a vigorous sport.

Let's discuss an example of how the different sensory receptors in the skin work. Keep in mind that more than one receptor will be sensing at any given time. Say you have a young kitten on your lap. Your **thermoreceptors** are sensing that the kitten is warmer than the surrounding air temperature. At the same time, your **mechanoreceptors** sense the texture of the fur and detect vibrations as the kitten purrs. **Other mechanoreceptors** located deeper in your hand sense that your hands are grasping the kitten, the way your hands are positioned around it, and how much pressure you are using to hold it. Finally, **proprioceptors** are sensing the stretching of the hands and fingers in relation to each other and the rest of the body. Hopefully you can see that quite a lot is going on in your nervous system when you are holding a kitten.

The **subcutaneous layer** is the bottom layer of the skin. It consists mostly of adipose tissue, or fat. The fat has two important roles. It helps *insulate* your body from changes in temperature. Here, you can make the comparison with the insulation in your home. You don't want your home to lose heat too quickly, especially on a cold winter day. Otherwise, your furnace would run constantly, which would be very expensive. Likewise, the body likes being at a constant temperature. Adipose tissue also protects the tissues and the organs lying beneath it by absorbing shocks. For example, if you fall down, the fat helps cushion the blow.

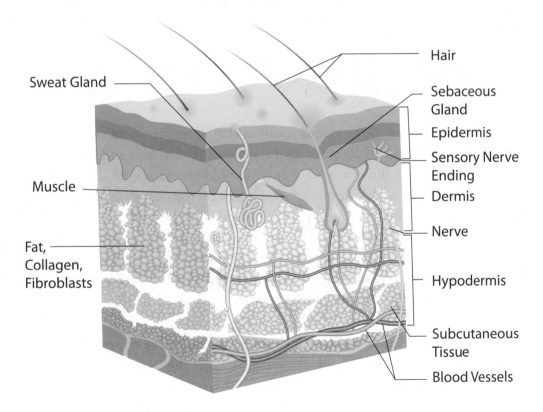

B. Taking Care of Your Skin

Bacteria and microbes are ever present on the surface of your skin. You remove many of these along with dead skin cells when you bathe or wash. However, in about 24 hours the bacteria return to the same pre-wash numbers. This is perfectly normal and part of *being human*.

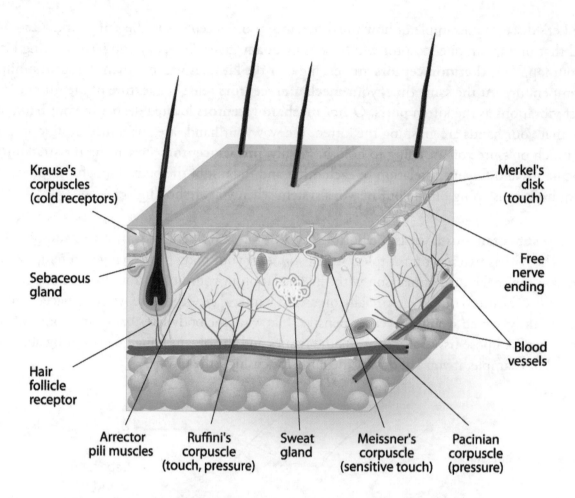

Everyone has had injuries to the skin, including chafes, scrapes, cuts, and punctures. These openings or wounds potentially serve as entry points for bacteria and other microbes, which would quickly colonize the wound and enter the bloodstream if we didn't take certain precautions. These precautions include washing all breaks in the skin with soap and warm water. Rinsing and allowing the wound to dry should be followed by the application of a disinfectant such as hydrogen peroxide. This can be fun to watch as the solution bubbles up, destroying microbes and reacting with the hemoglobin in your red blood cells. It might sting a little, though. Apply bandages and/or gauze as necessary. Of course, if the cuts are severe, seek first aid and visit your local emergency room or family doctor.

Doctors will tell you that any prolonged exposure to sunlight is not good for you. Some people heed these warnings; others do not. Sunburn damages the skin. Solar radiation penetrates the skin and potentially causes changes that include wrinkles, dark spots, leathery skin, and even cancer. You may have seen people who spent almost their entire lives in the sun. Their skin has an abnormal appearance, as described above.

When you plan some activity that requires prolonged exposure to sunlight (for example, the beach, a picnic, or the zoo), make sure that you bring along a sunblock. Sunblocks are rated with sun protection factors (SPFs), and many dermatologists (skin doctors) recommend using those that have an SPF of 30 and are water resistant. You should also wear lip balm to protect your lips from the sun and help keep them from drying out. If possible, wear a wide-brimmed hat that helps protect the face, nose, ears, and neck. Healthy skin is important for overall good health. Use common sense. A little sunlight is good for you and helps produce Vitamin D. You will live with your skin the rest of your life. Take care of it and avoid sunburns!

More information about sunblocks and the effects of sun on the skin is available at your local library or on the Internet.

Joshua Commands the Sun, **by March**

Chapter 11 Summary

1. The eye sits in a bony socket, called an orbit, which is lined with fat tissue.

2. There are six extrinsic eye muscles and two intrinsic eye muscles.

3. The eyebrow, eyelashes, and eyelids protect the eye from dirt and injury.

4. Lacrimal (or tear) glands are found underneath the eyelids.

5. The cornea is in the center of the eye and is the window through which we see.

6. The iris is the colored part of the eye, and changes the size of the pupil, the round black opening that allows light to pass through to the lens.

7. The retina is tissue that lines the back of the eye, and contains tiny photoreceptors which capture light and convert it to electrical impulses.

8. There are about 120 million rods in the retina, which allow us to see black and white and even have night vision when it is dark.

9. There are about 6 million cones in the retina, which help us to see color.

10. The outer ear, also called the auricle, collects, amplifies, and funnels sound to other parts of the ear. Sound then travels to the ear canal, which is lined with glands to make cerumen or earwax, which lubricates the ear canal and protects the ear from germs.

11. The tympanic membrane, or eardrum, is a tight piece of skin that vibrates from sound waves. The vibrations pass on to three bones: the malleus (or hammer), the incus (or anvil), and the stapes (or stirrup).

12. The auditory (eustachian) tube is part of the middle ear. The auditory tube maintains pressure between the outer and inner surfaces of the tympanic membrane.

13. Sound vibrations pass from the stapes or stirrup through a tiny membrane called the oval window. The cochlea, which looks like a snail's shell, lies on the other side of the oval window.

14. The process of hearing: sound energy or vibrations are transmitted by the outer and middle ear, where the vibrations cause pressure differences within a fluid, which then activates nerves that carry electrical impulses to the brain.

15. A sense of balance come from the semicircular canals in the inner ear.

16. Listening to music through headphones can damage your hearing, which can never be healed or returned.

17. The nose consists of the nostrils, the septum, and the nasal cavity, which contains the olfactory sense organs for our sense of smell.

18. We can distinguish about 10,000 different odors.

19. The tongue allows speech, allows us to taste food, and helps us to swallow food.

20. The tongue has three major salivary glands. The bumps on the tongue are called papillae. Taste buds are in folds among the papillae. Scientists now recognize five kinds of taste buds, among them being sweet and salty.

21. For fresh breath and fewer germs and cavities, brush your teeth.

22. The skin protects us against germs, regulates our body temperature, and manufactures Vitamin D.

23. The epidermis is the outer layer of skin and contains melanin, the pigment that gives our skin color.

24. Below the epidermis lies the dermis, which contains blood vessels, oil glands, sweat glands, nerve endings, and skin receptors, which allow us to feel touch, pressure, warmth, cold, and pain.

25. Thermoreceptors are hot and cold receptors found throughout the body.

26. There are more than three million pain receptors throughout the human body.

27. Proprioceptors sense the position of different parts of the body in relation to one another and the surrounding environment. They are found in our muscles, tendons, and joints.

28. The subcutaneous layer is the bottom layer of the skin, which helps insulate the body from changes in temperature.

29. Sunburn damages the skin.

30. A little sunlight is good and helps produce Vitamin D.

J.M.J.

Questions for Review

1. The _____ is the window through which we see.

2. The _____ changes the size of the pupil.

3. The _____ capture light and convert it to electrical impulses.

4. _____ in the retina allow us to have night vision.

5. _____ in the retina allow us to see color.

6. The _____ is a membrane that vibrates sound waves.

7. Vibrations pass on to three bones: the hammer, the anvil, and the _____.

8. The _____ looks like a snail's shell.

9. A sense of balance comes from the semicircular canals in the _____.

10. Listening to music through _____ can damage your hearing.

11. People can distinguish about _____ different odors.

12. The bumps on the tongue are called _____.

13. The skin manufactures _____.

14. The pigment that gives our skin color is called _____.

15. There are more than _____ pain receptors throughout the body.

16. The bottom layer of the skin helps insulate the body from changes in _____.

17. Sunburn _____ the skin.

18. Thermoreceptors are found with high concentration on the face and _____.

19. Skin _____ allow us to feel touch and pain.

20. We brush our teeth for fewer germs and _____.